MONSTERS!

& Other Stories

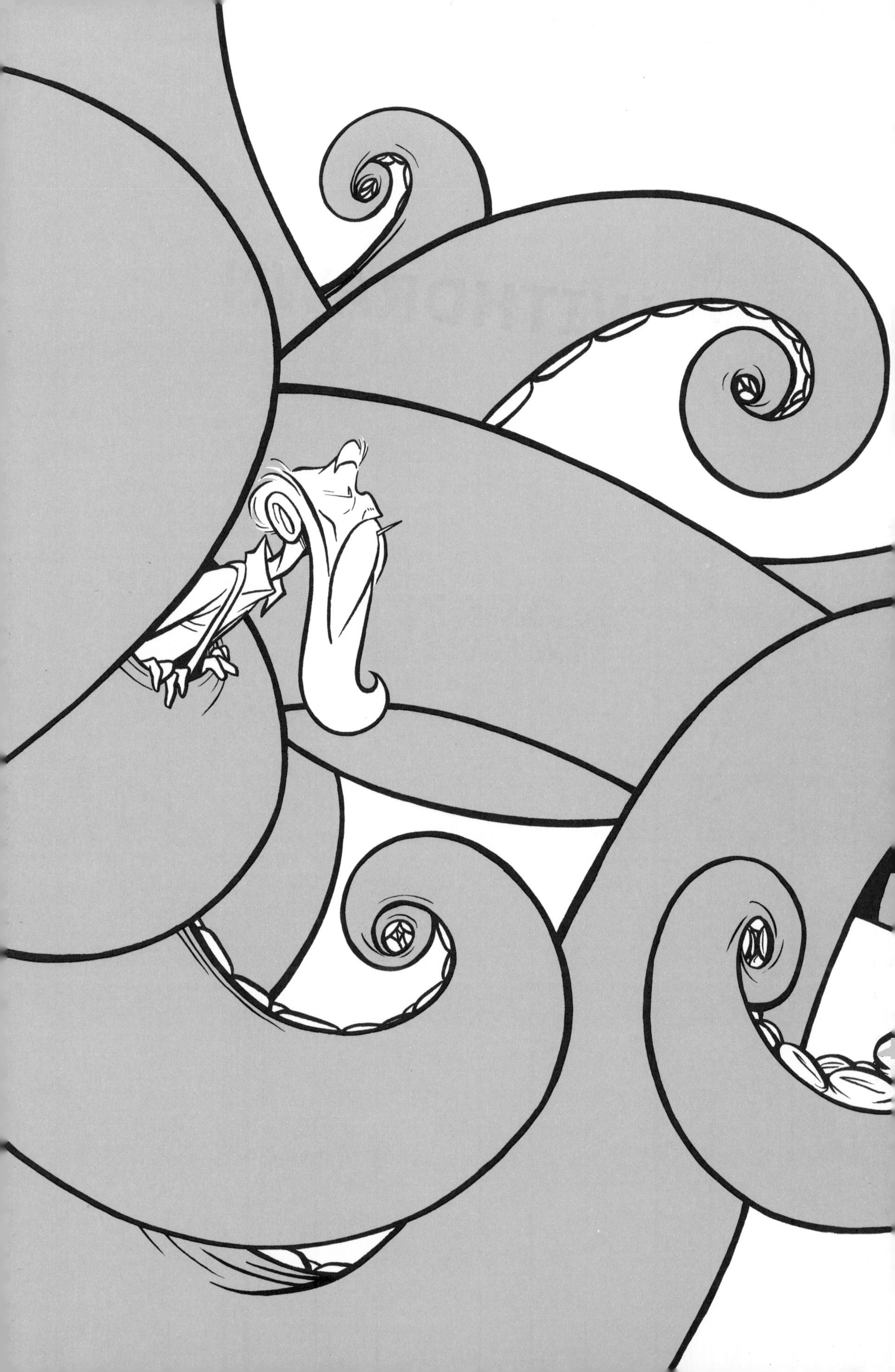

[*Contents*]

CÓ!

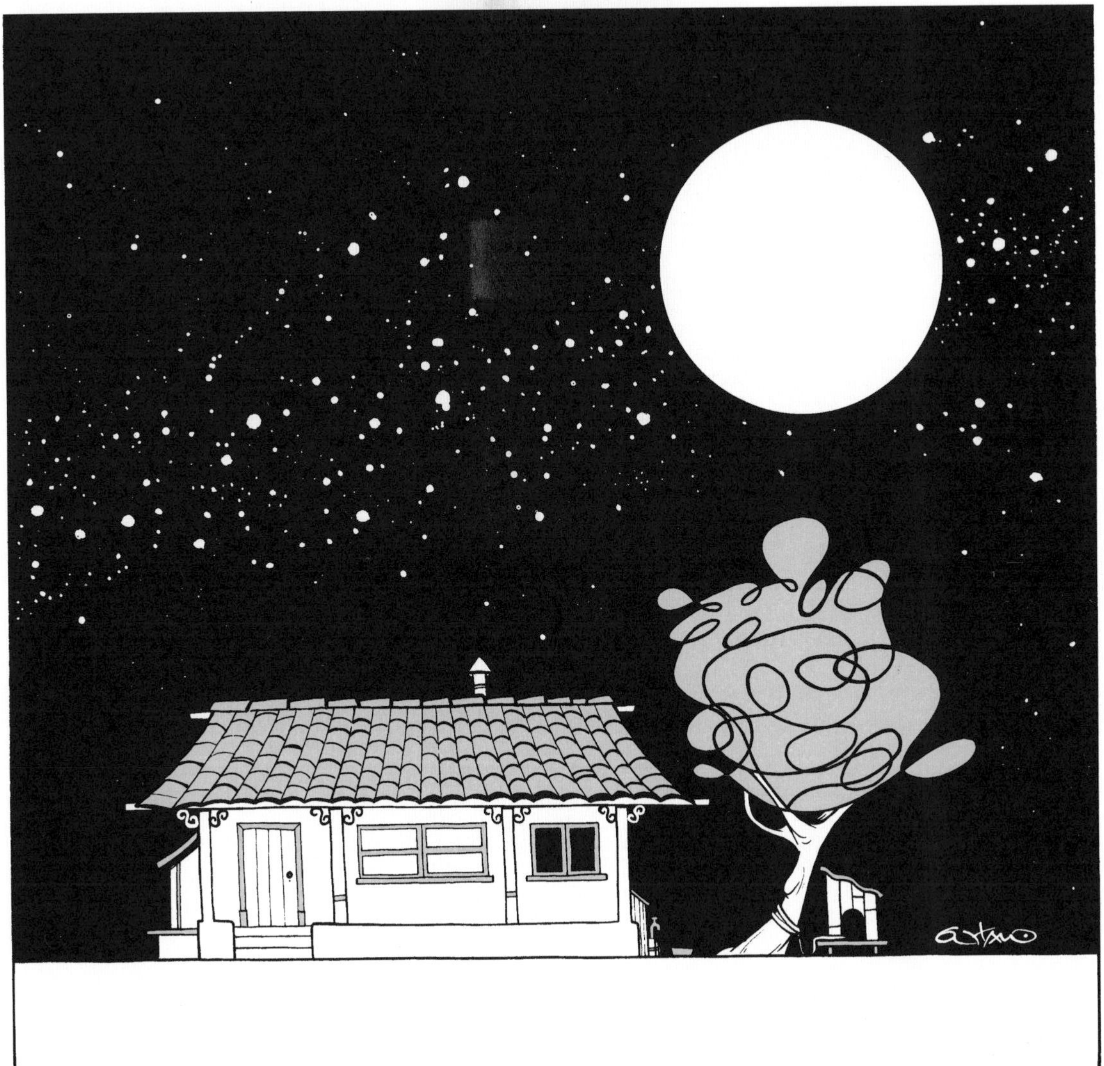

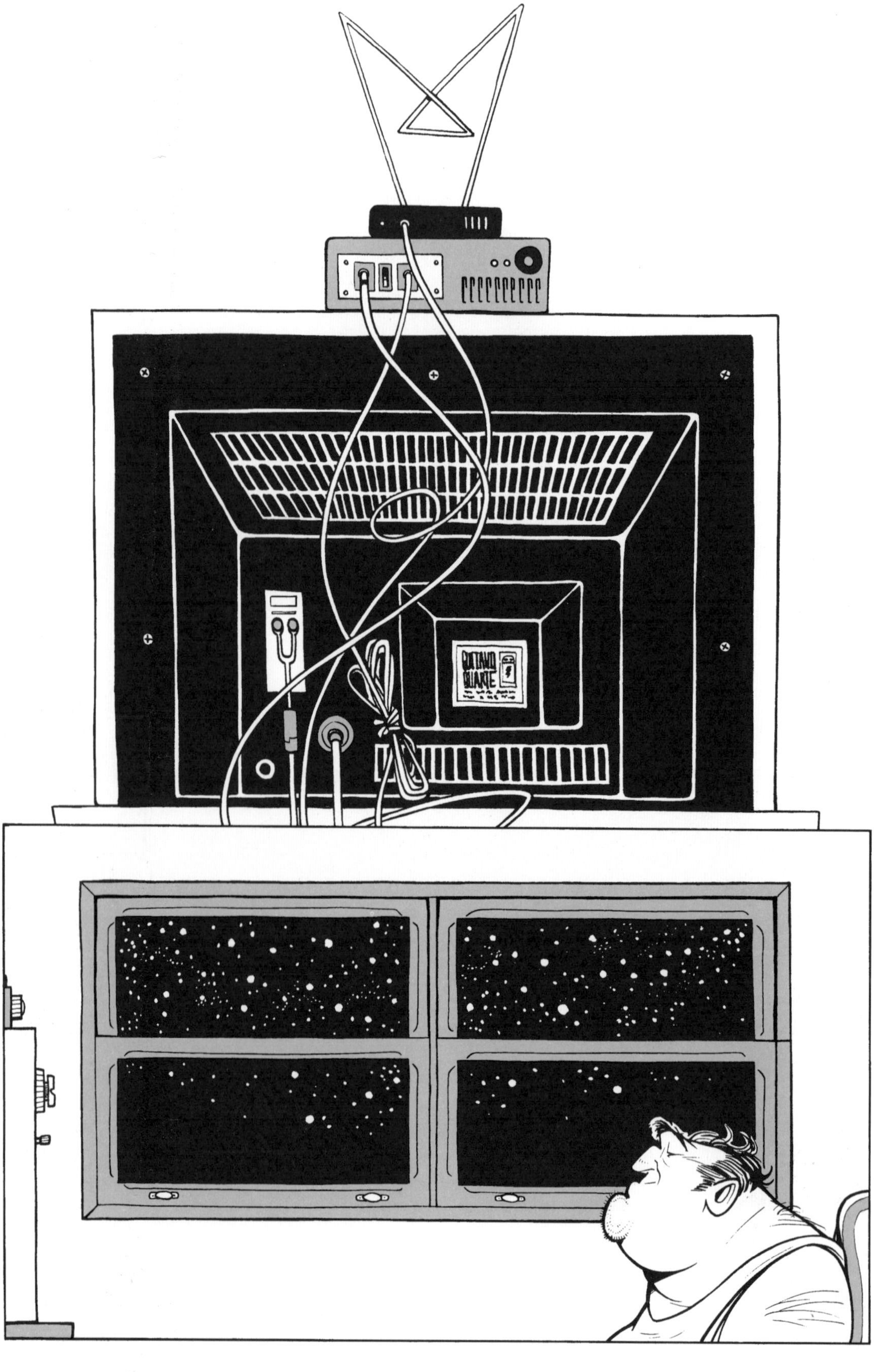
GUSTAVO DUARTE

[*Introduction*]

Ever since I started cartooning at an early age, I've had a fascination with pantomime, maybe because a great majority of animated cartoons that I watched as a kid were silent, or because it was easy for me to understand the humor in printed cartoons without words. As I grew older and started to draw, I realized that what I enjoyed the most was pantomime. I learned from cartoonists like Chaval, Tetsu, Mose, François, Dubout—all masters of the world of silent humor—and today, after a lifetime of drawing wordless cartoons, I still love that difficult and wonderful art form.

And that's why, when I received Gustavo Duarte's *Monsters! & Other Stories* in the mail, it was with great pleasure that I realized there is a new generation of cartoonists with the same love and passion that I have for that genre. Not only is Duarte a very good craftsman; he is also an excellent storyteller. Following a great tradition of Brazilian artists like Ziraldo, Jaguar, and, in a different way, Henfil, Duarte draws with a well-balanced composition and a very expressive style that do not distract from the message. His twisted approach to horror, his humor, and his surprise endings allow his stories to belong to the short story genre with a perfect fit.

The tradition of telling stories without words is centuries old. In medieval times, plaza and market storytellers would display placards with sequential drawings, depicting events that related to the town, a crime of passion, a recent fire, tales of war, etc. . . . Words were not necessary, as almost all the people didn't know how to read.

In the 1920s, in Europe, wordless novels were quite popular, usually woodcuts. In North America, Lynd Ward published a series of novels without words, also woodcuts, that he called pictorial narratives. Then came the mimes and the "art of silence": Chaplin, Jean-Louis Barrault, Marcel Marceau, and Alejandro Jodorowsky. There was Milt Gross with his long, silent graphic novel, *He Done Her Wrong*. The comic strips, such as Otto Soglow's *The Little King*, Carl Anderson's *Henry*, and Antonio Prohías's *Spy vs. Spy*. And the new generation of Lewis Trondheim, Jim Woodring, and now Gustavo Duarte will join us to continue delighting readers—well, viewers!—with well-crafted stories that, as you can tell, are universal, without need of translation . . .

Enjoy this book as I did.

Sergio Aragonés
Ojai, California 2013

Sergio Aragonés is the recipient of the National Cartoonists Society's Reuben Award and the Will Eisner Hall of Fame Award. He is a longtime contributor to *Mad* magazine and the cocreator of *Groo the Wanderer*, with Mark Evanier. He's currently working on *Sergio Aragonés Funnies*. You can explore his incredible works at his website, SergioAragones.com.

To Dr. Gori

GUSTAVO DUARTE

MONSTERS!

& Other Stories

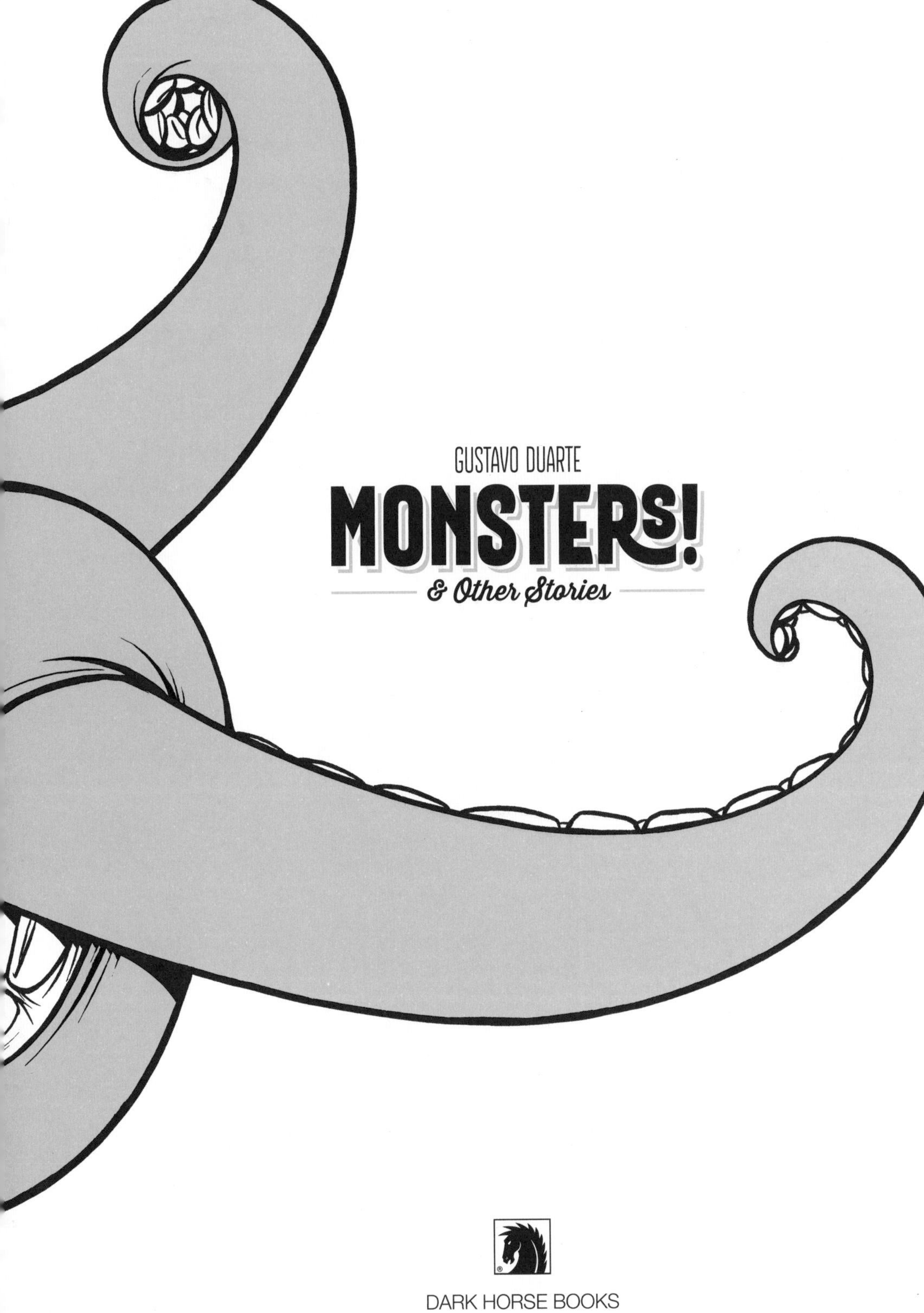

DARK HORSE BOOKS

Mike Richardson [president & publisher]

Sierra Hahn [collection editor]

Freddye Lins [collection assistant editor]

Gustavo Duarte [book designer]

Neil Hankerson Executive Vice President • Tom Weddle Chief Financial Officer • Randy Stradley Vice
President of Publishing • Michael Martens Vice President of Book Trade Sales • Anita Nelson Vice President
of Business Affairs • Scott Allie Editor in Chief • Matt Parkinson Vice President of Marketing • David Scroggy
Vice President of Product Development • Dale LaFountain Vice President of Information Technology • Darlene
Vogel Senior Director of Print, Design, and Production • Ken Lizzi General Counsel • Davey Estrada Editorial
Director • Chris Warner Senior Books Editor • Diana Schutz Executive Editor • Cary Grazzini Director of Print
and Development • Lia Ribacchi Art Director • Cara Niece Director of Scheduling • Tim Wiesch Director of
International Licensing • Mark Bernardi Director of Digital Publishing

MONSTERS! & OTHER STORIES

Published by Dark Horse Books
A division of Dark Horse Comics, Inc.
10956 SE Main Street
Milwaukie, OR 97222

DarkHorse.com
GustavoDuarte.com.br

International Licensing: (503) 905-2377
To find a comics shop in your area, call the Comic Shop Locator Service toll-free at 1-888-266-4226.

First edition: January 2014
ISBN 978-1-61655-309-8

10 9 8 7 6 5 4 3 2 1
Printed in China

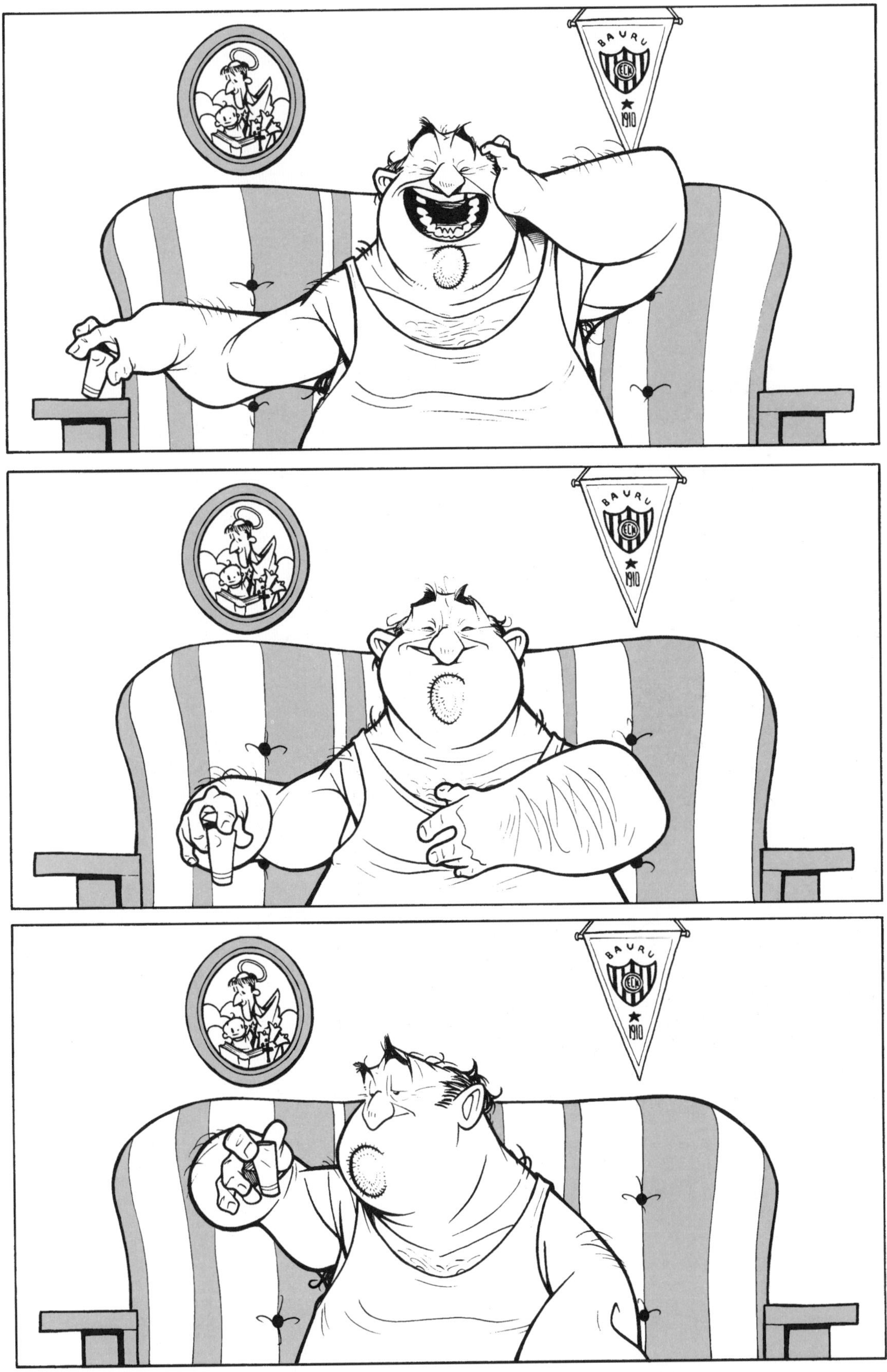
BAURU
1910

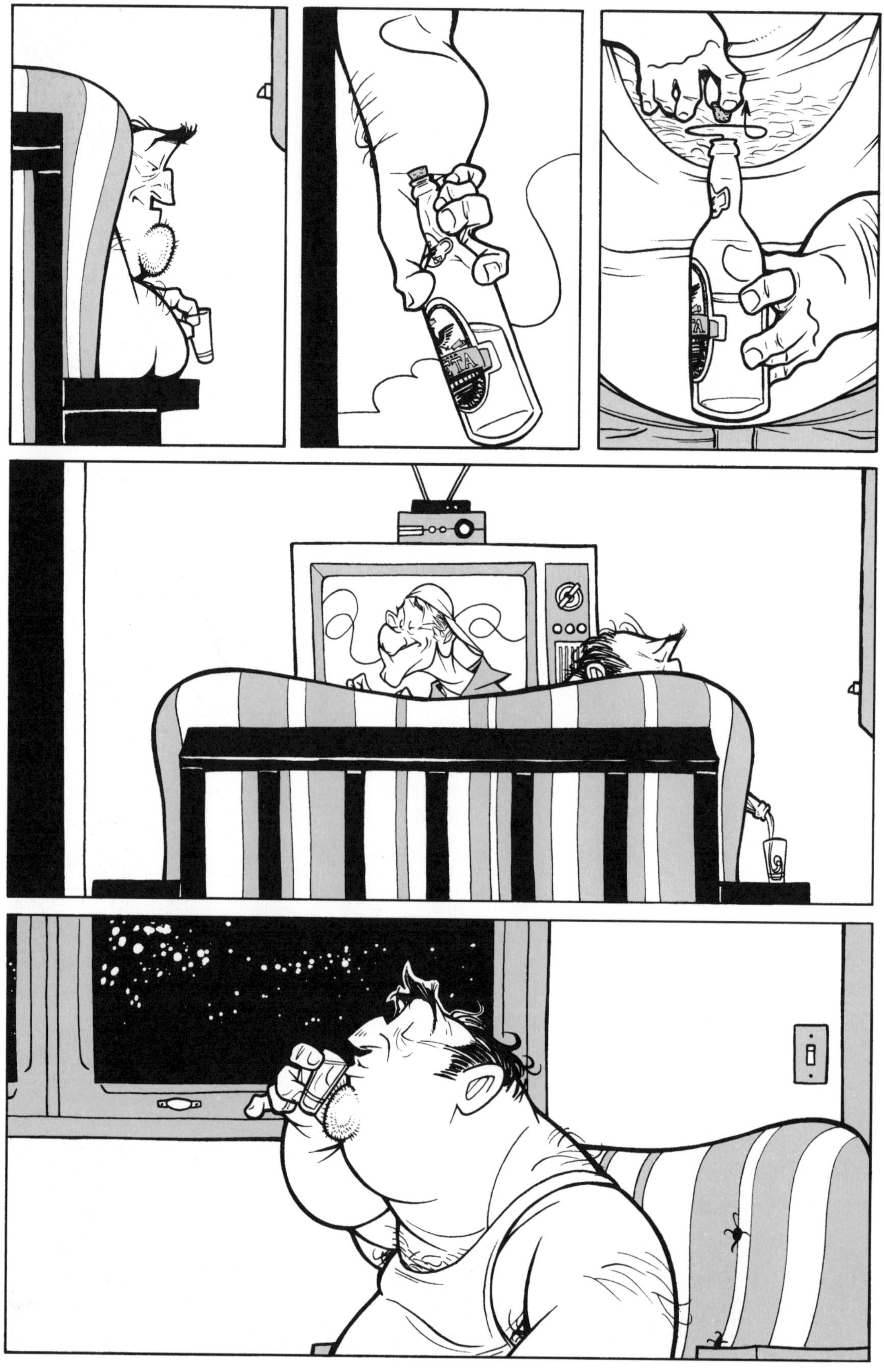

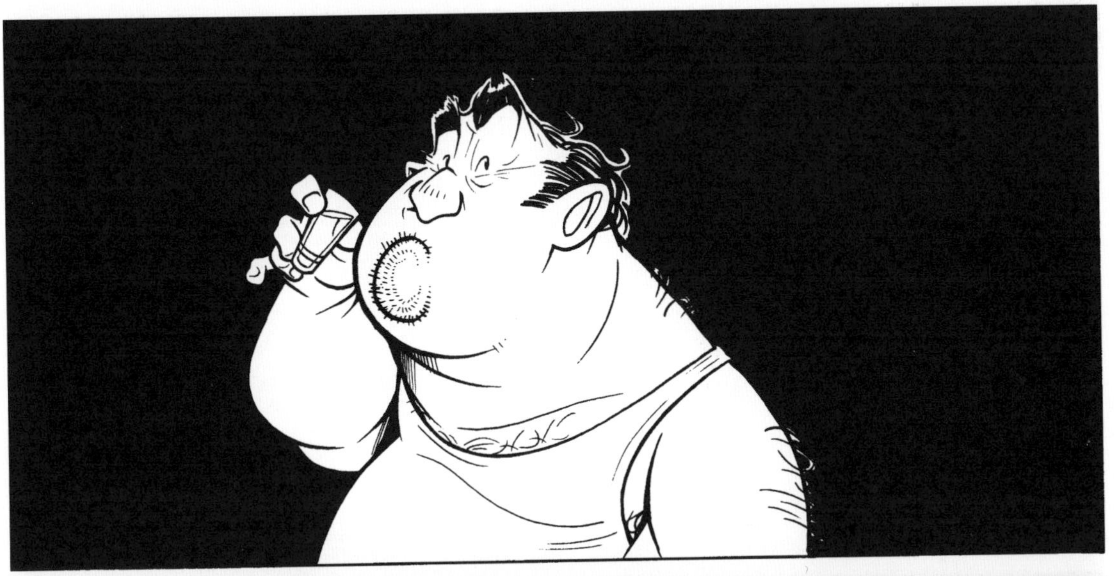
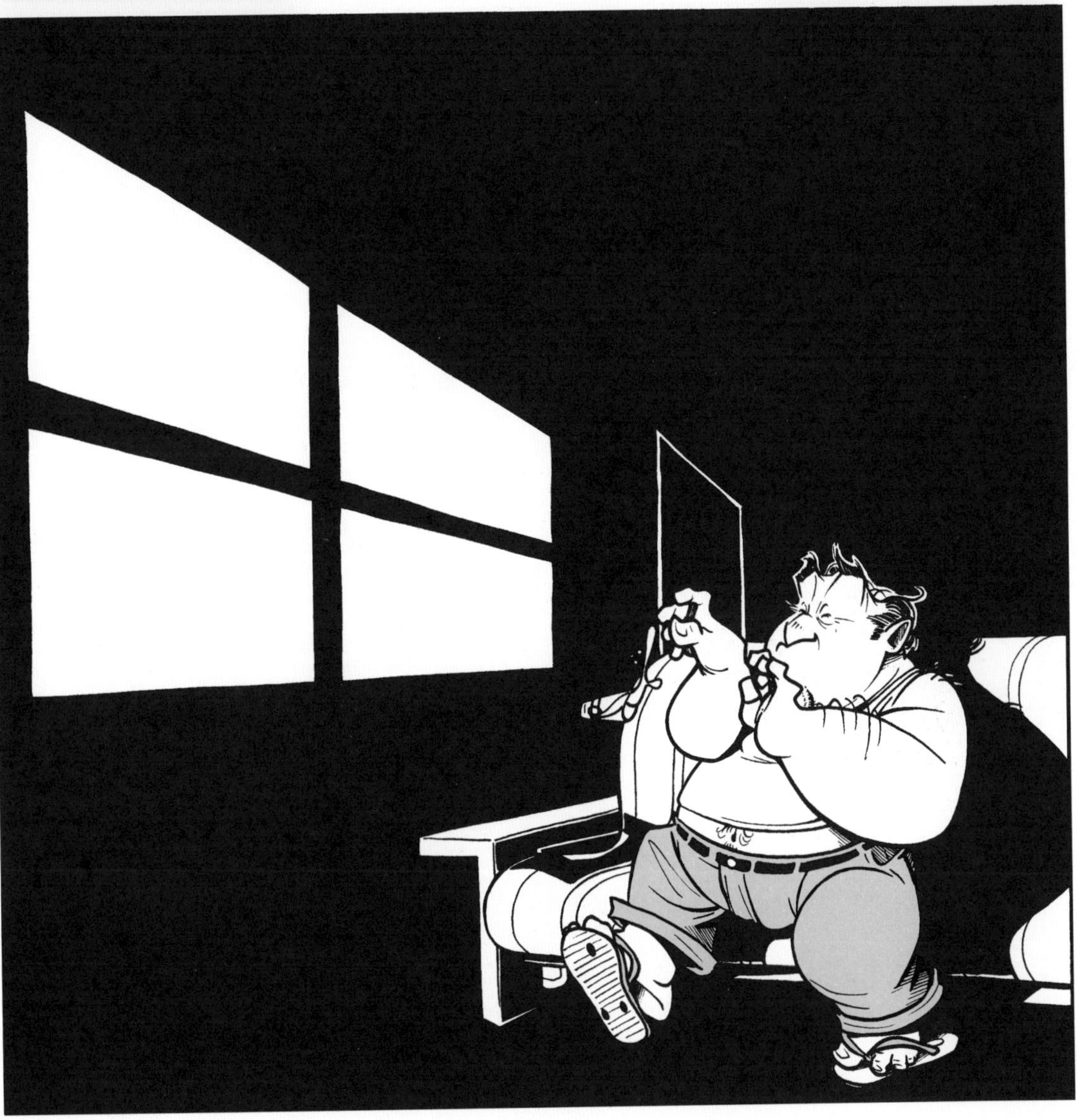

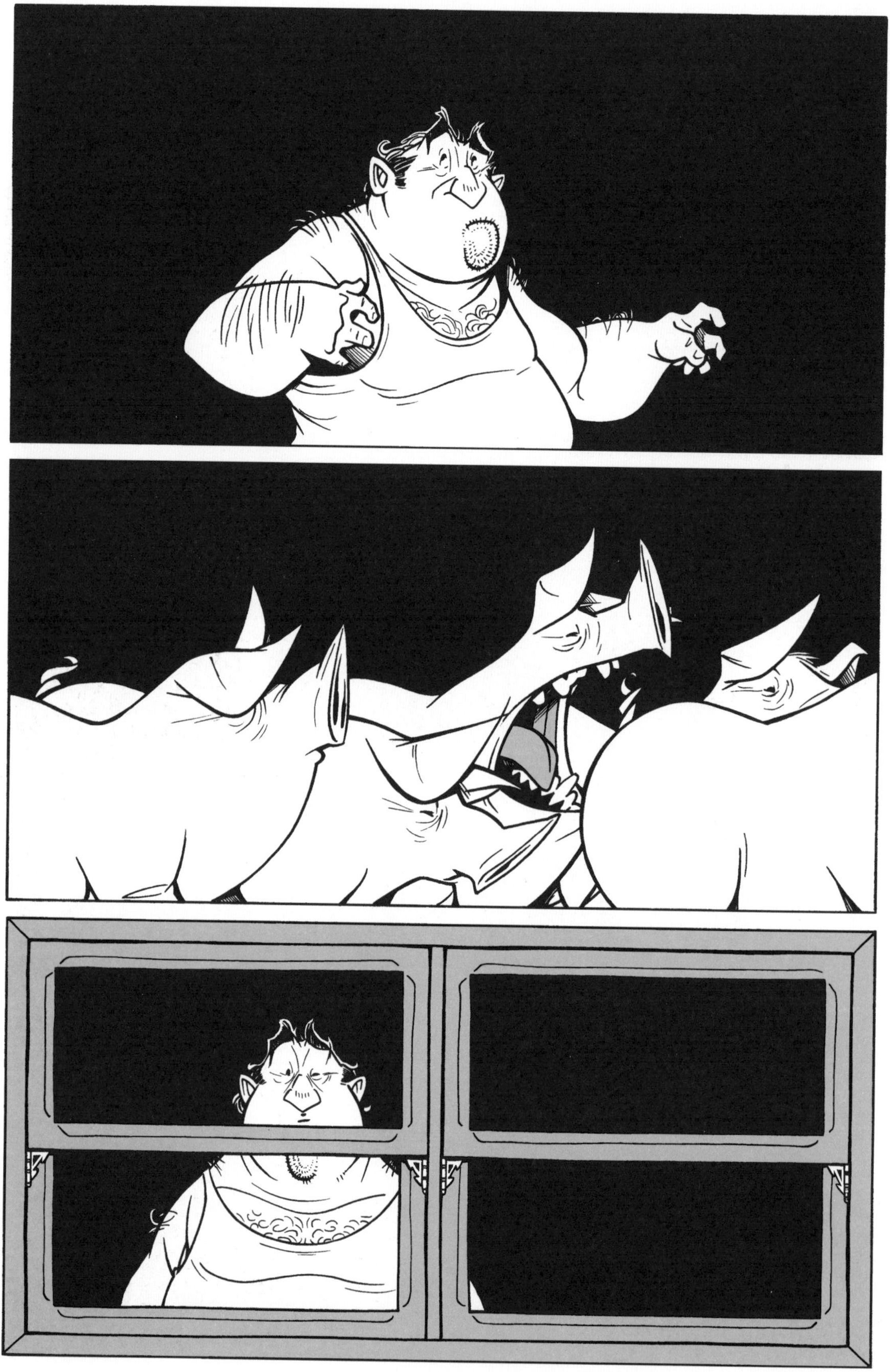

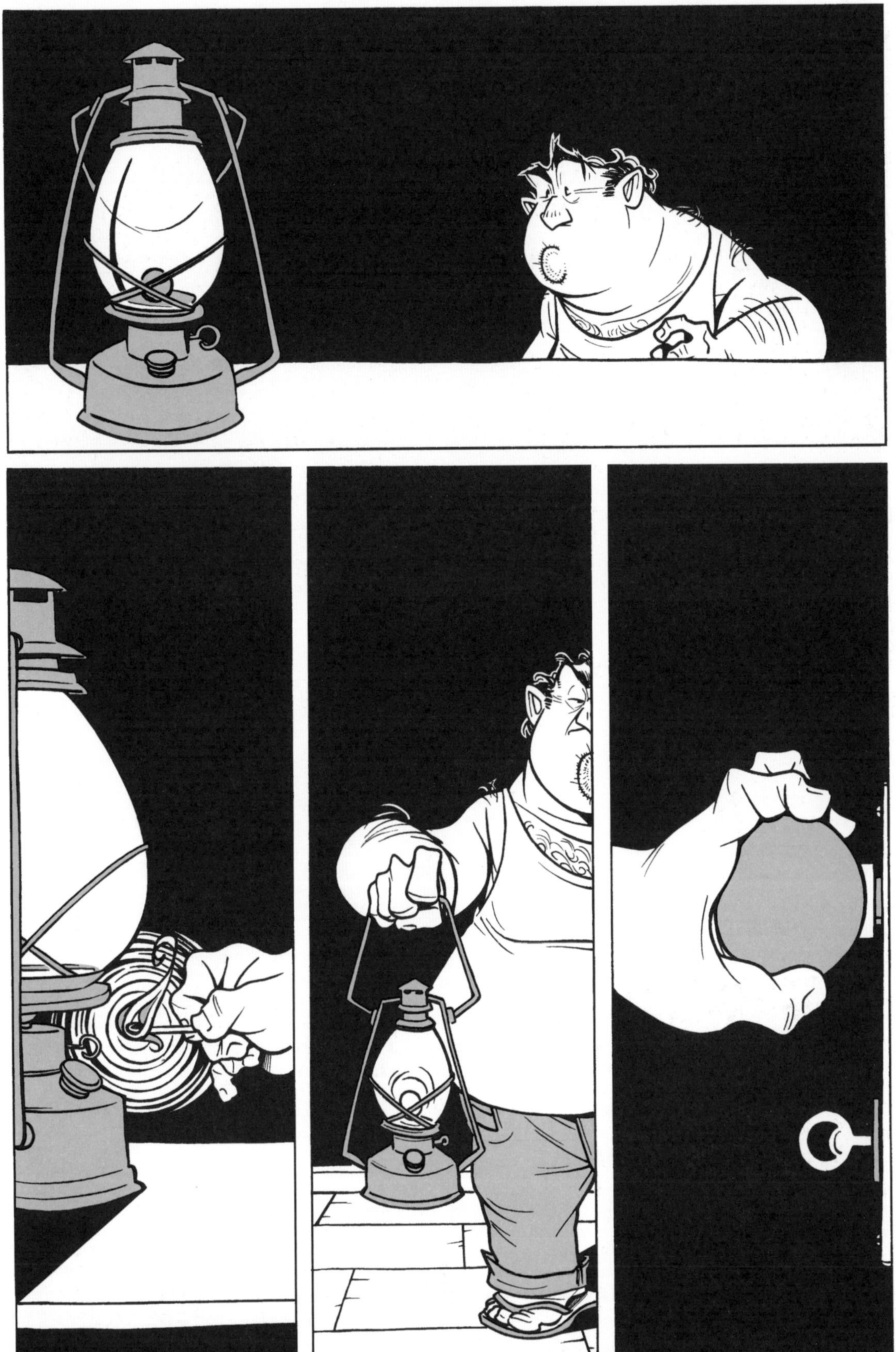

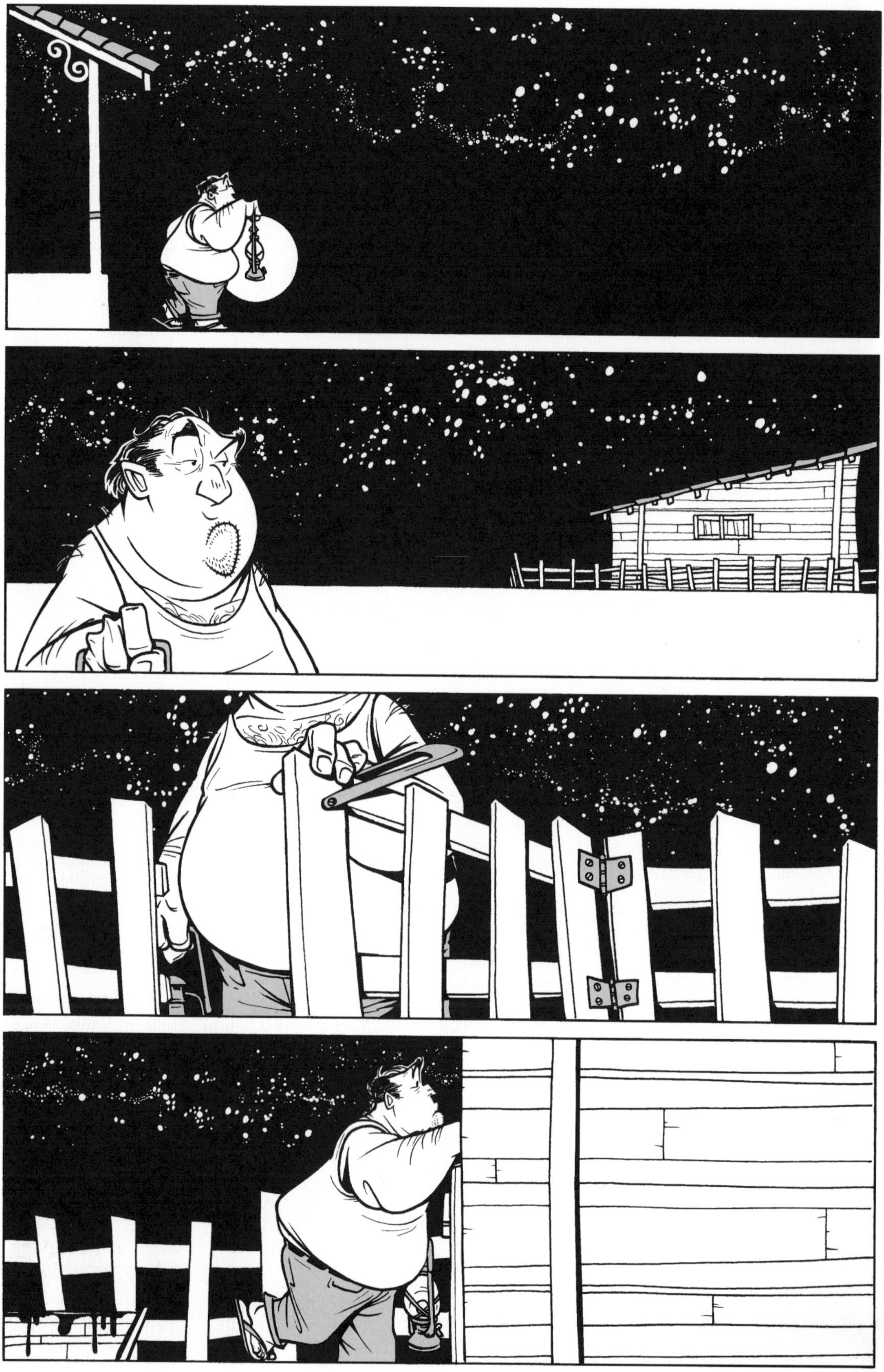

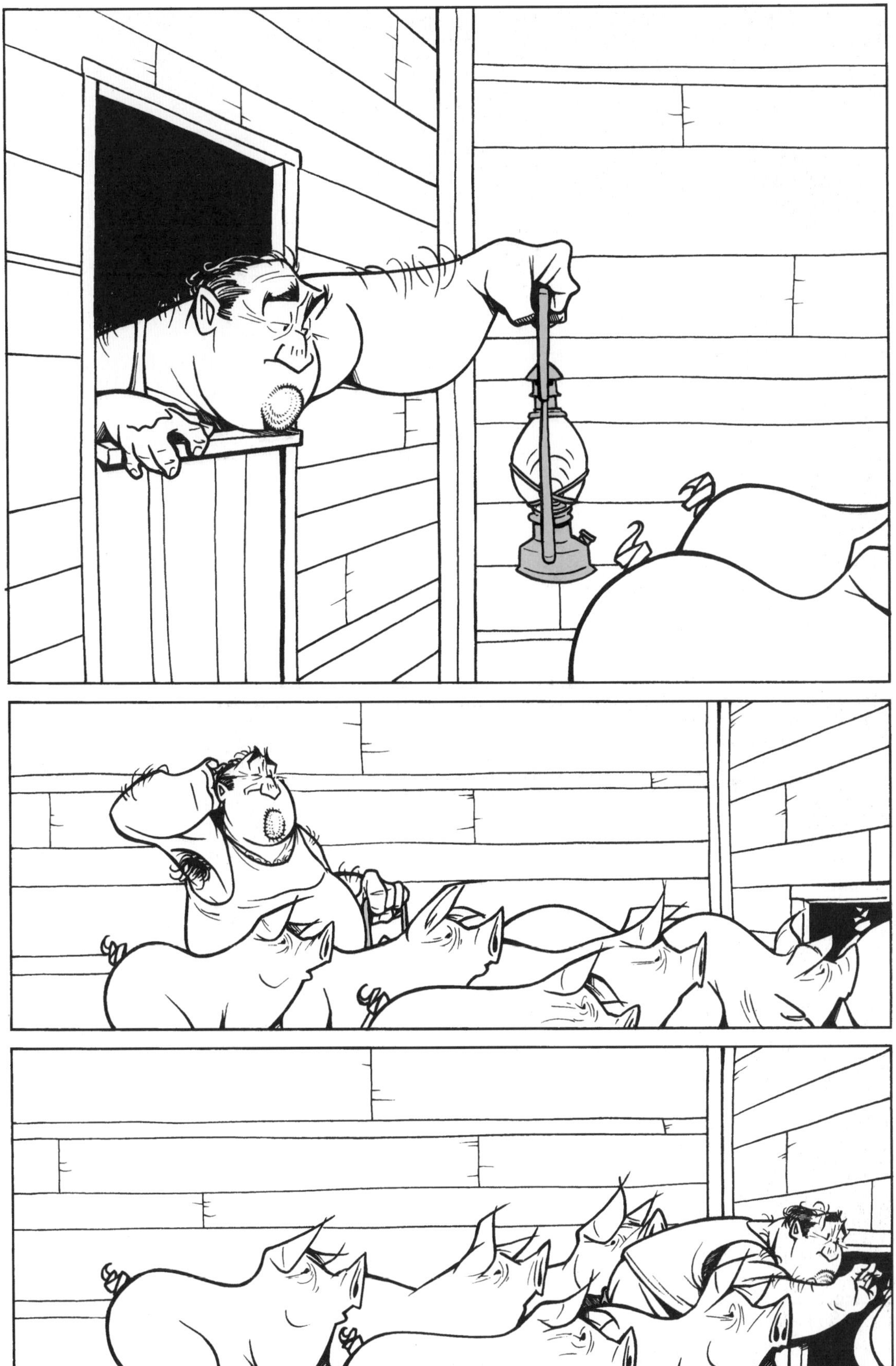

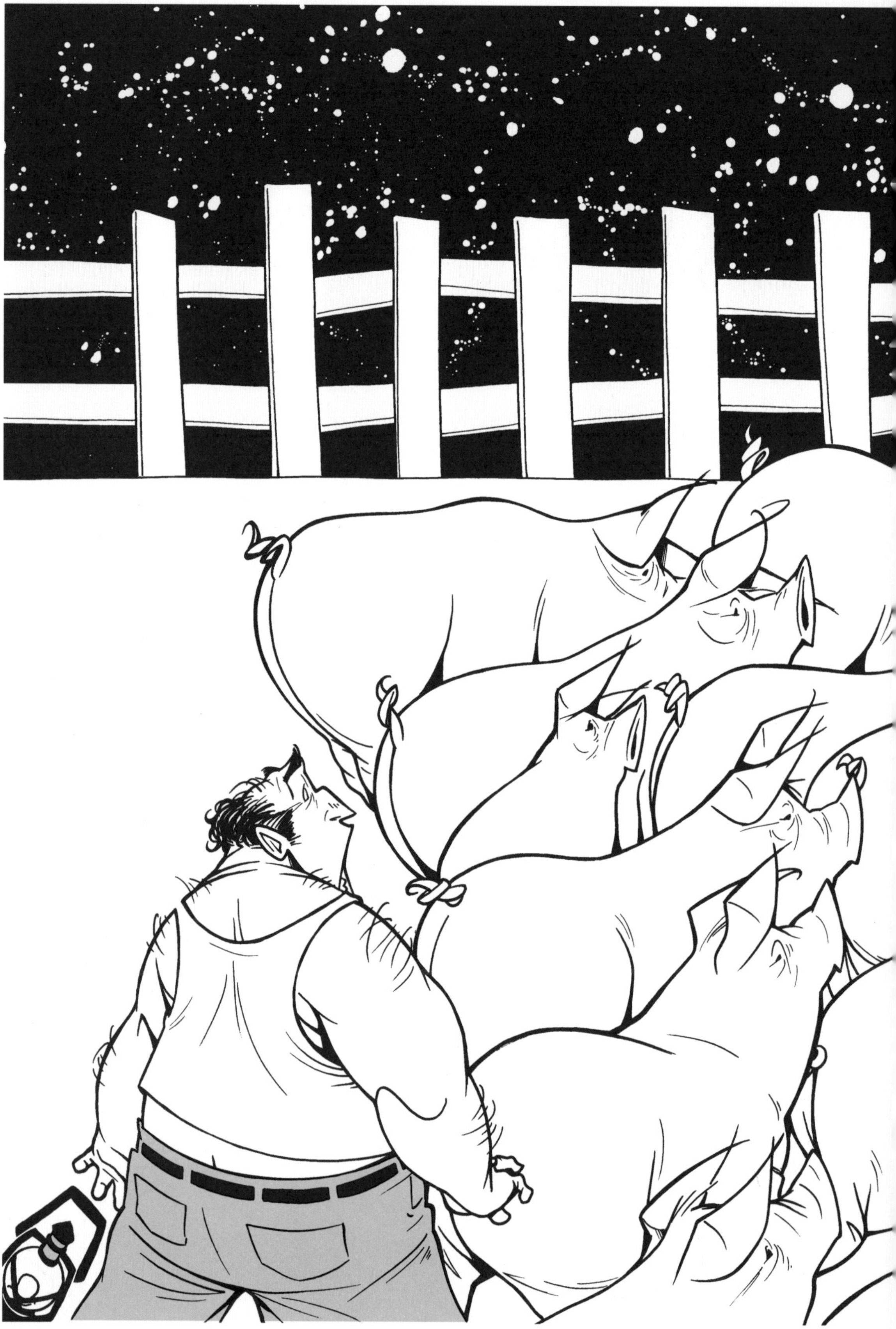

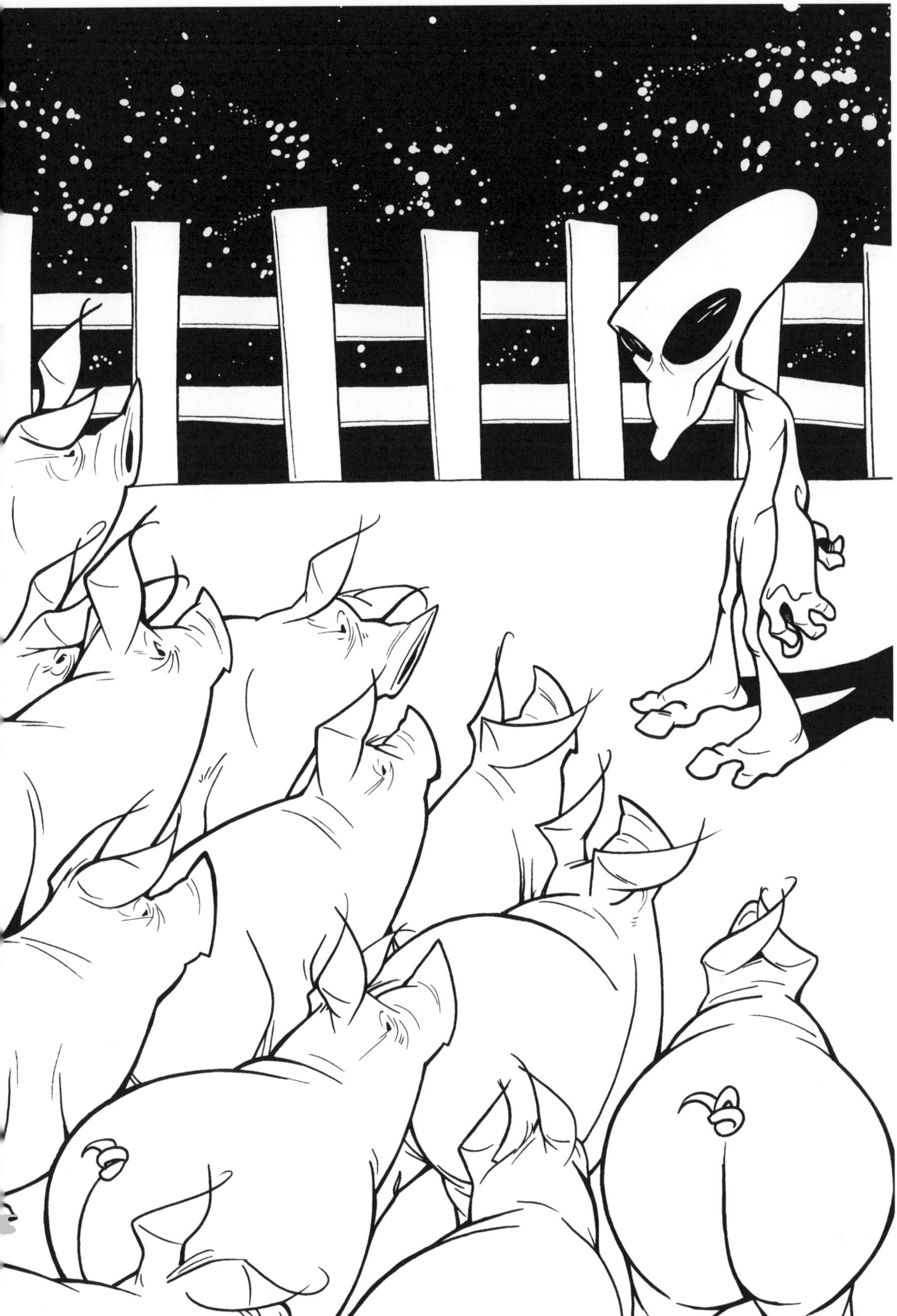

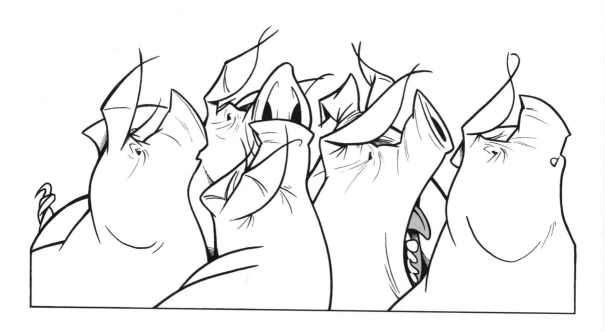

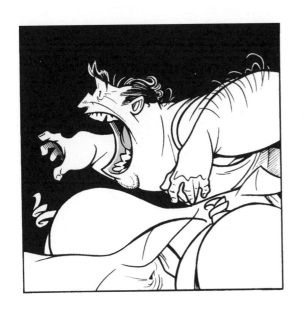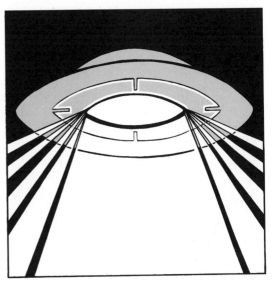

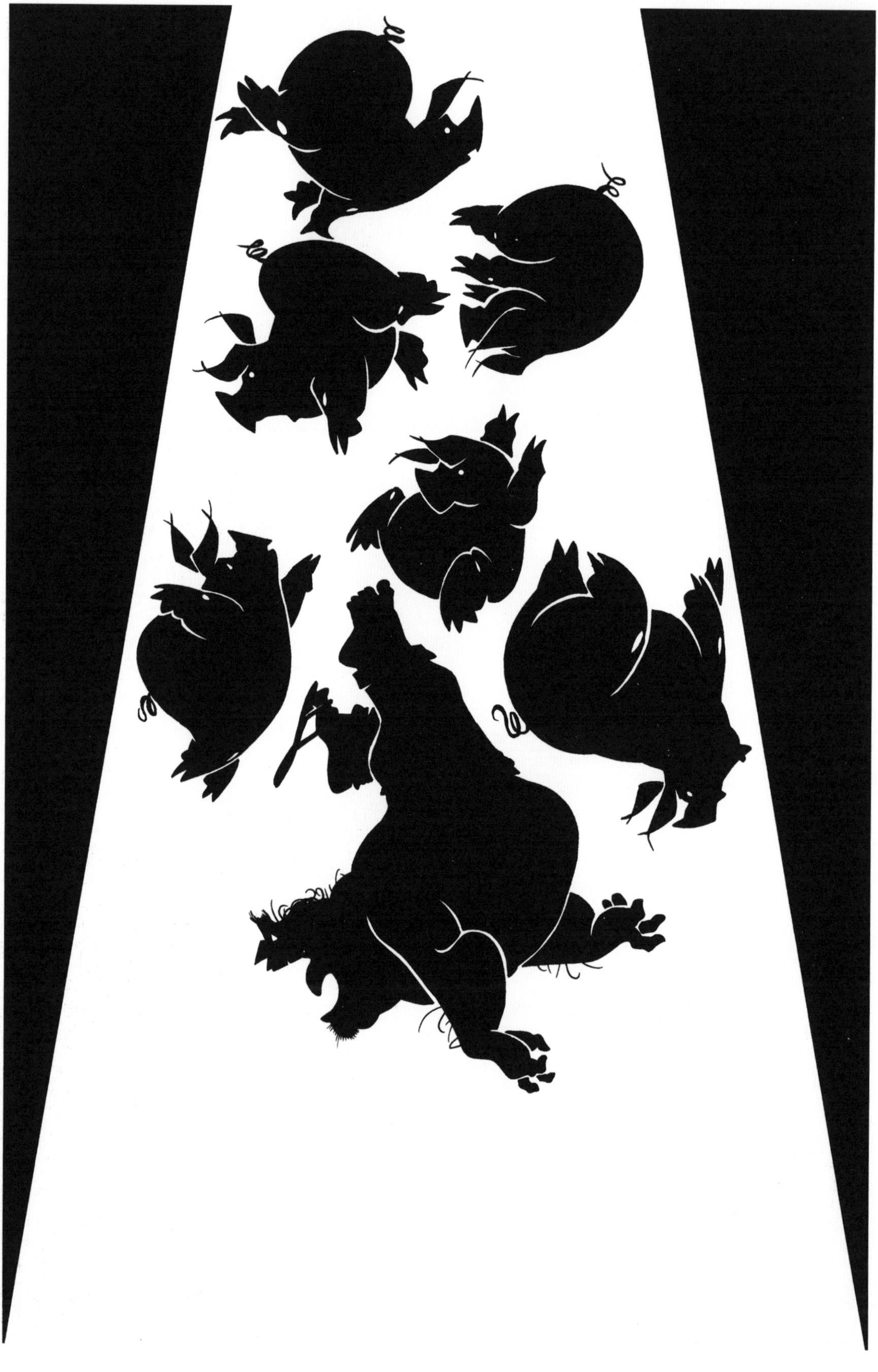

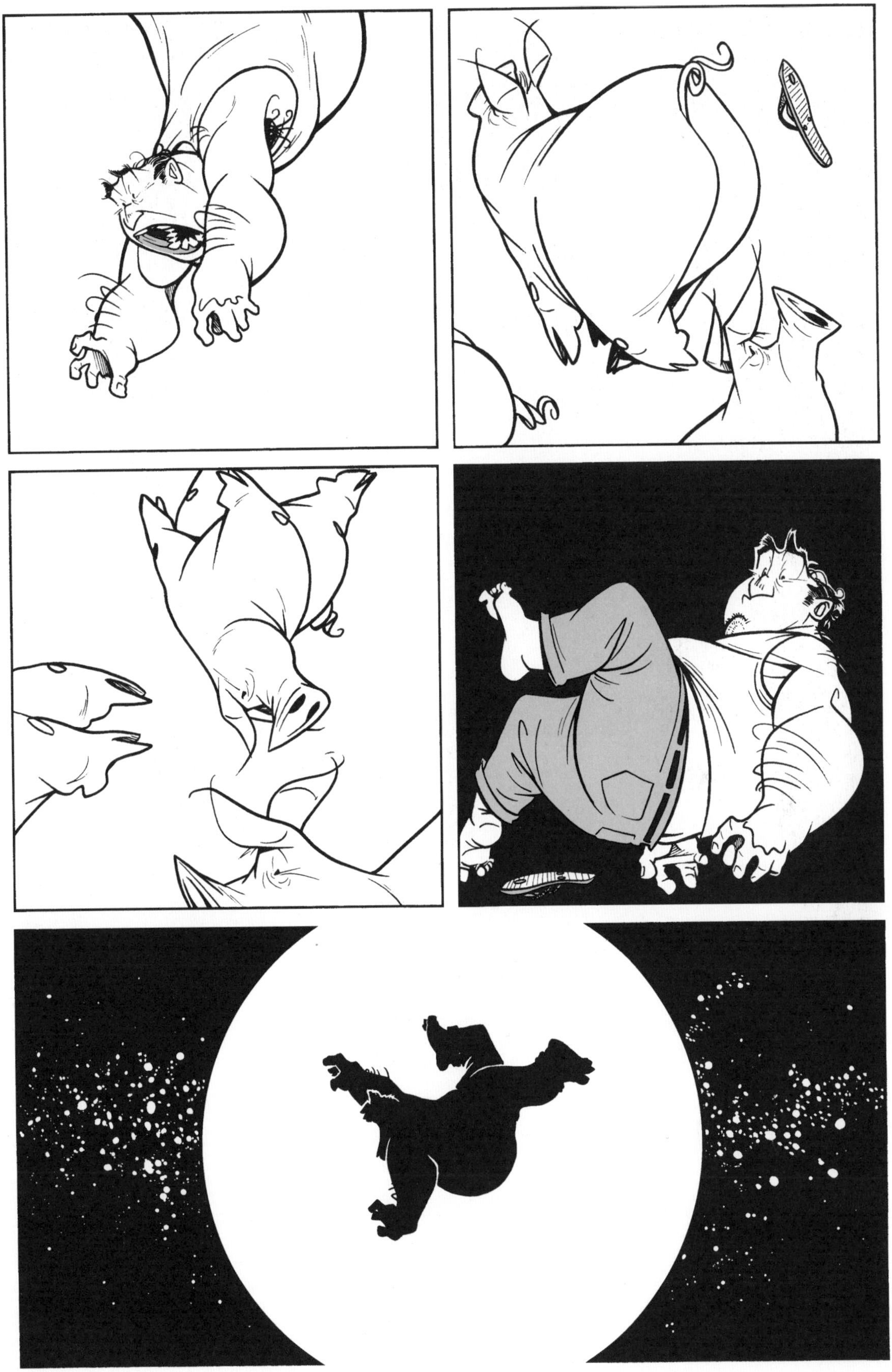

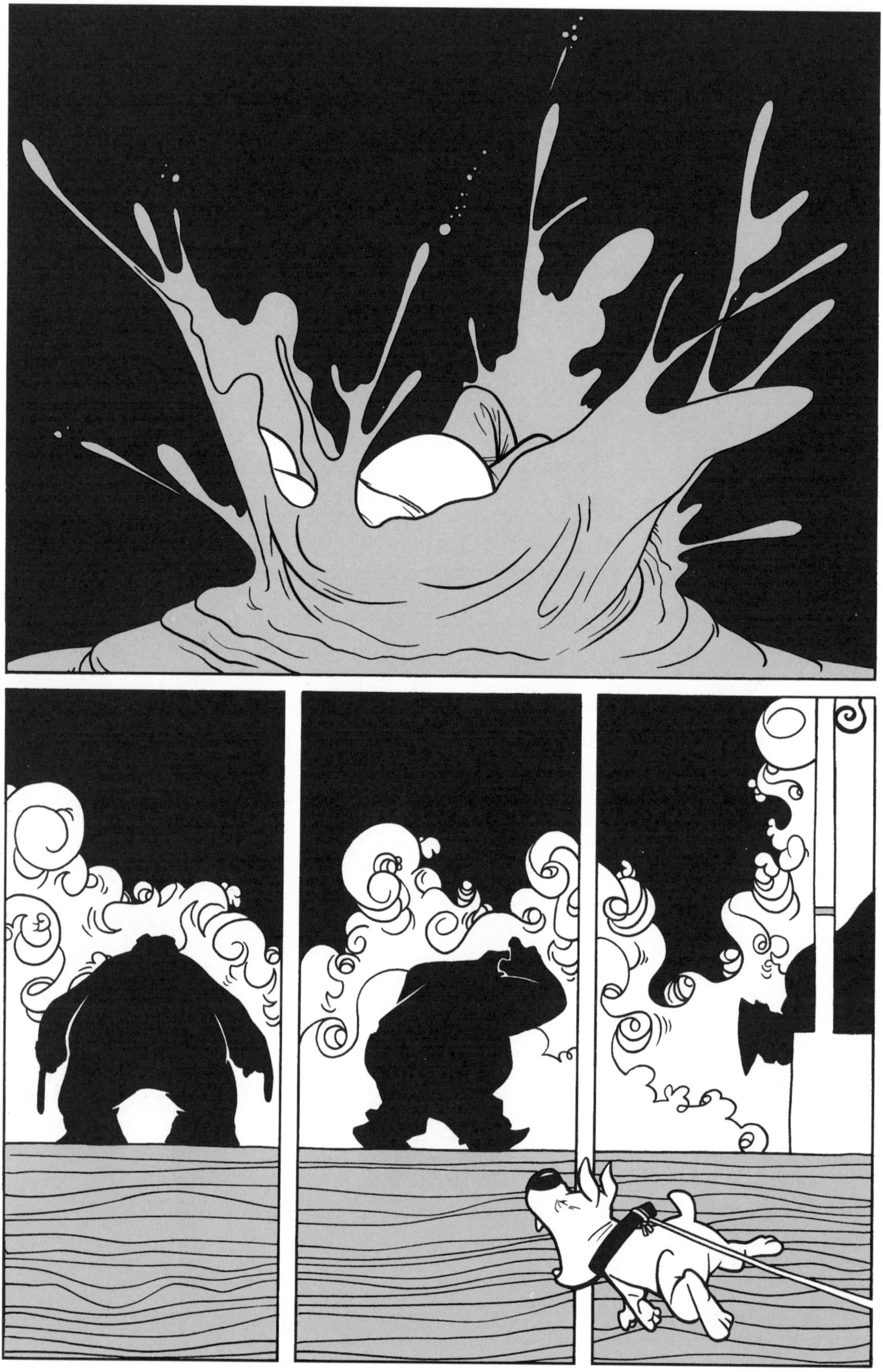

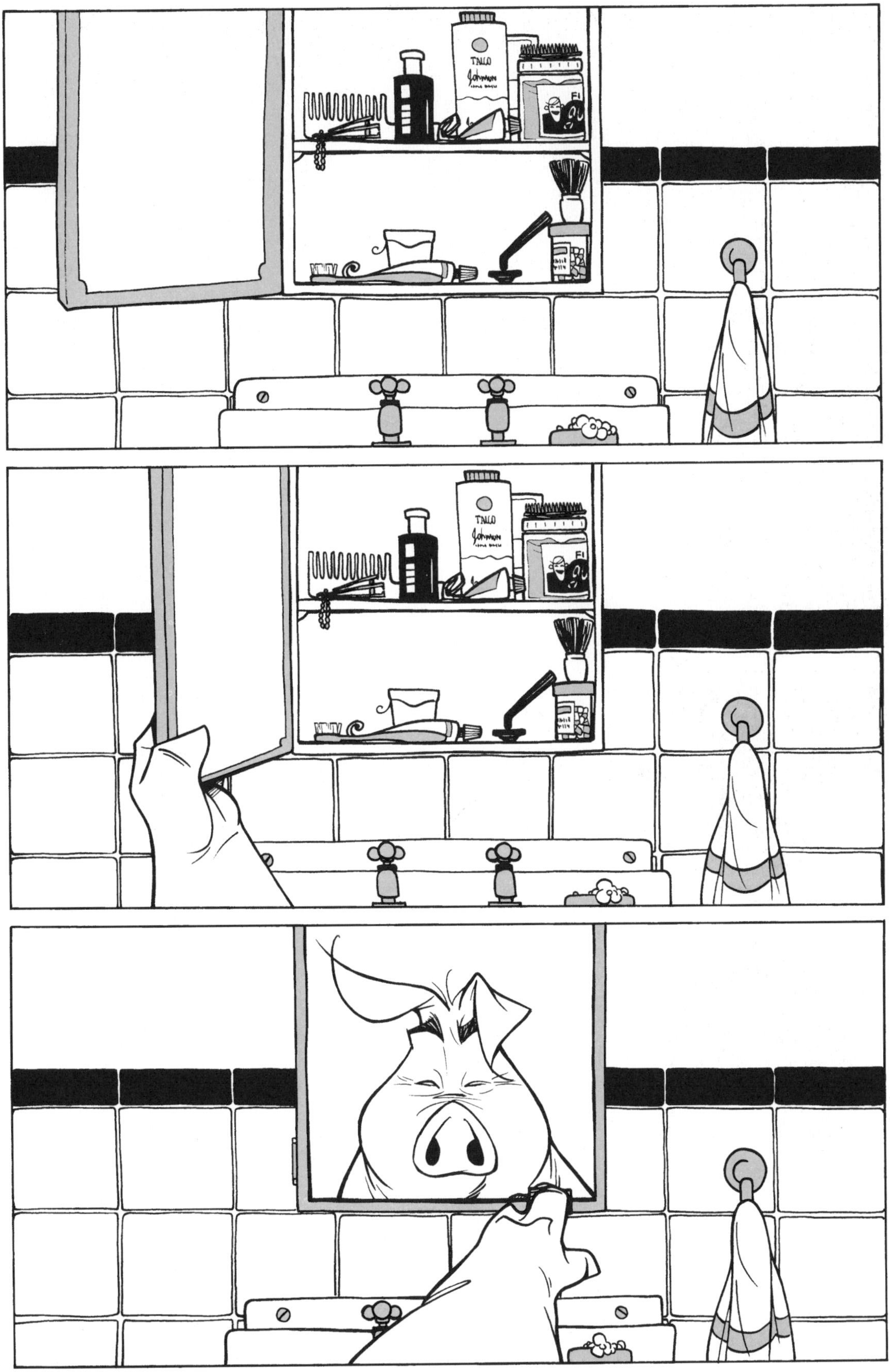

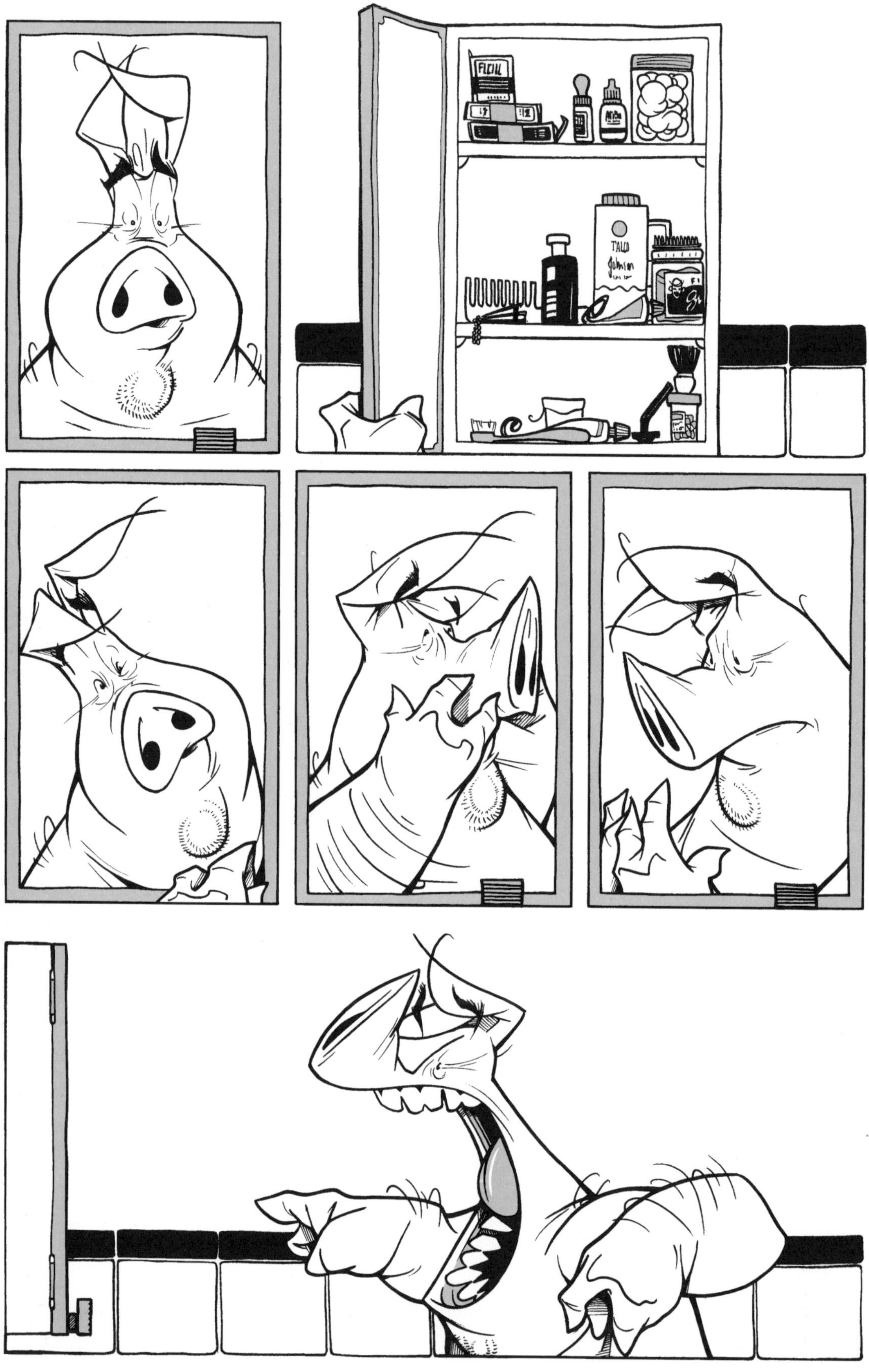
TALCO
Johnson

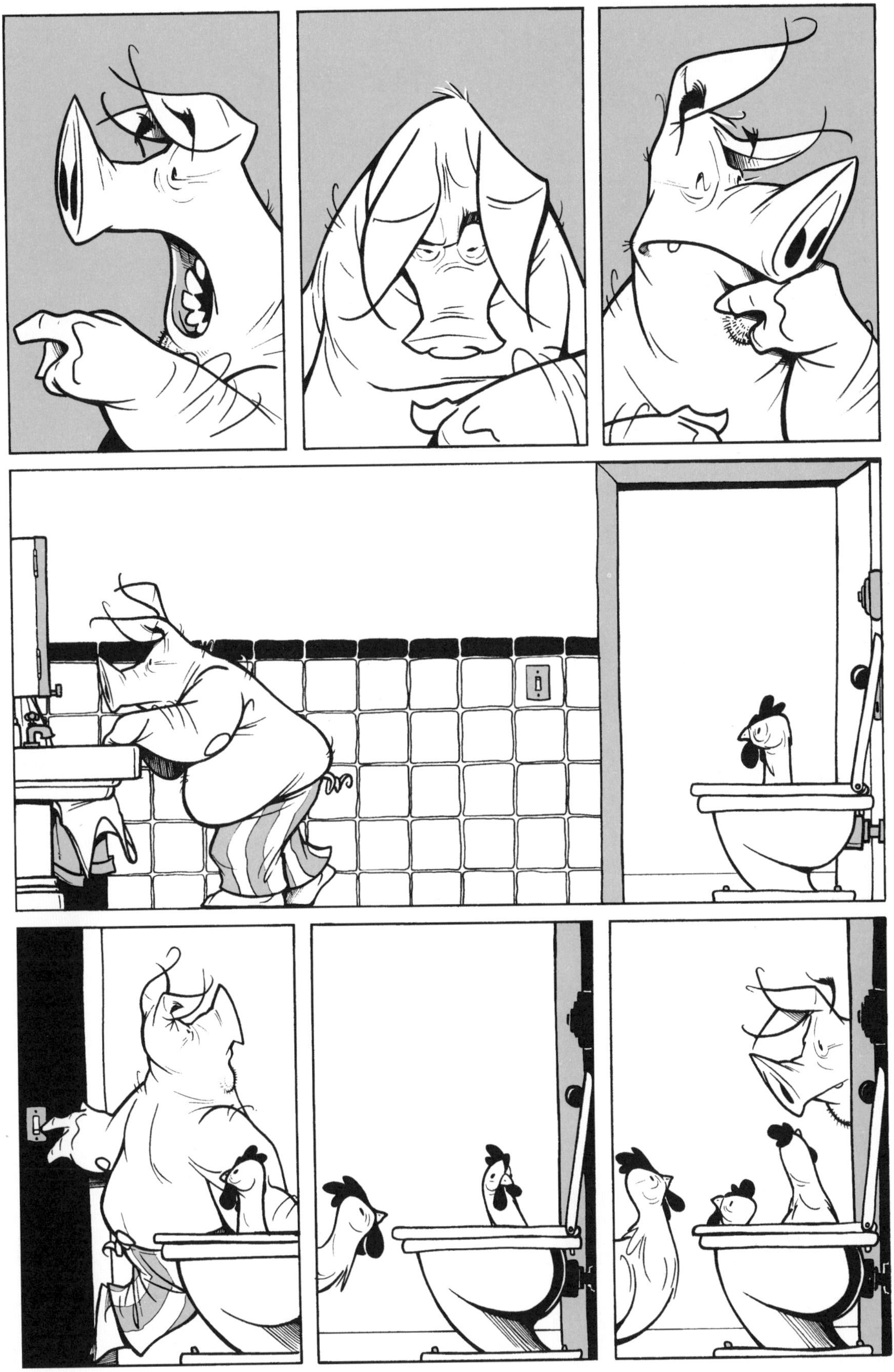

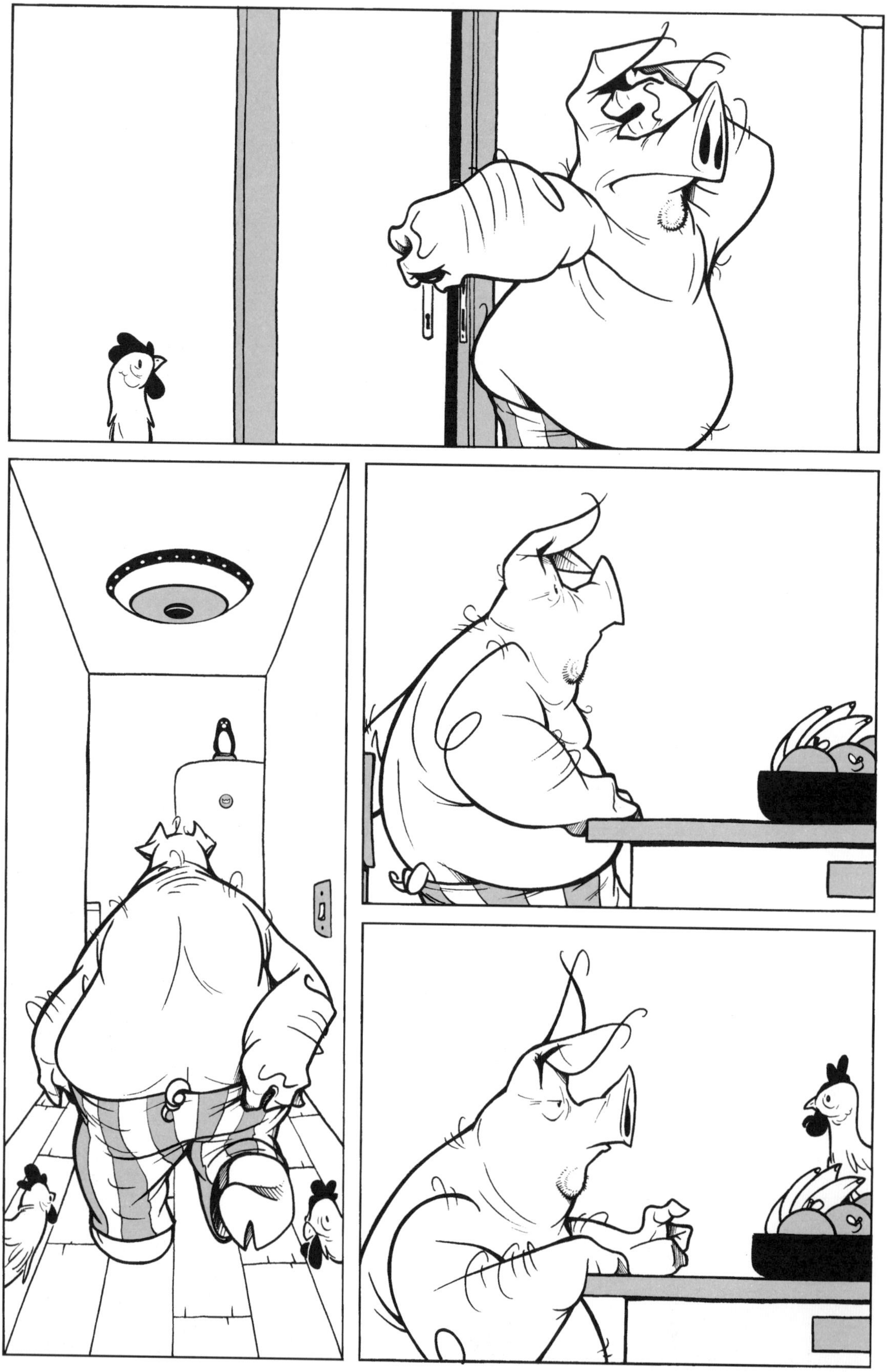

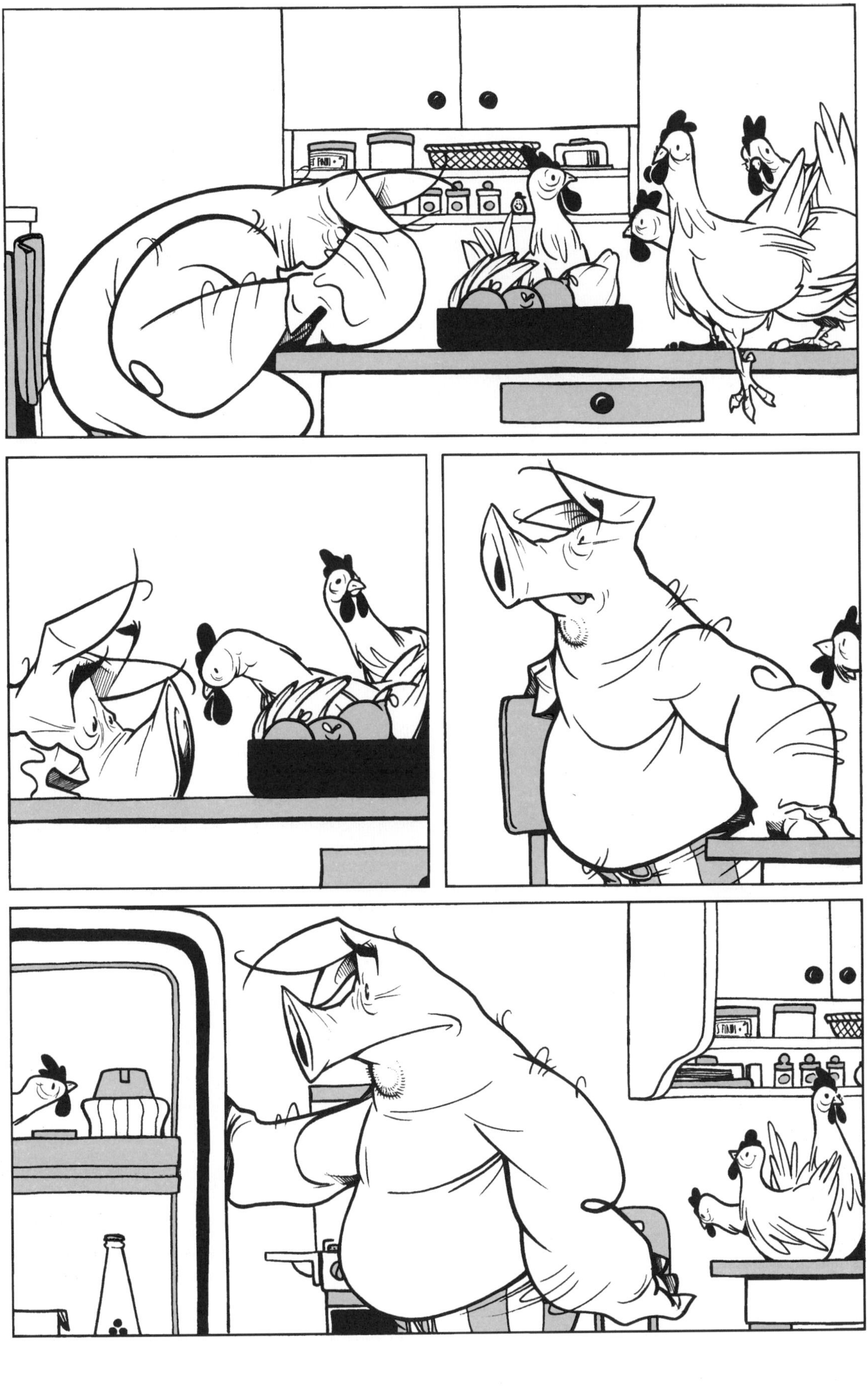

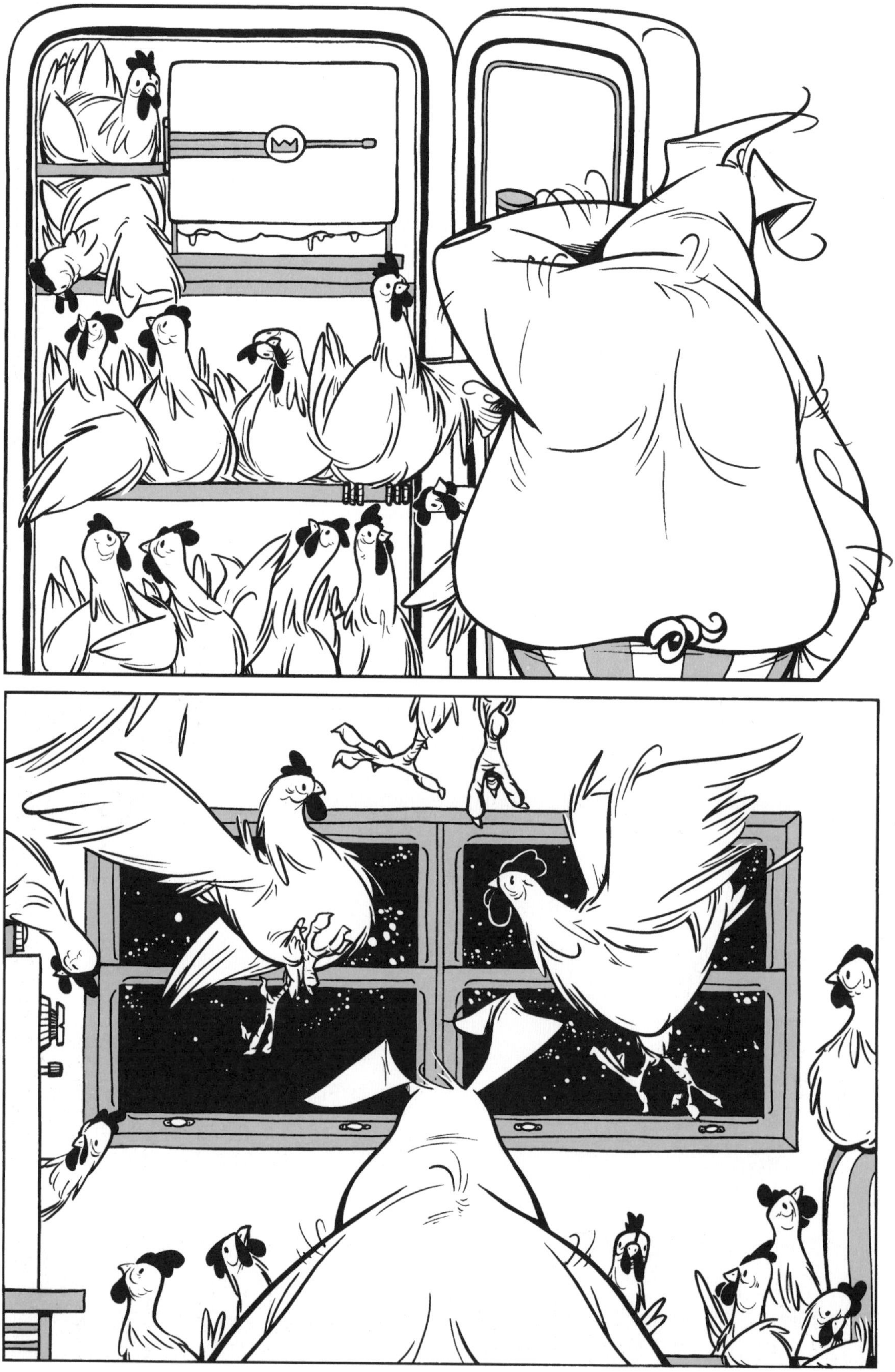

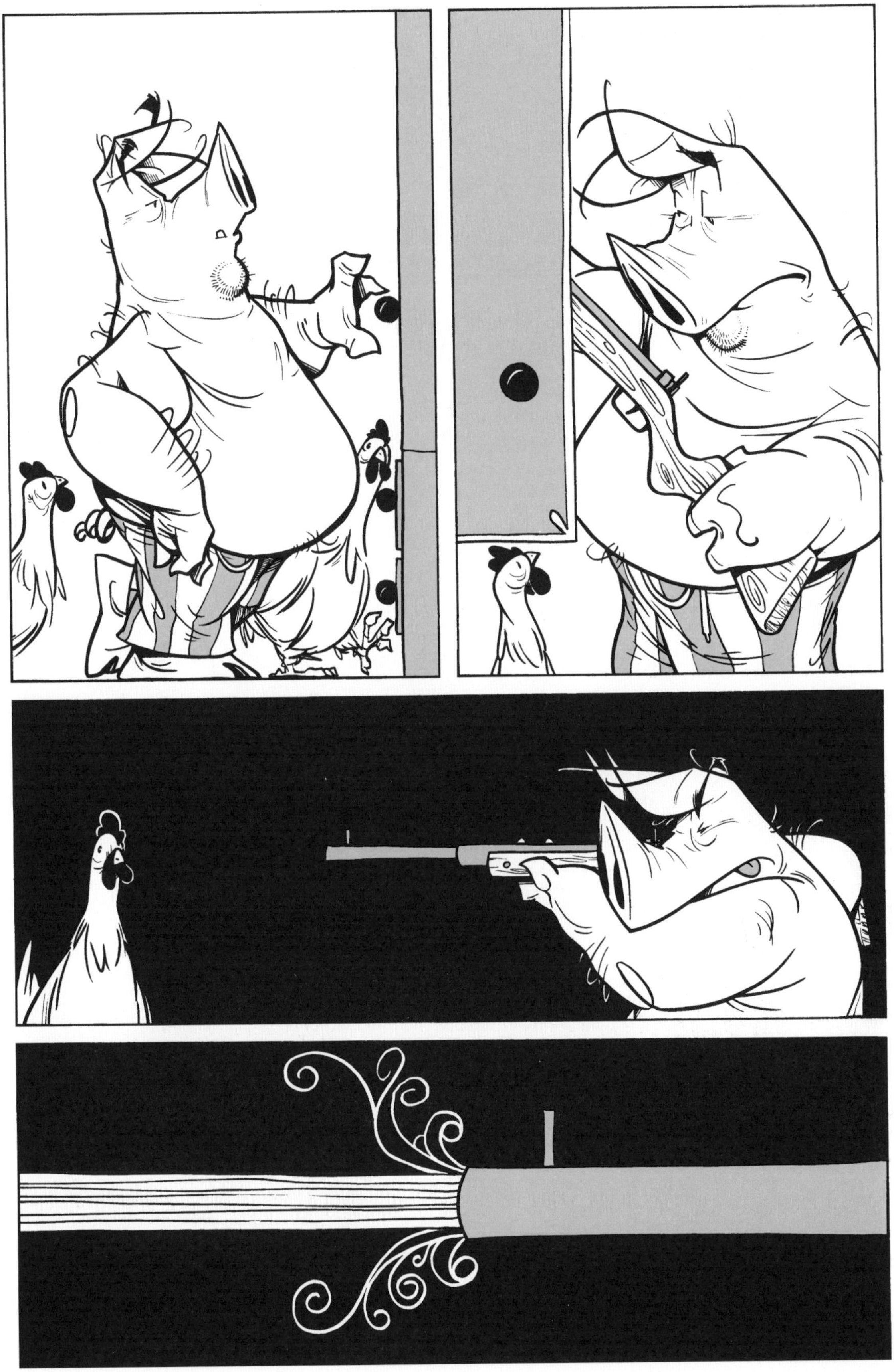

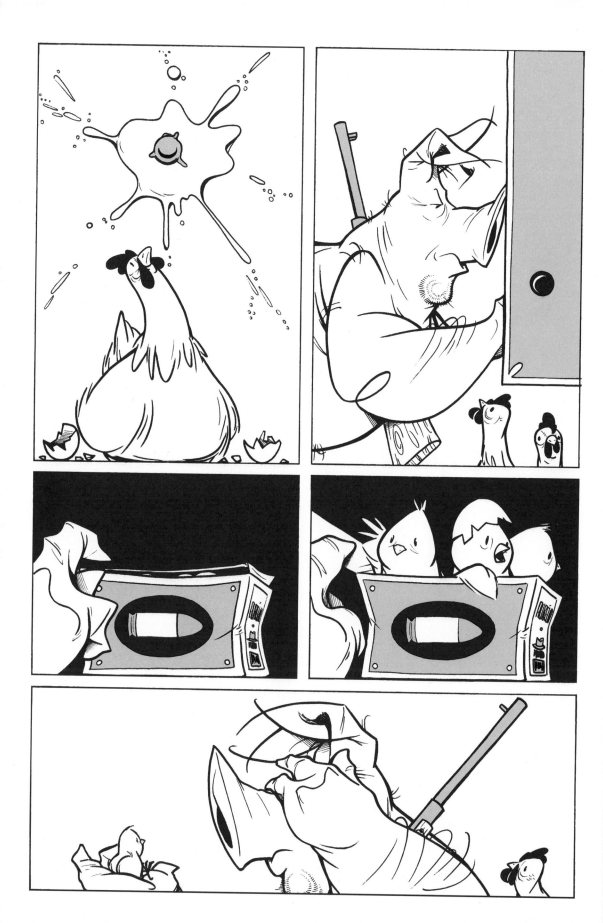

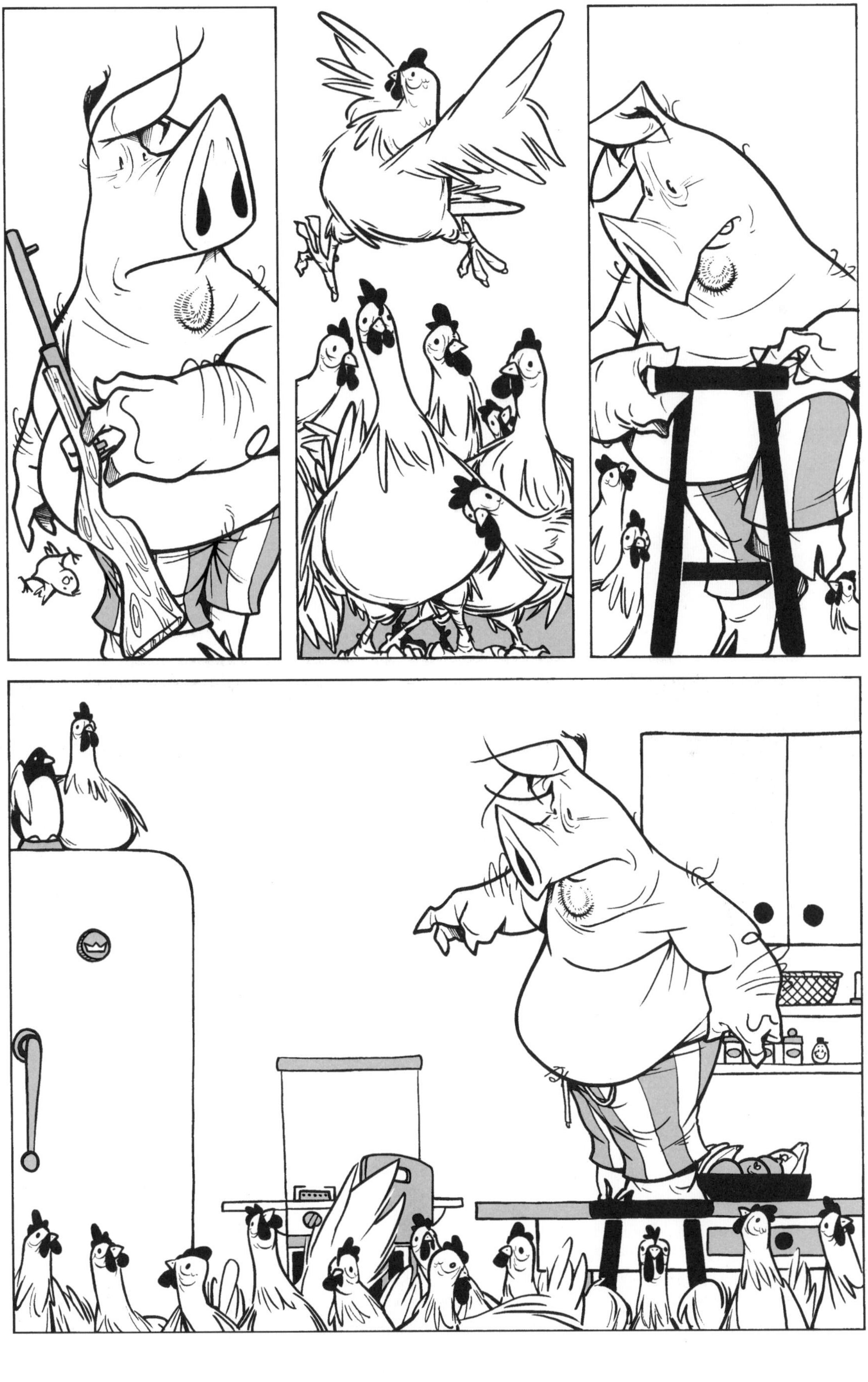

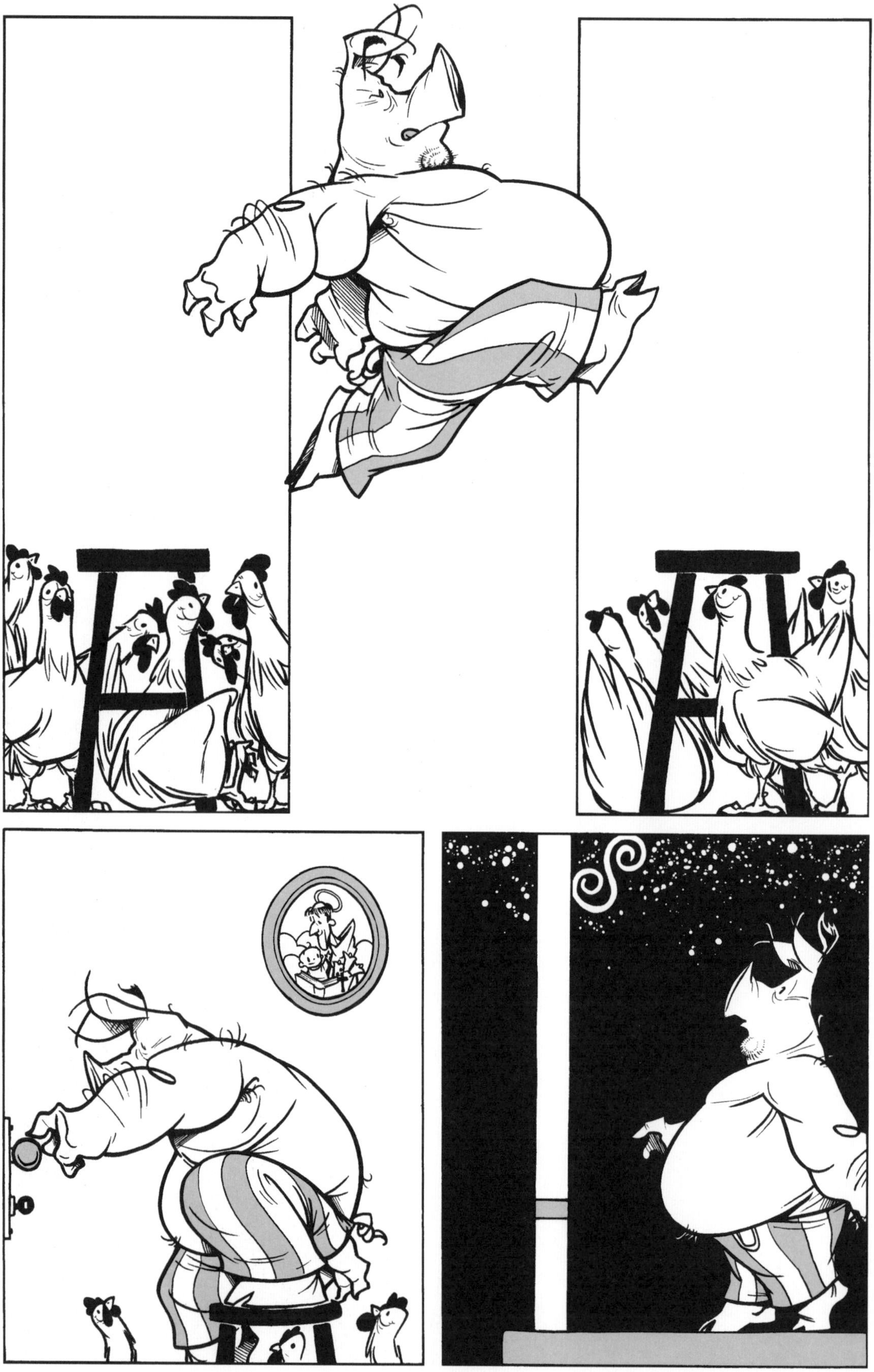

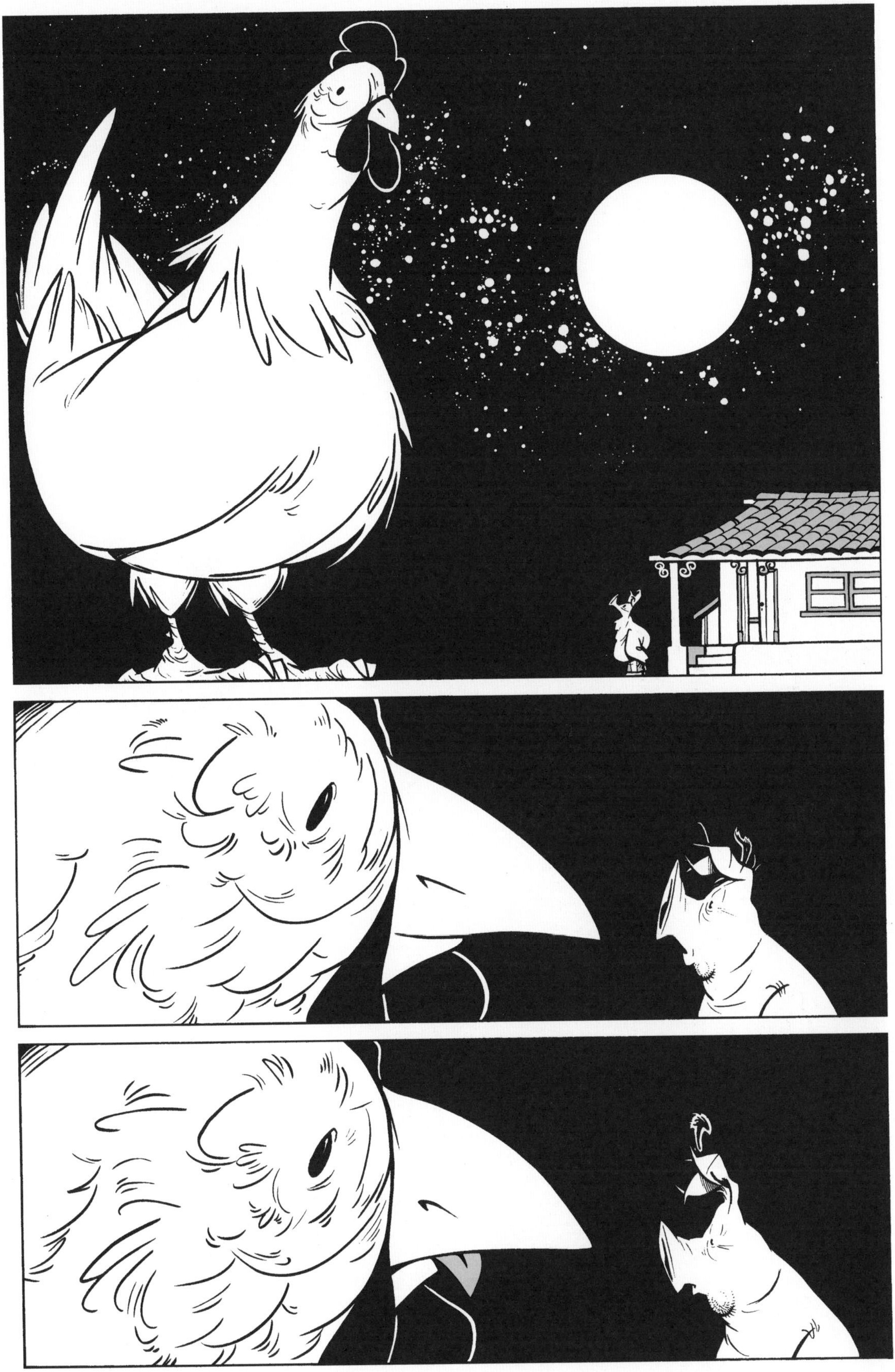

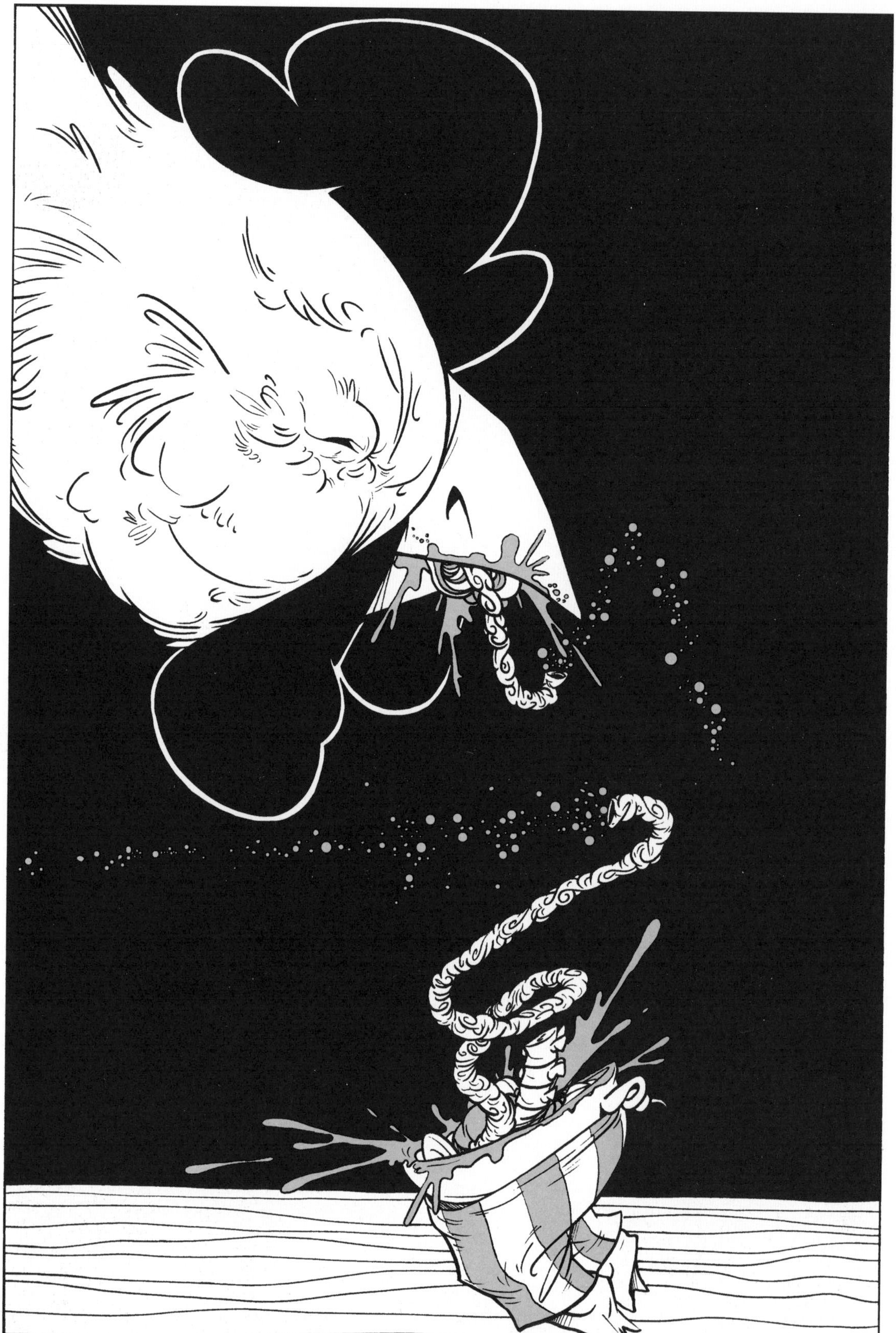

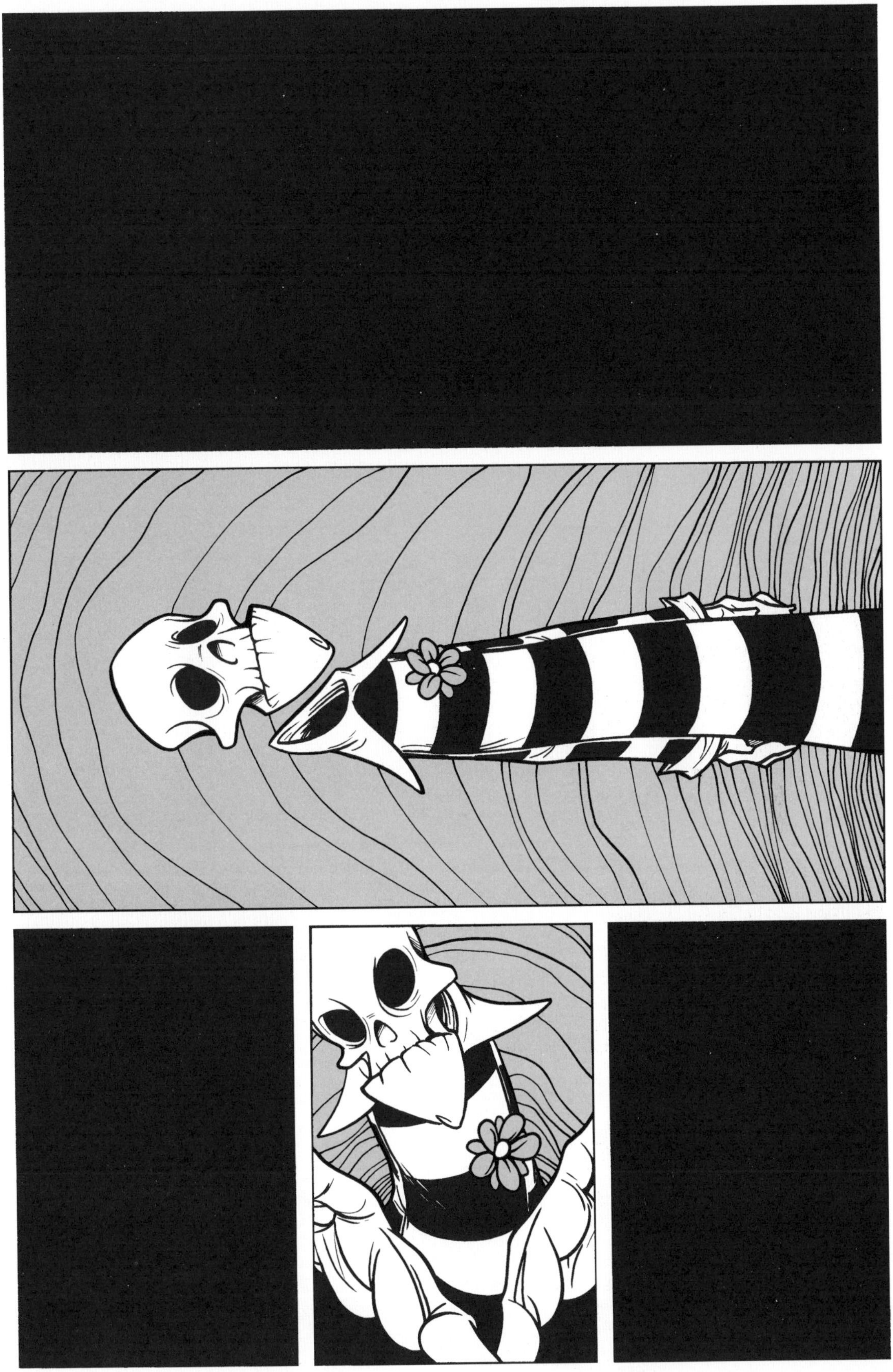

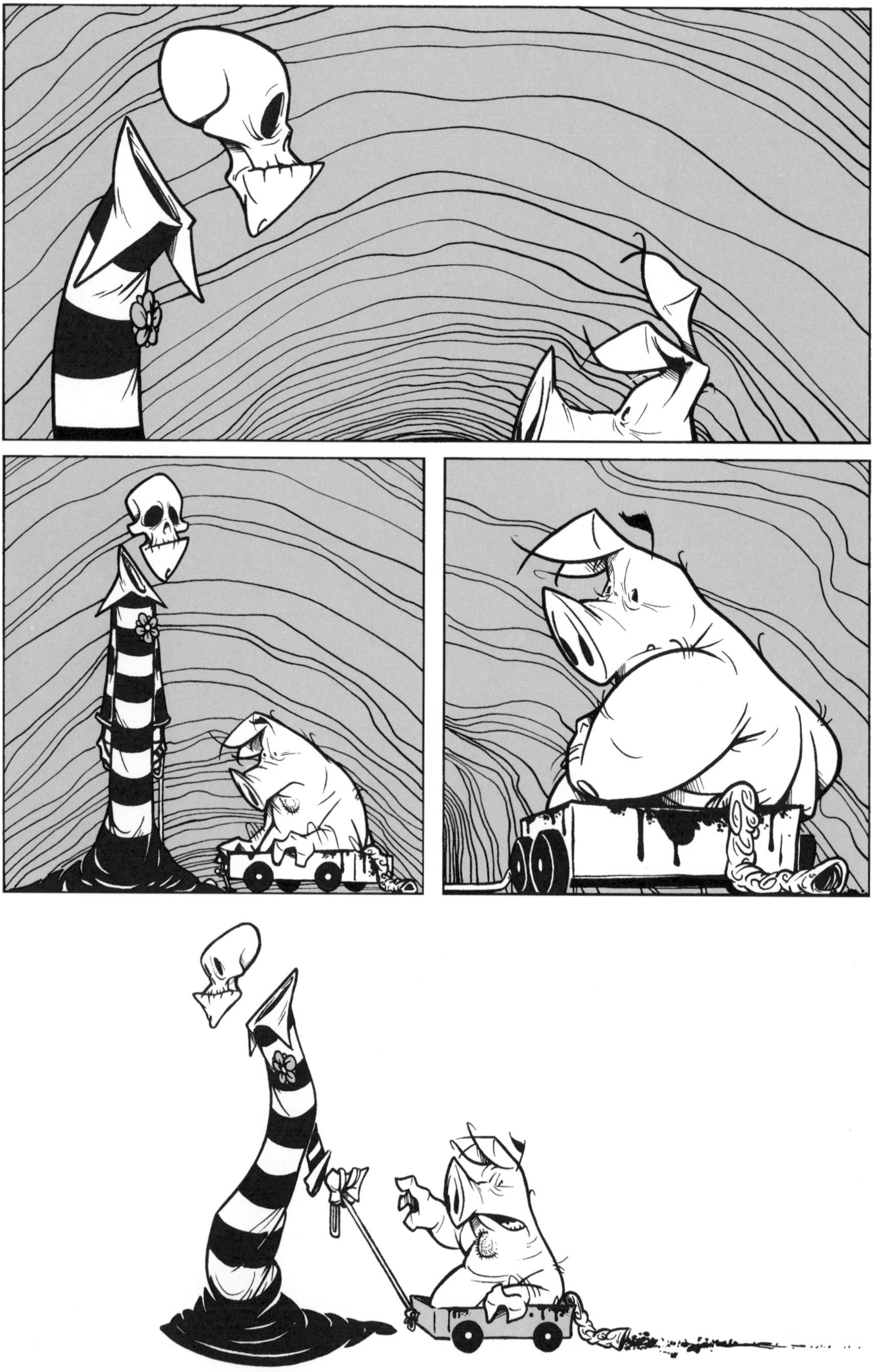

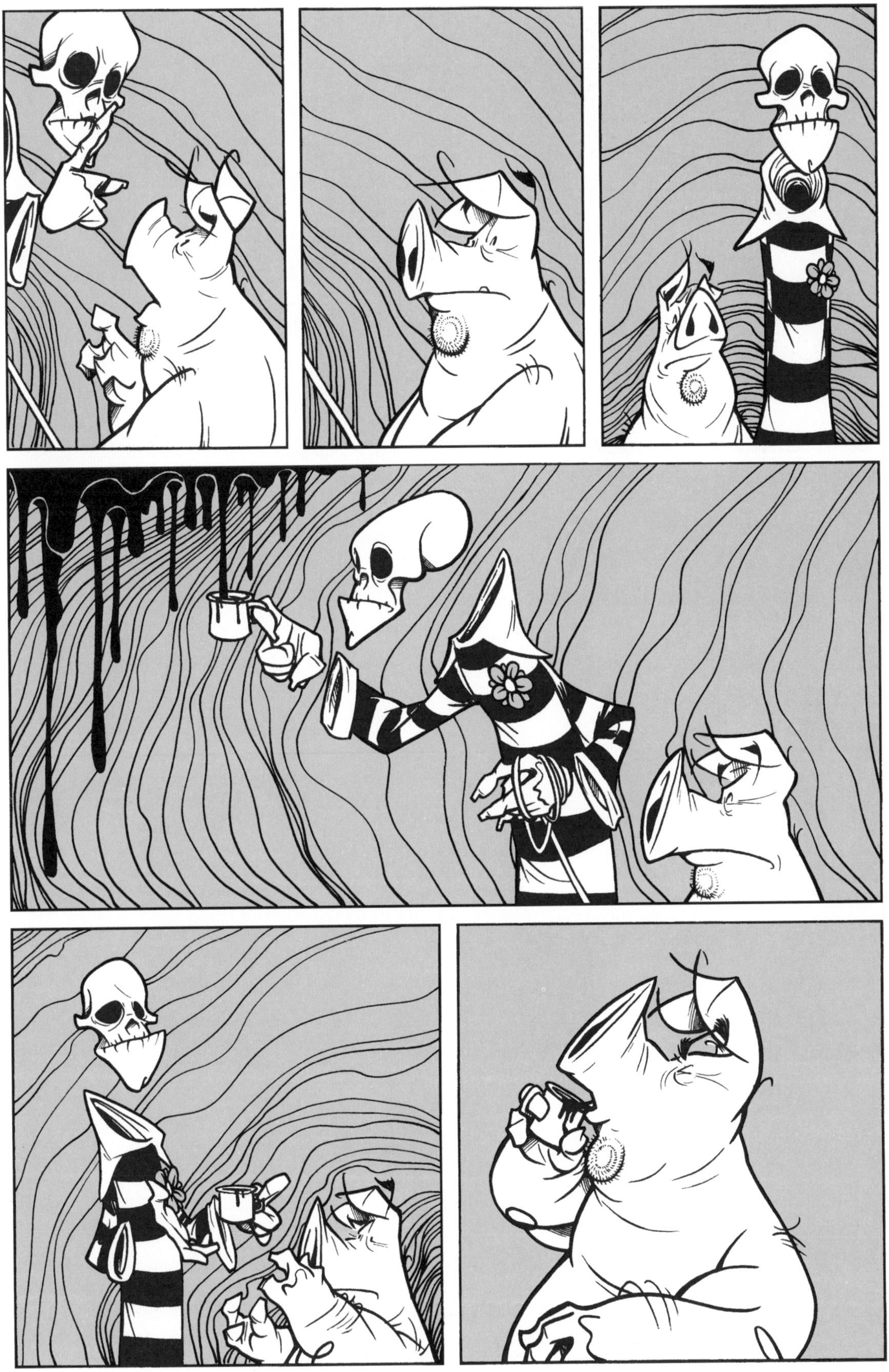

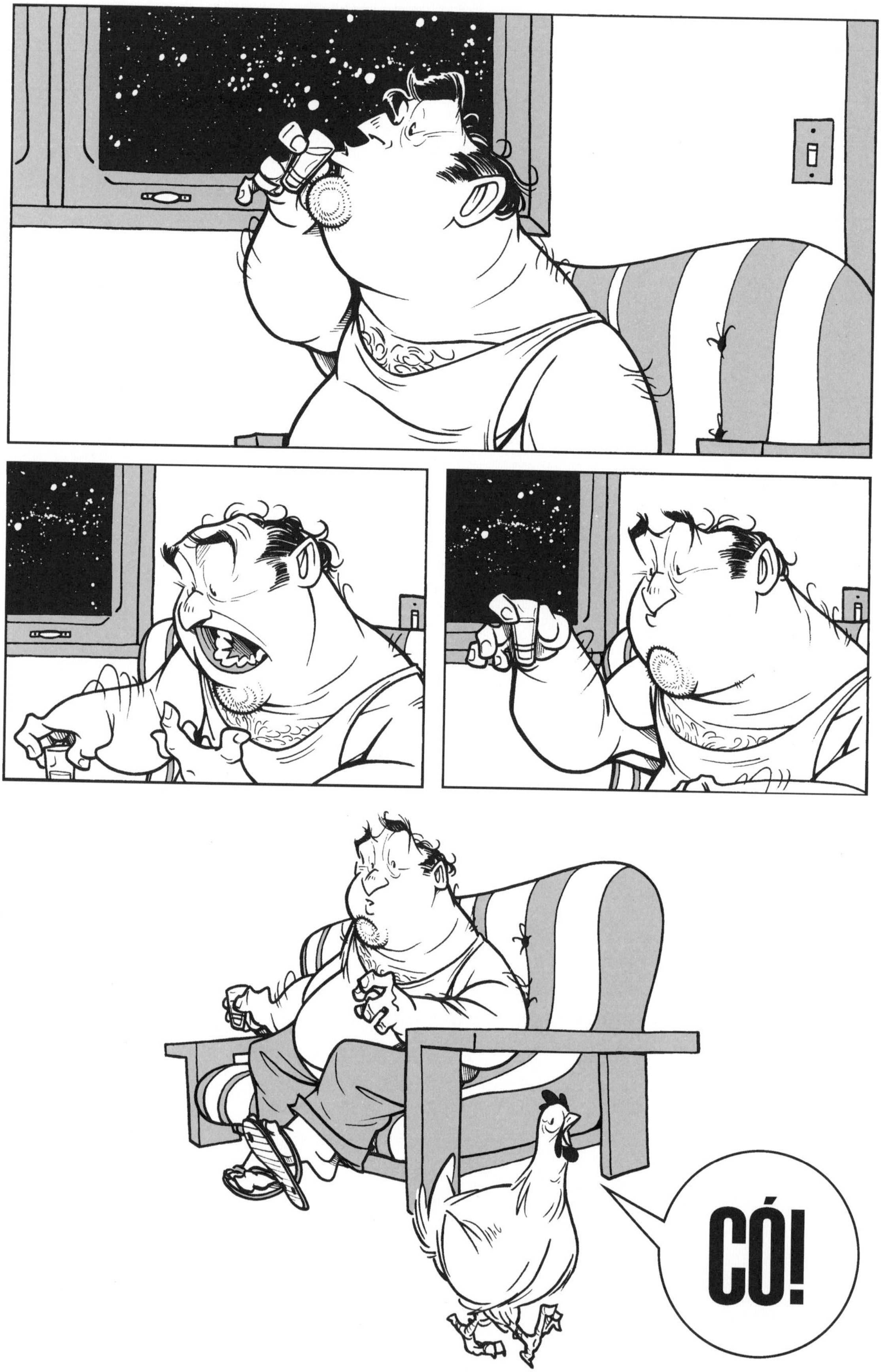
CÓ!

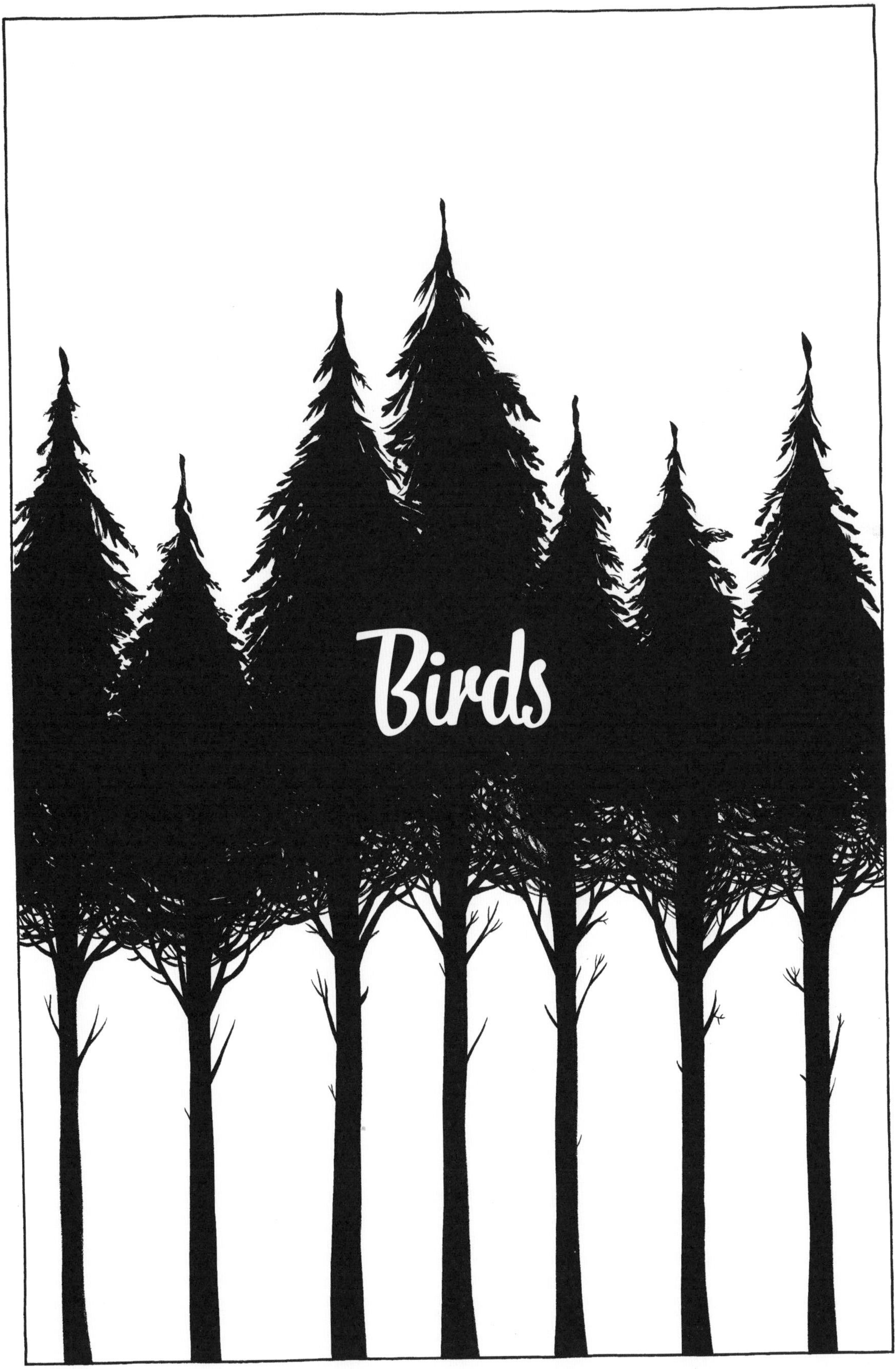
Birds

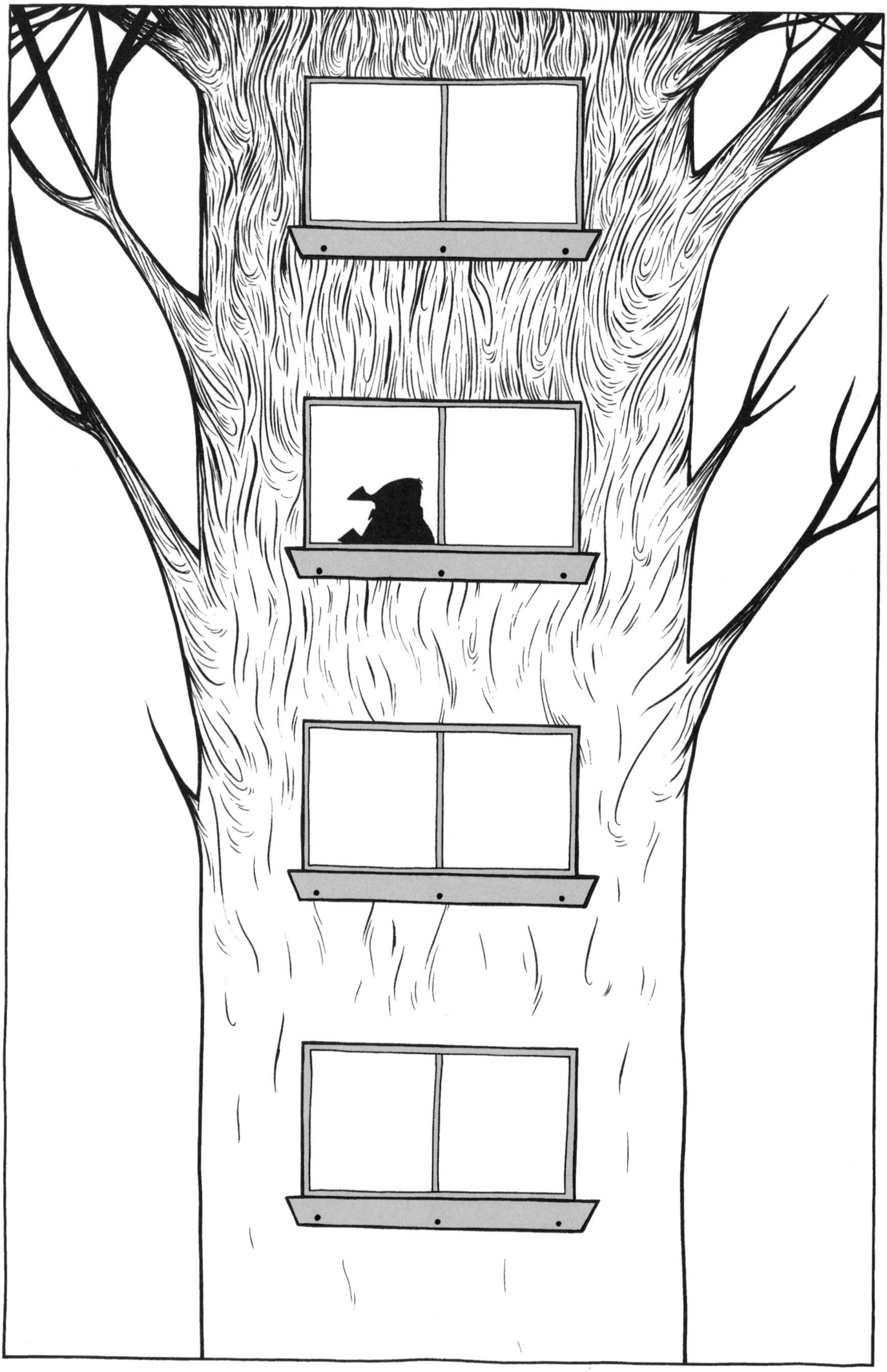

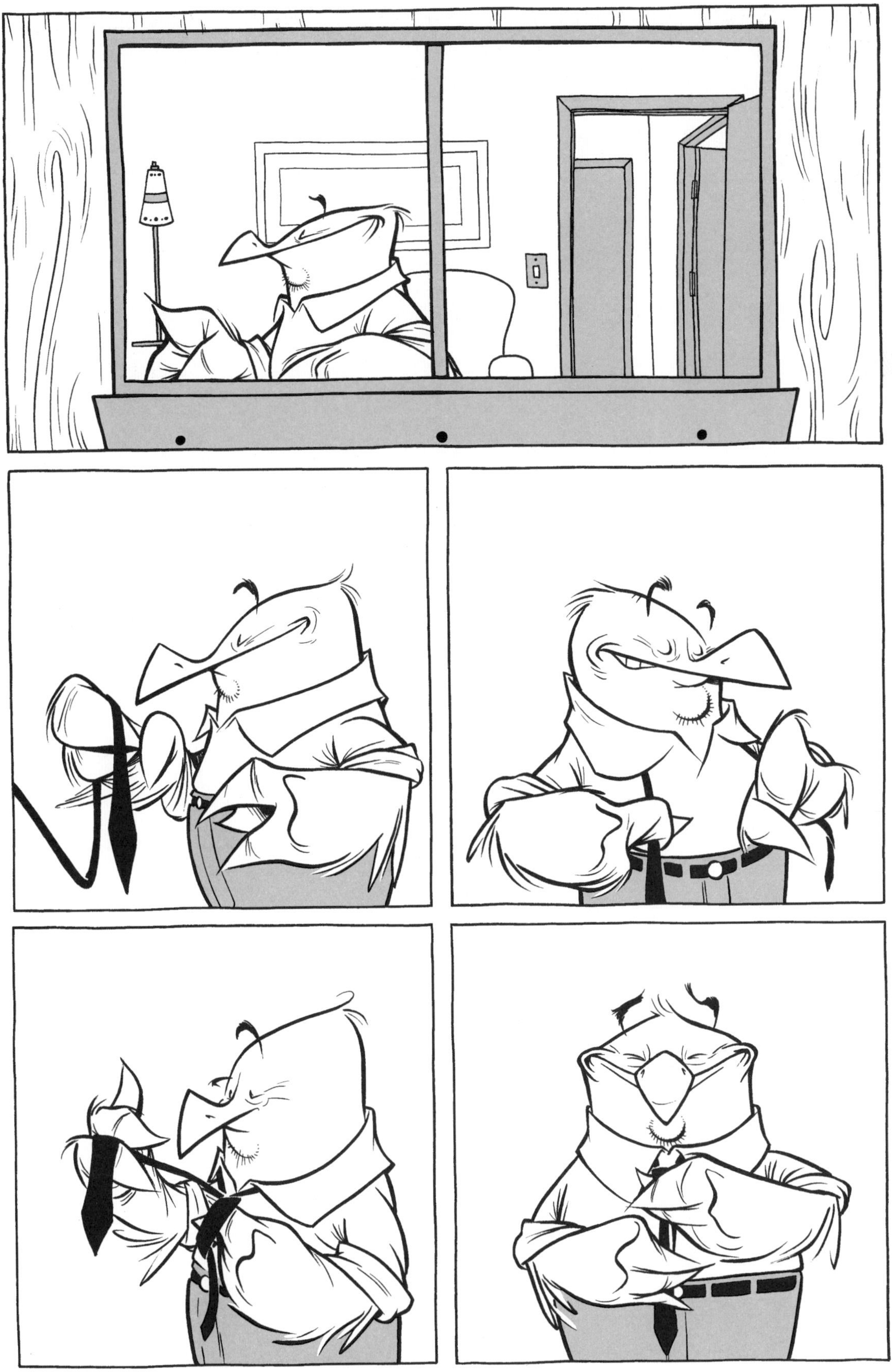

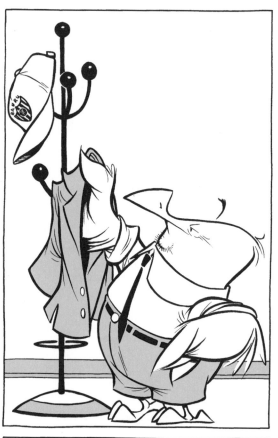

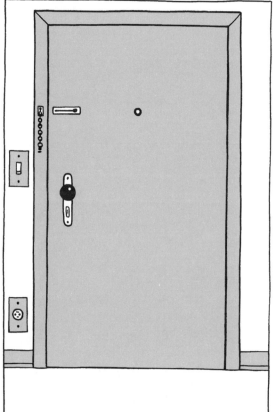
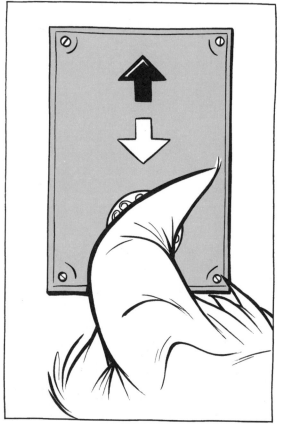

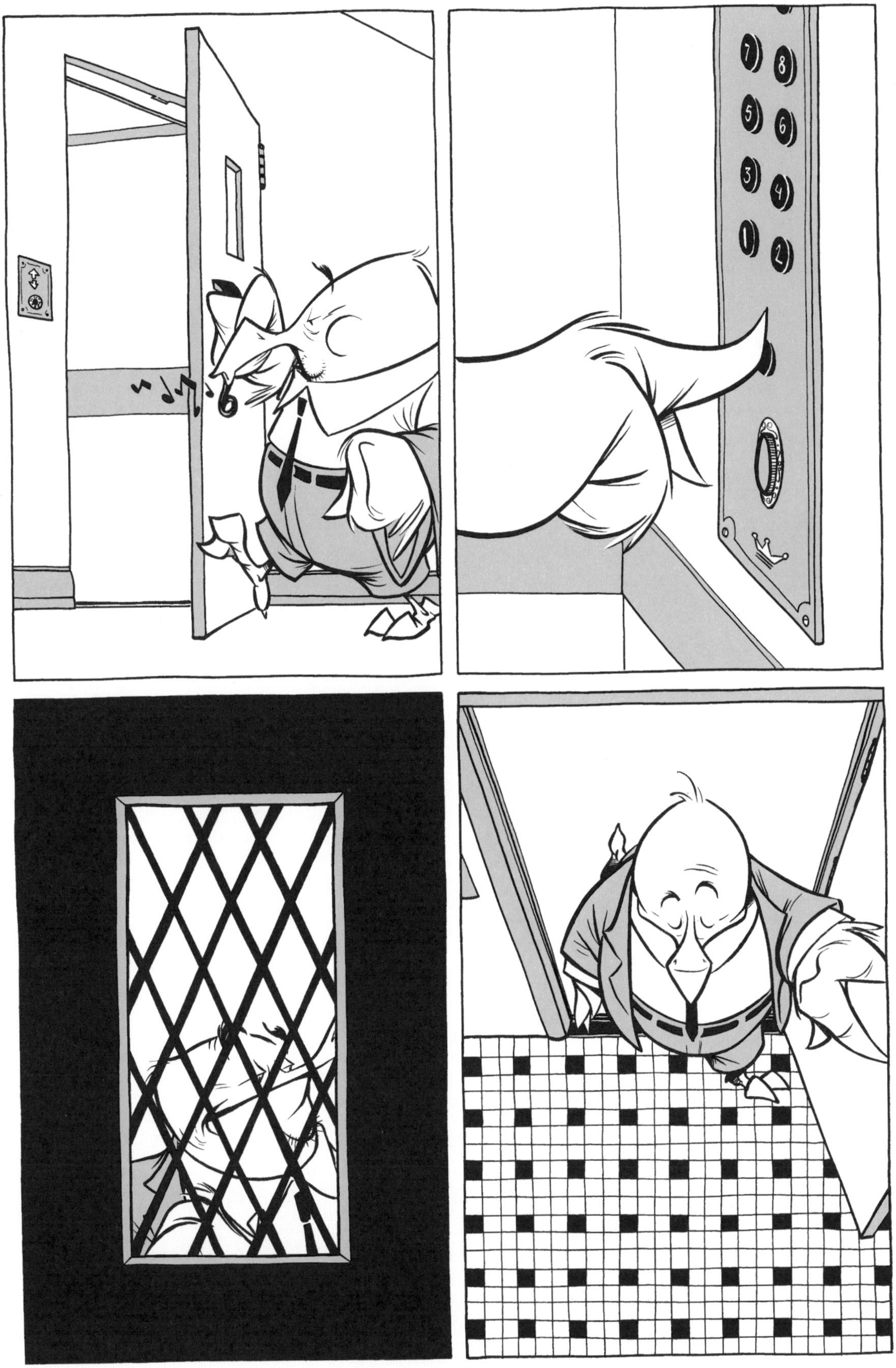

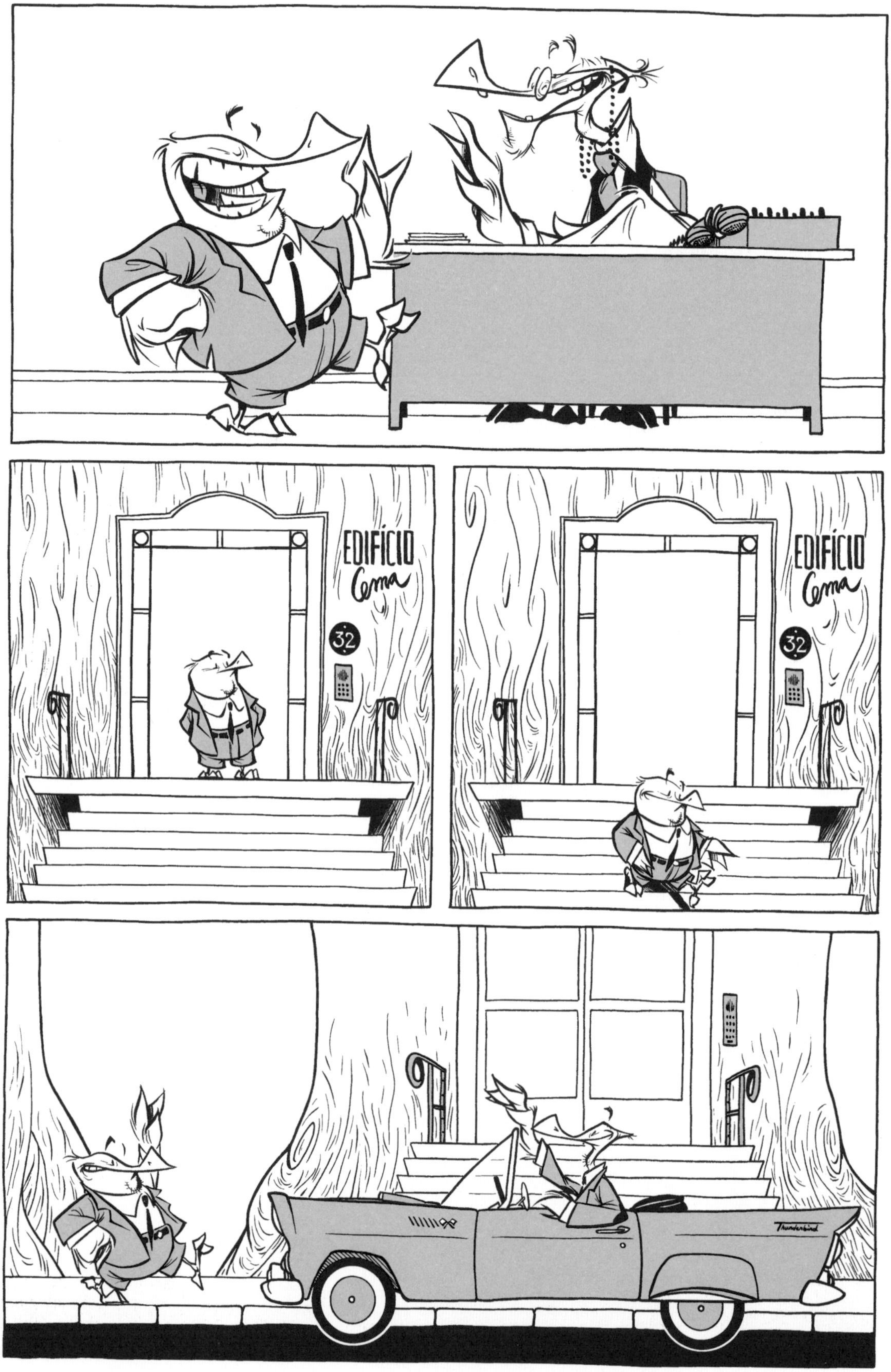
EDIFÍCIO
Cema
32
EDIFÍCIO
Cema
32
Thunderbird

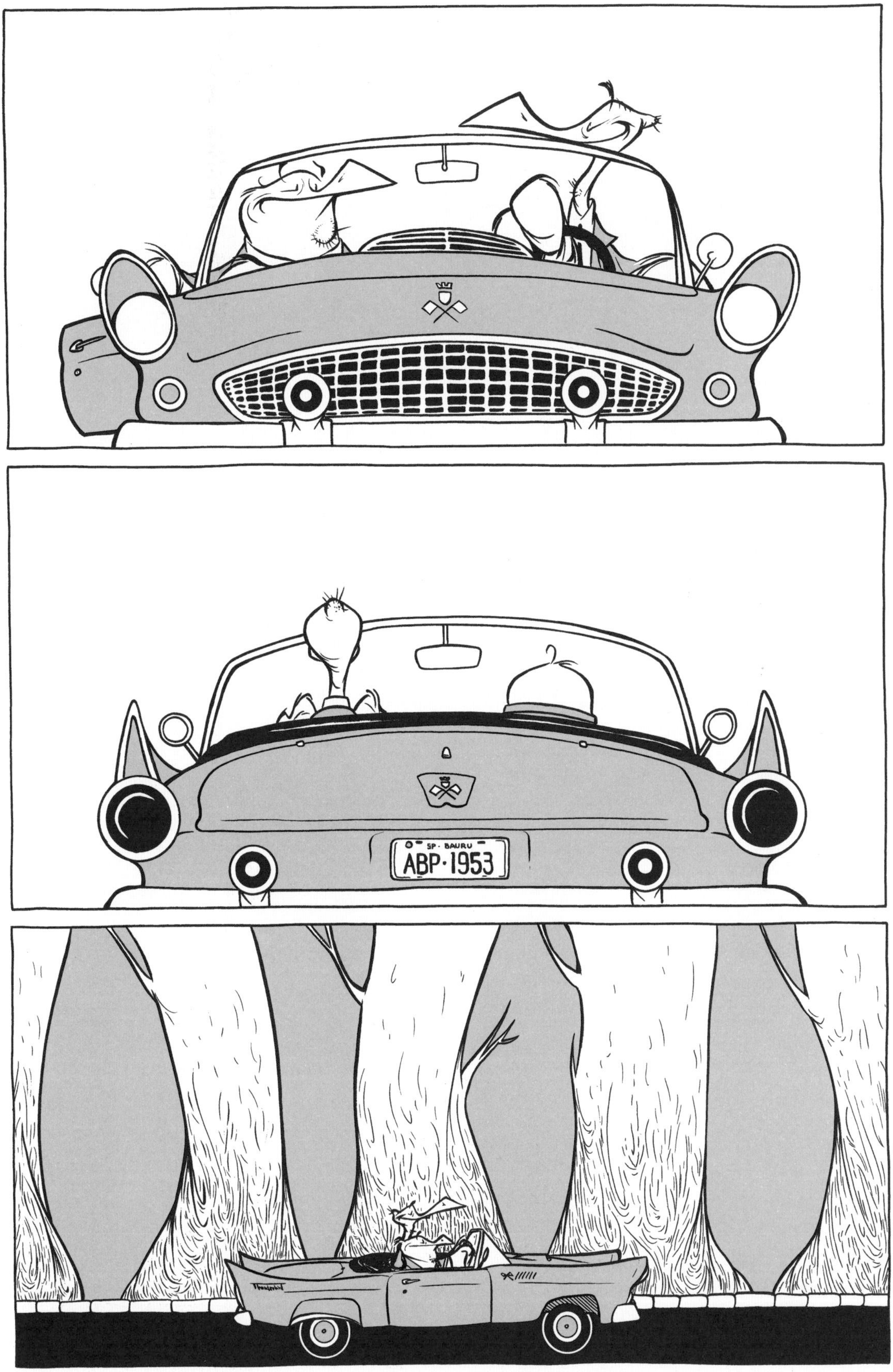
SP · BAURU
ABP·1953

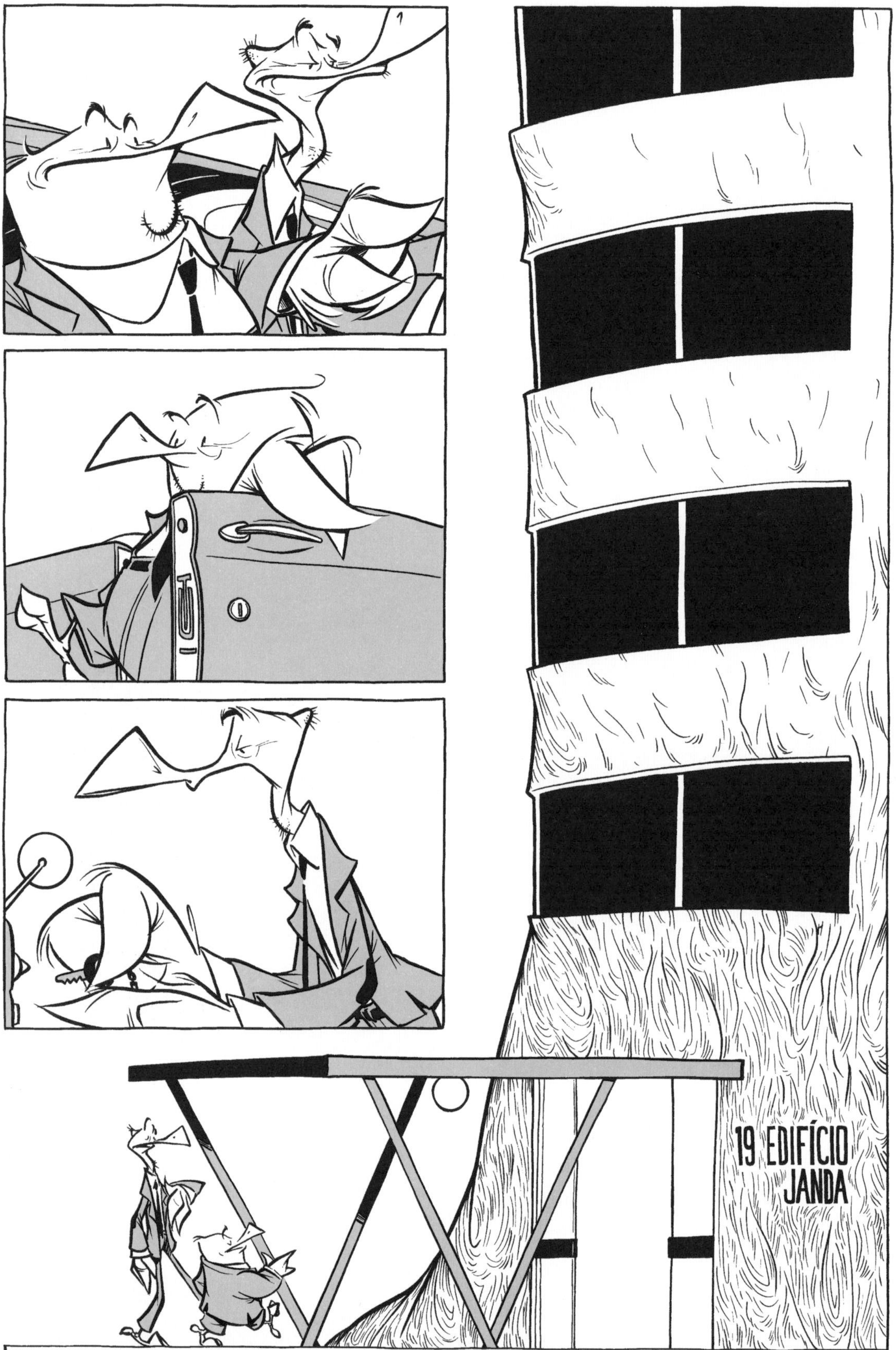
19 EDIFÍCIO
JANDA

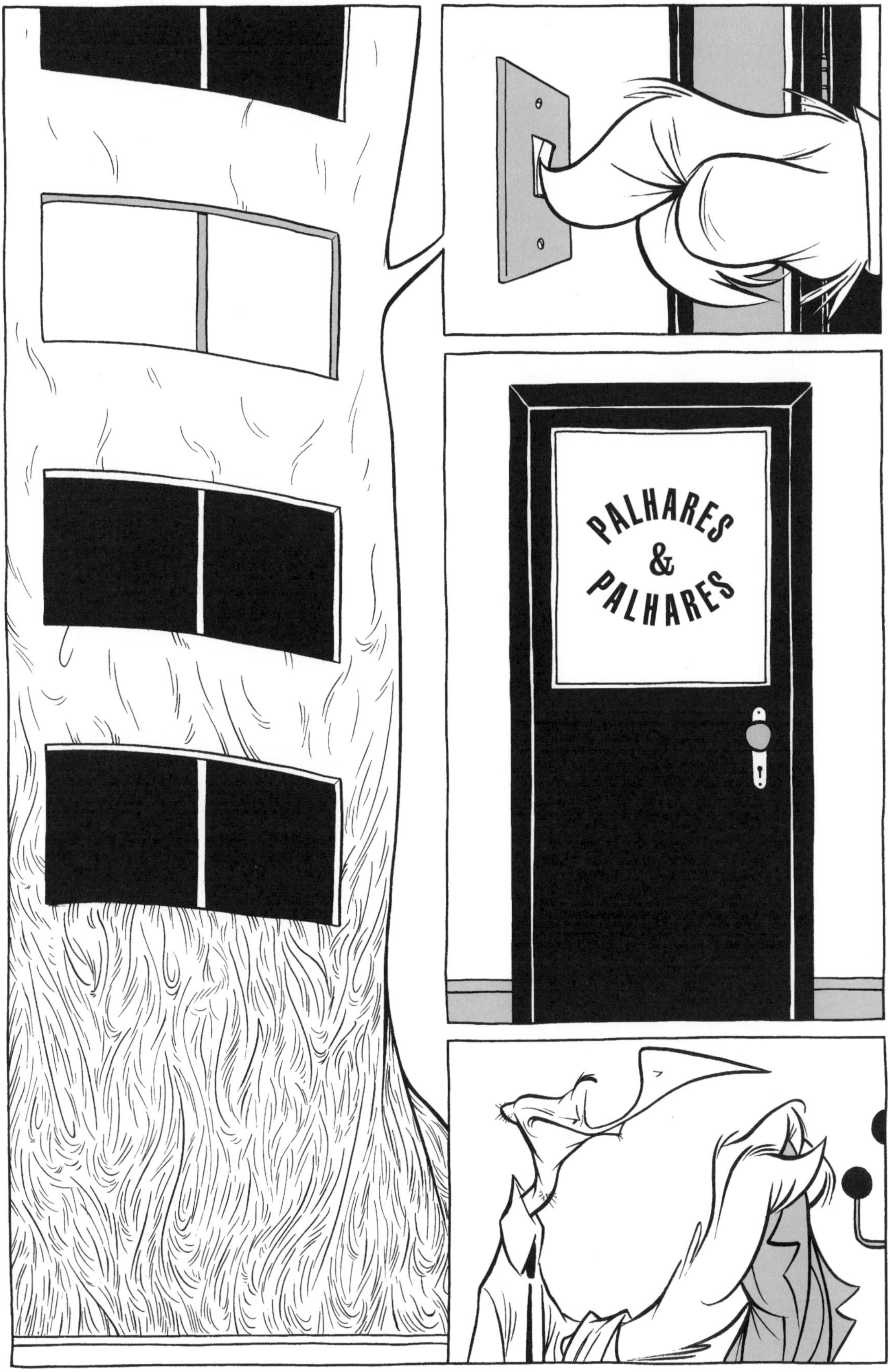
PALHARES
&
PALHARES

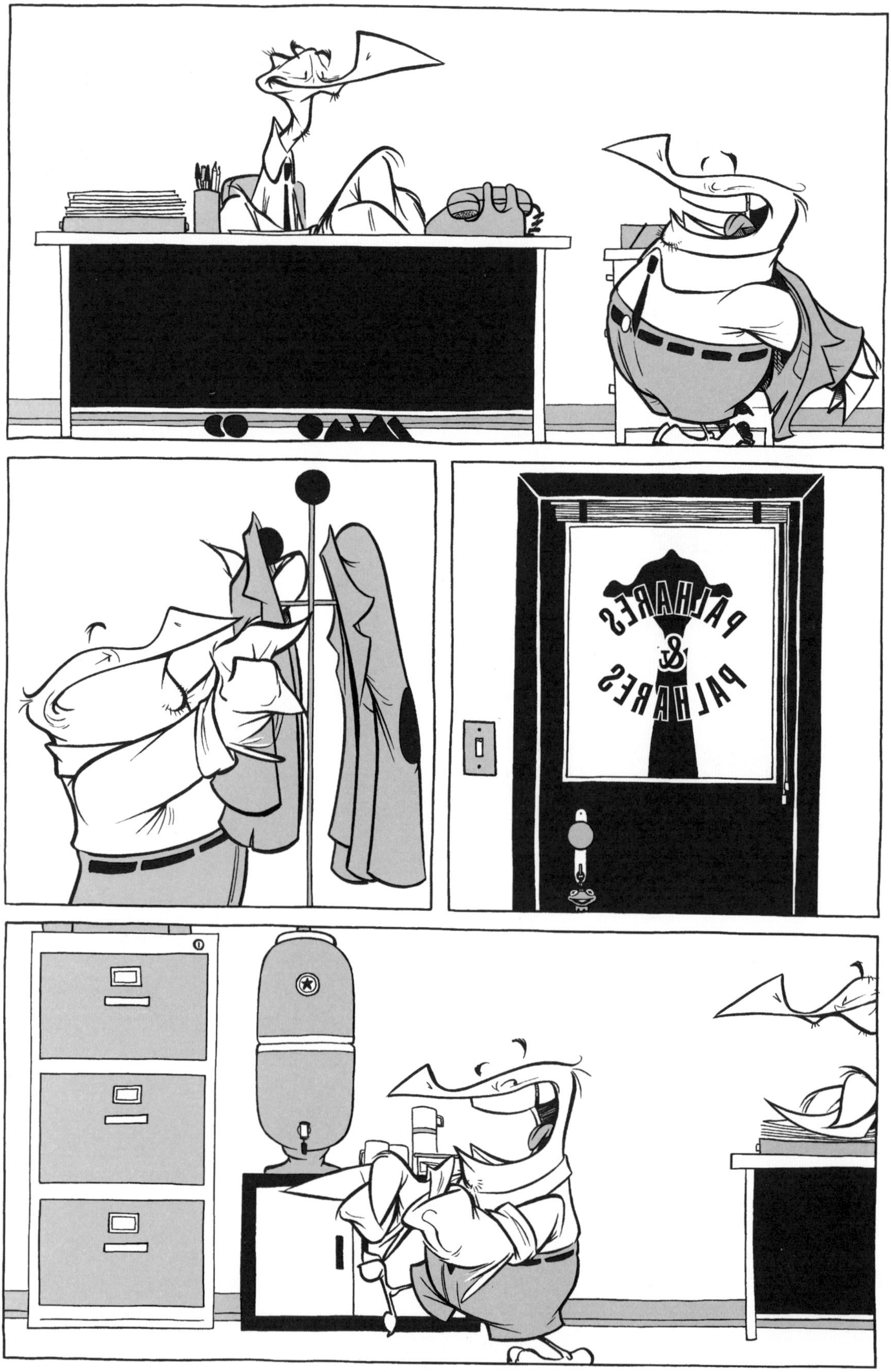
PALHARES
&
PALHARES

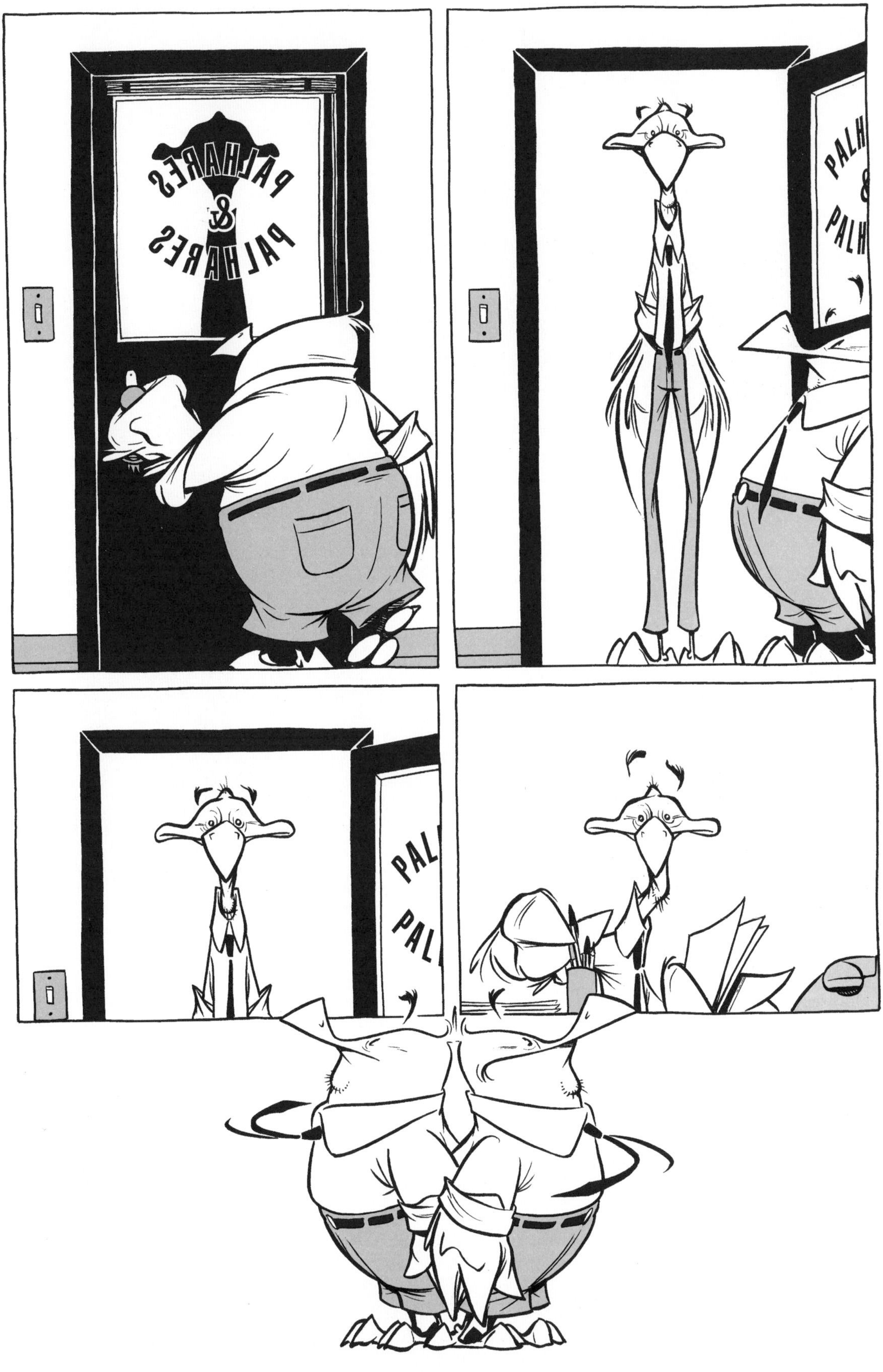

PALHARES
&
PALHARES
PALH
&
PALHA
PAL
PAL

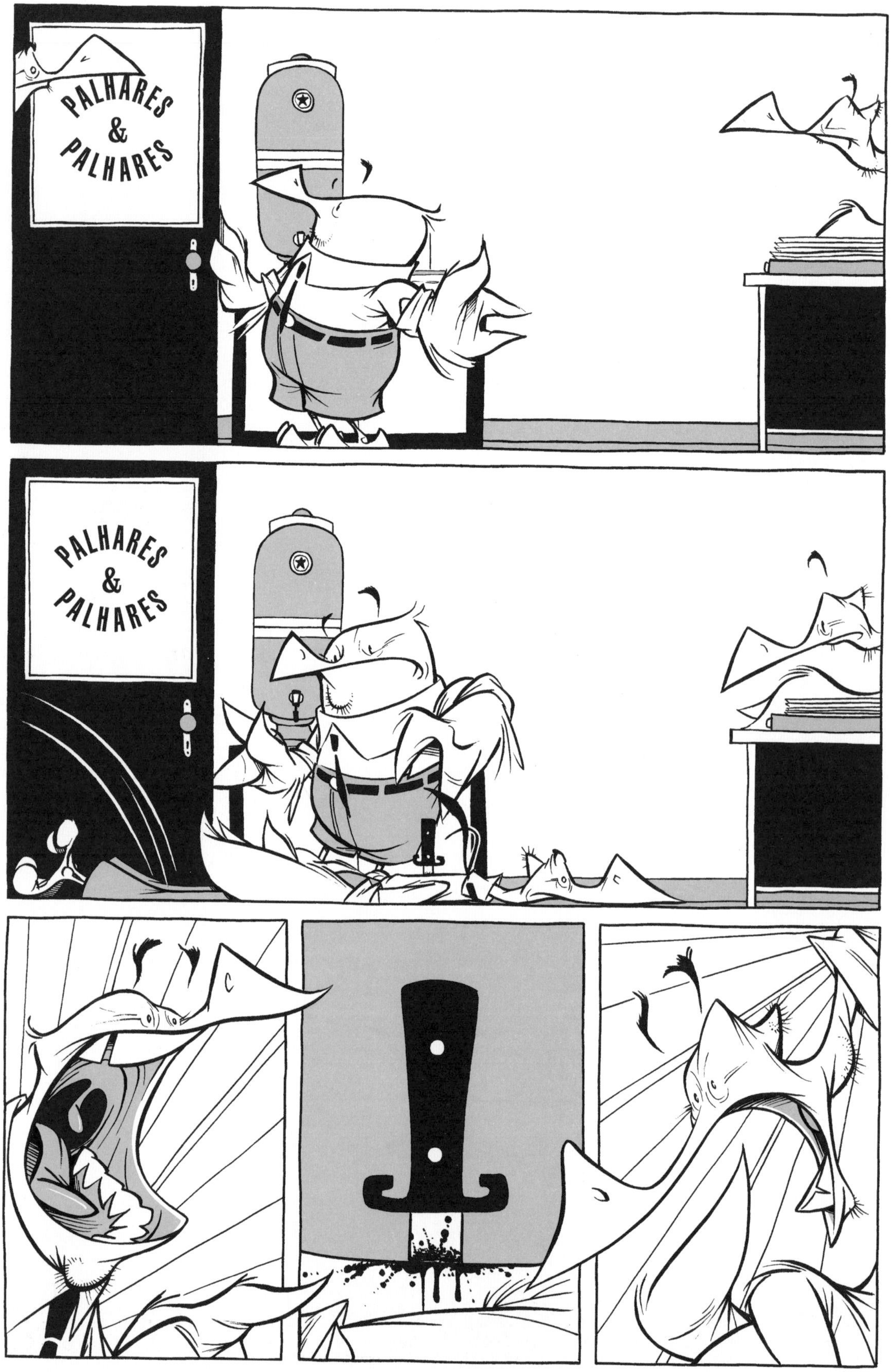
PALHARES & PALHARES
PALHARES & PALHARES

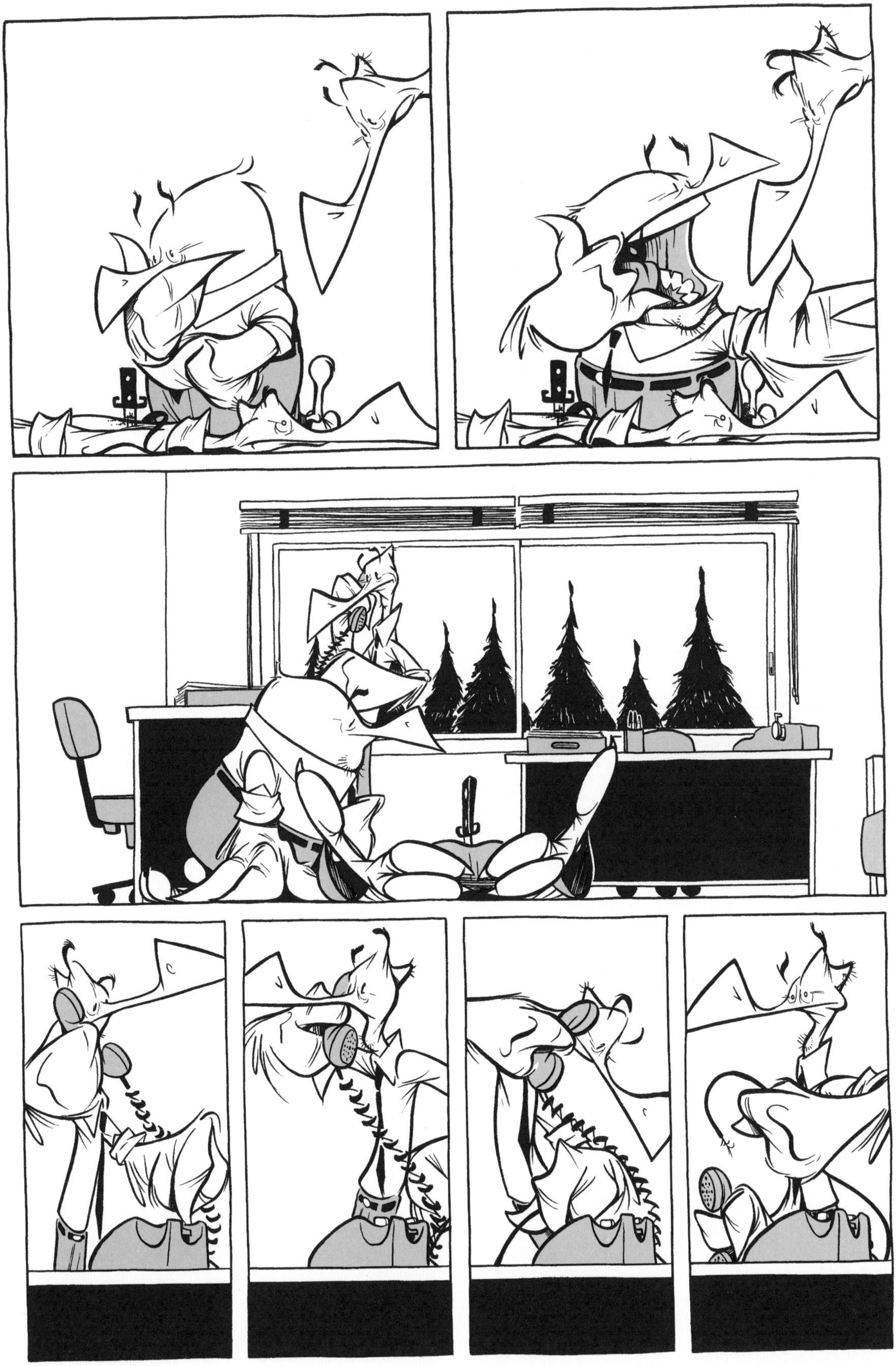

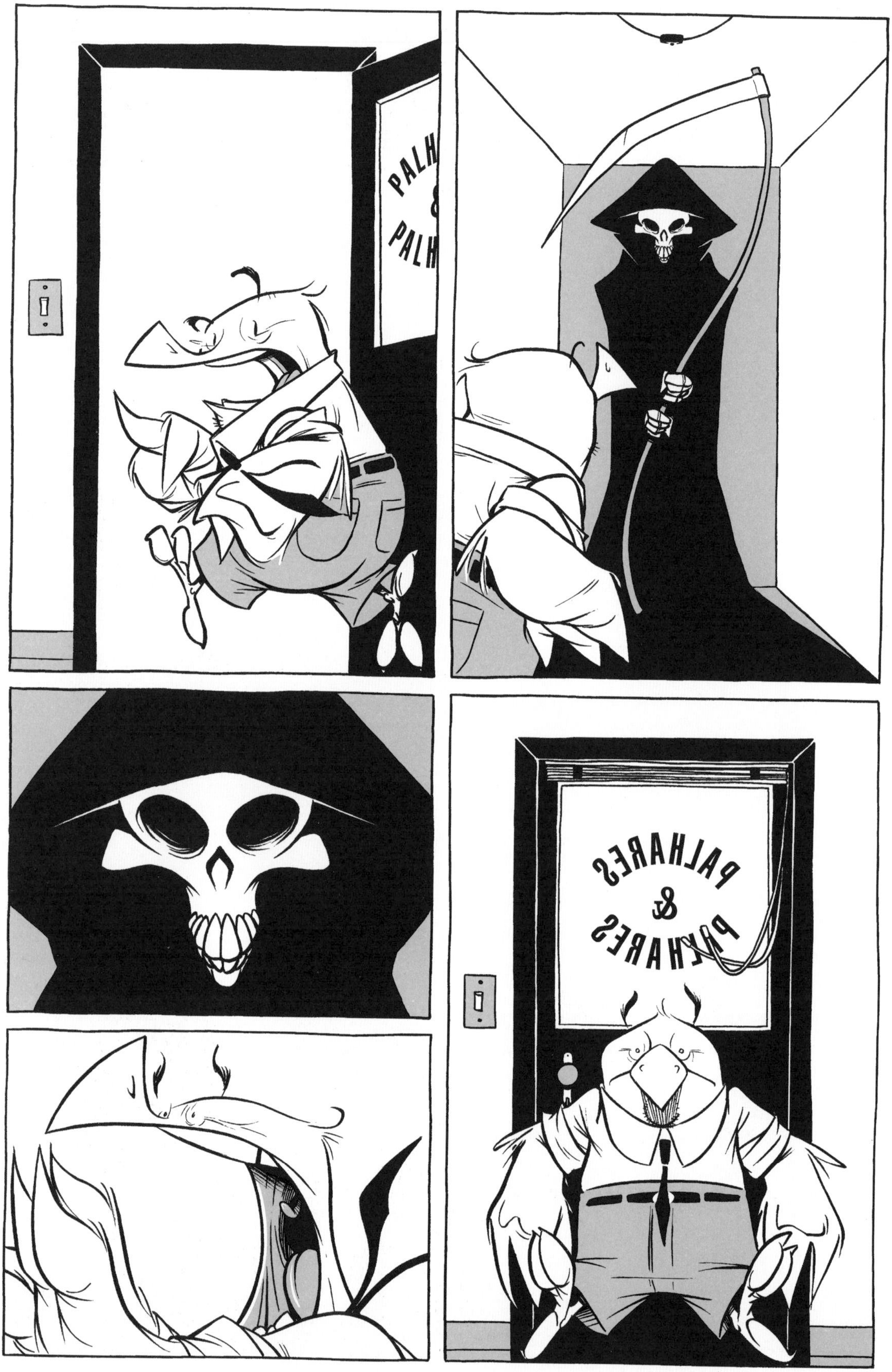
PALH
&
PALH
PALHARES
&

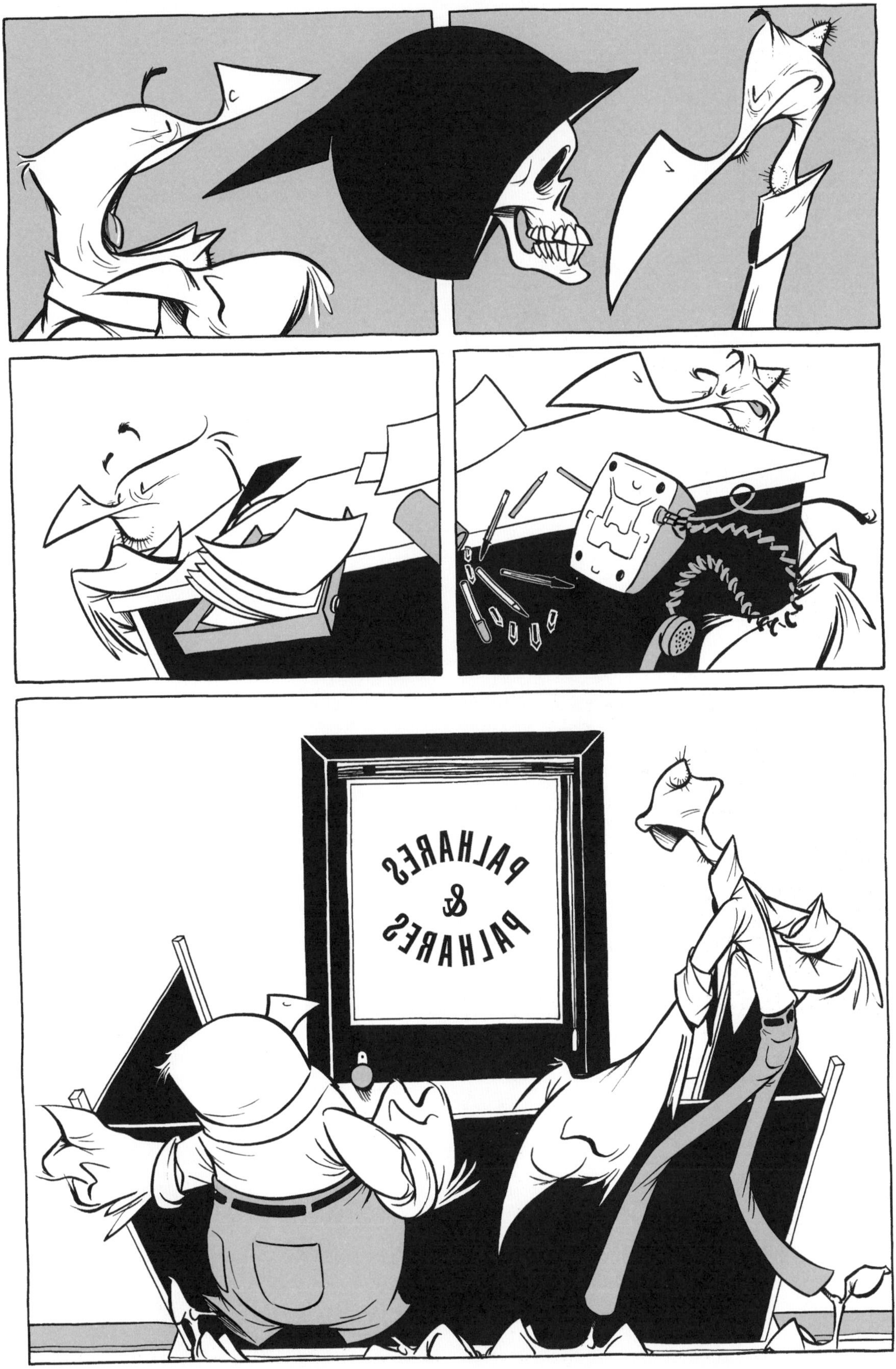
PALHARES
&
PALHARES

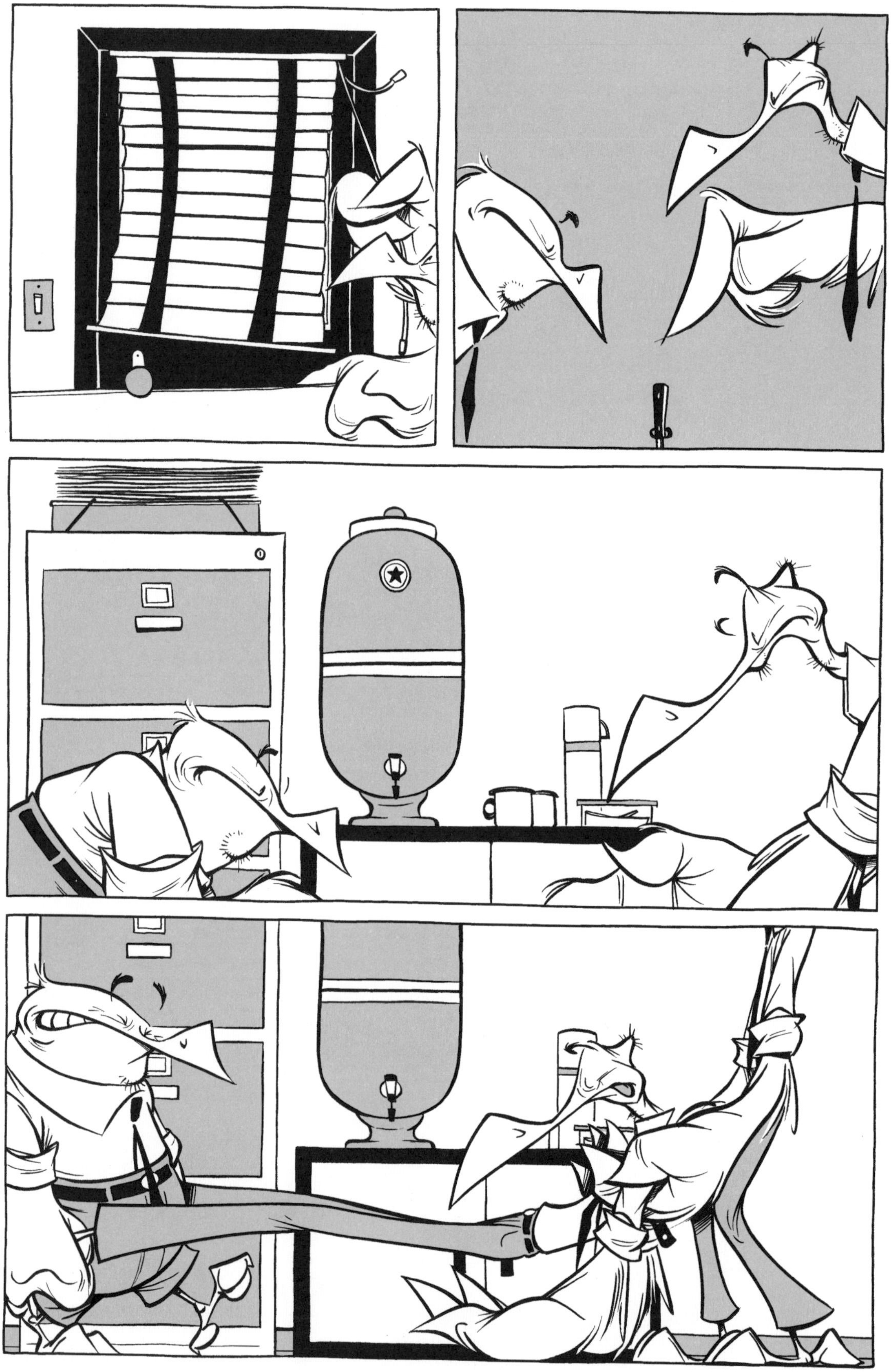

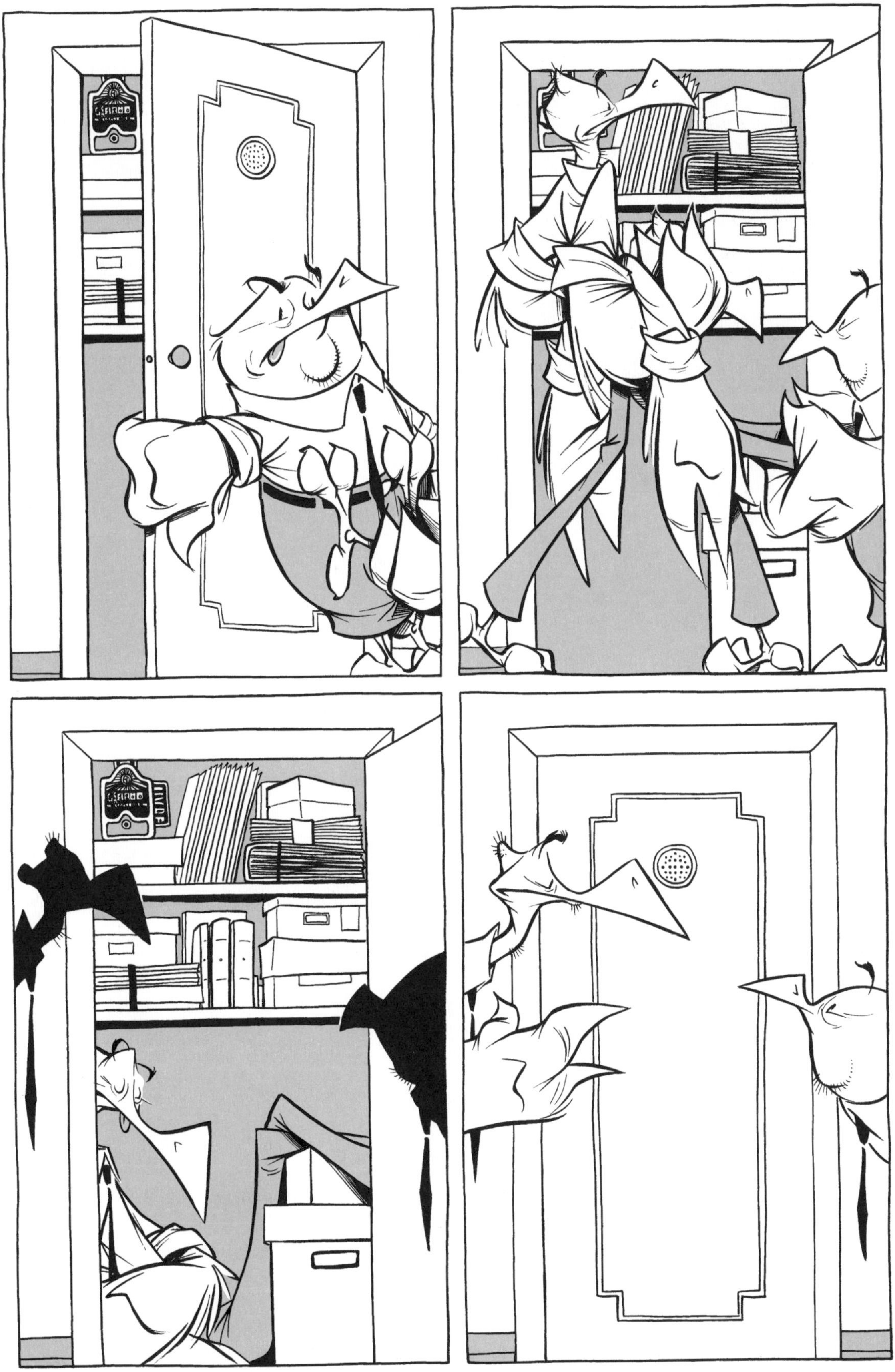

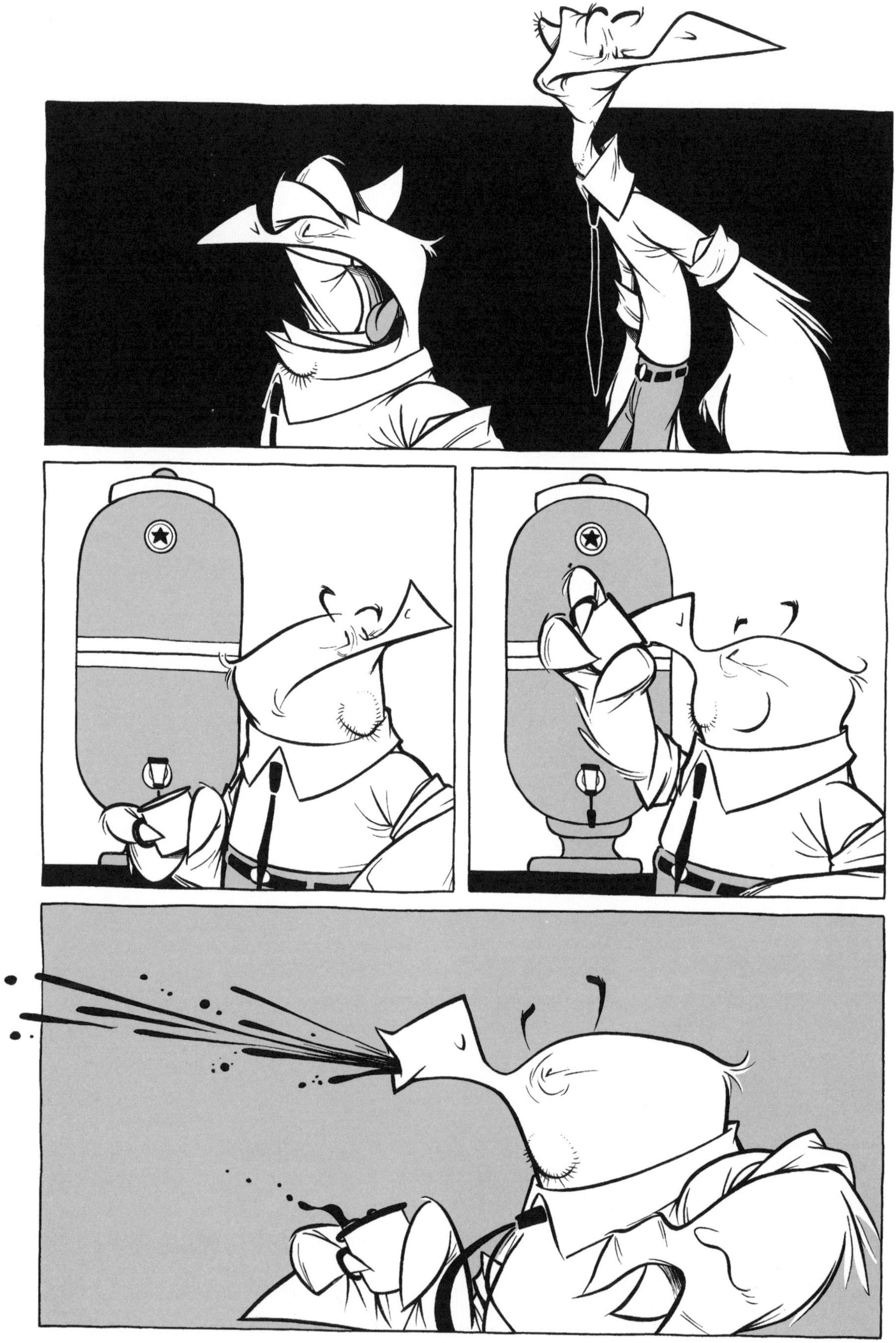

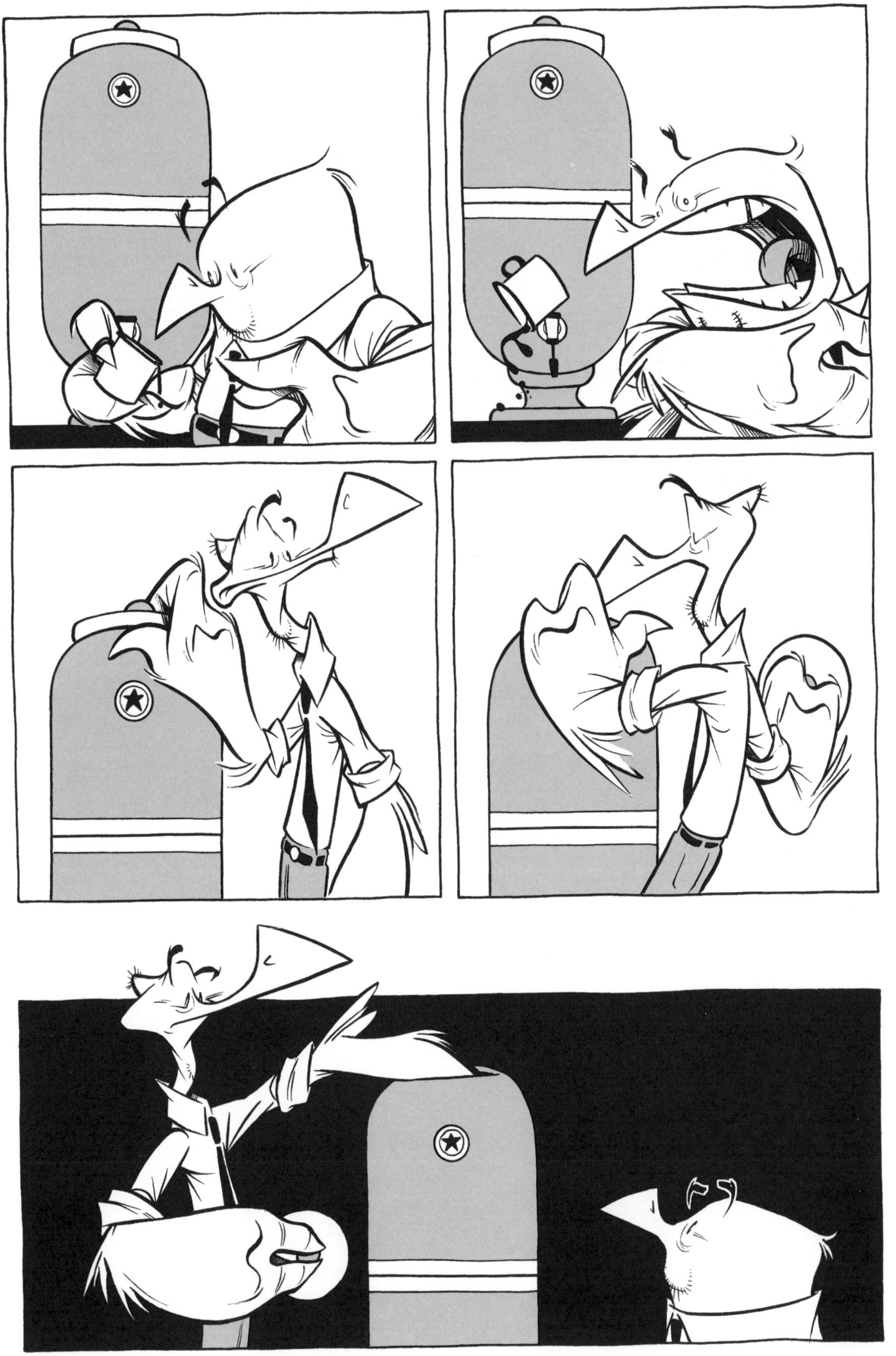

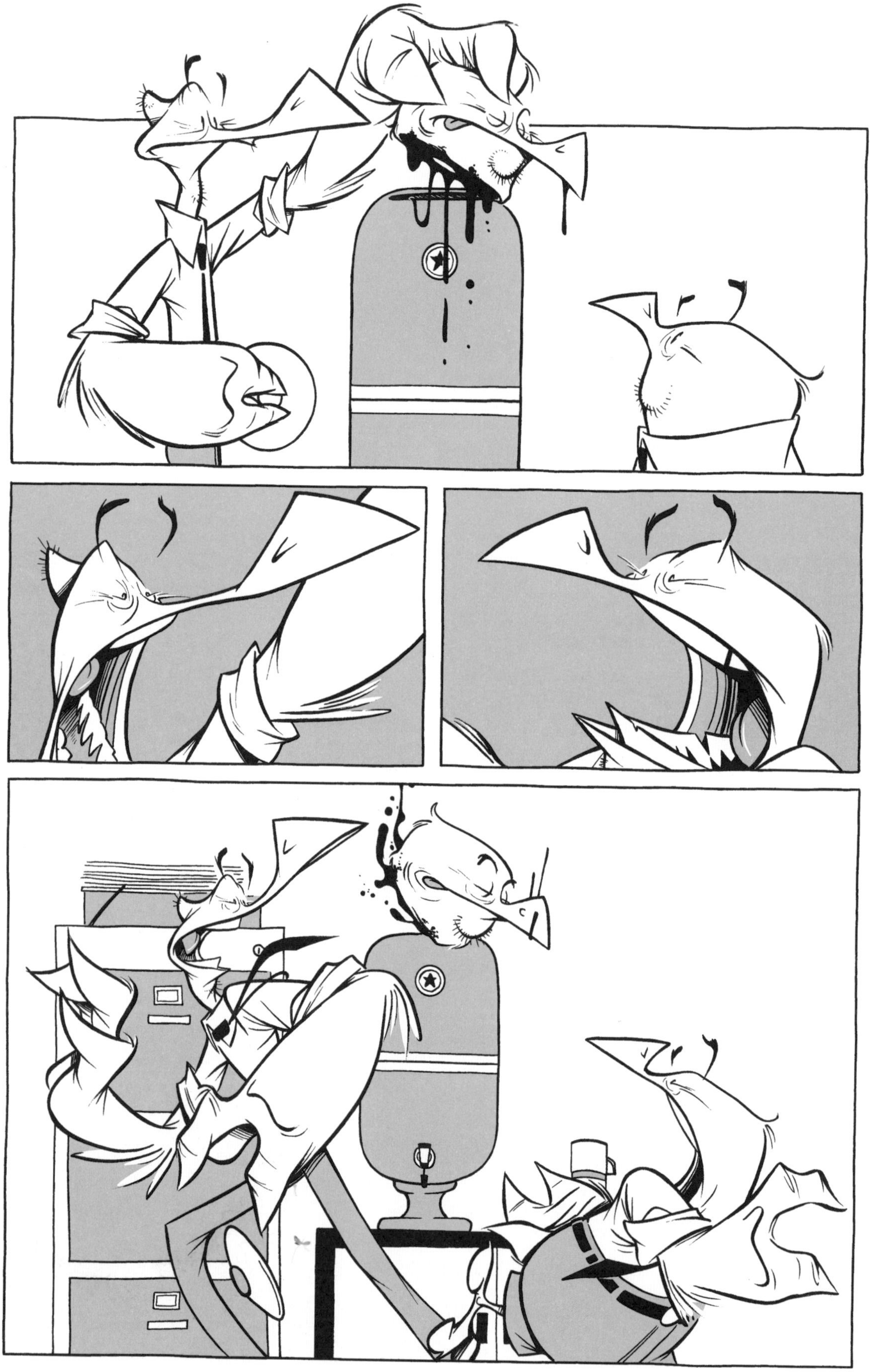

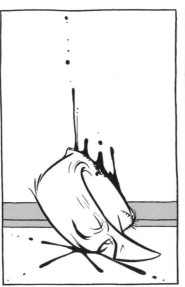

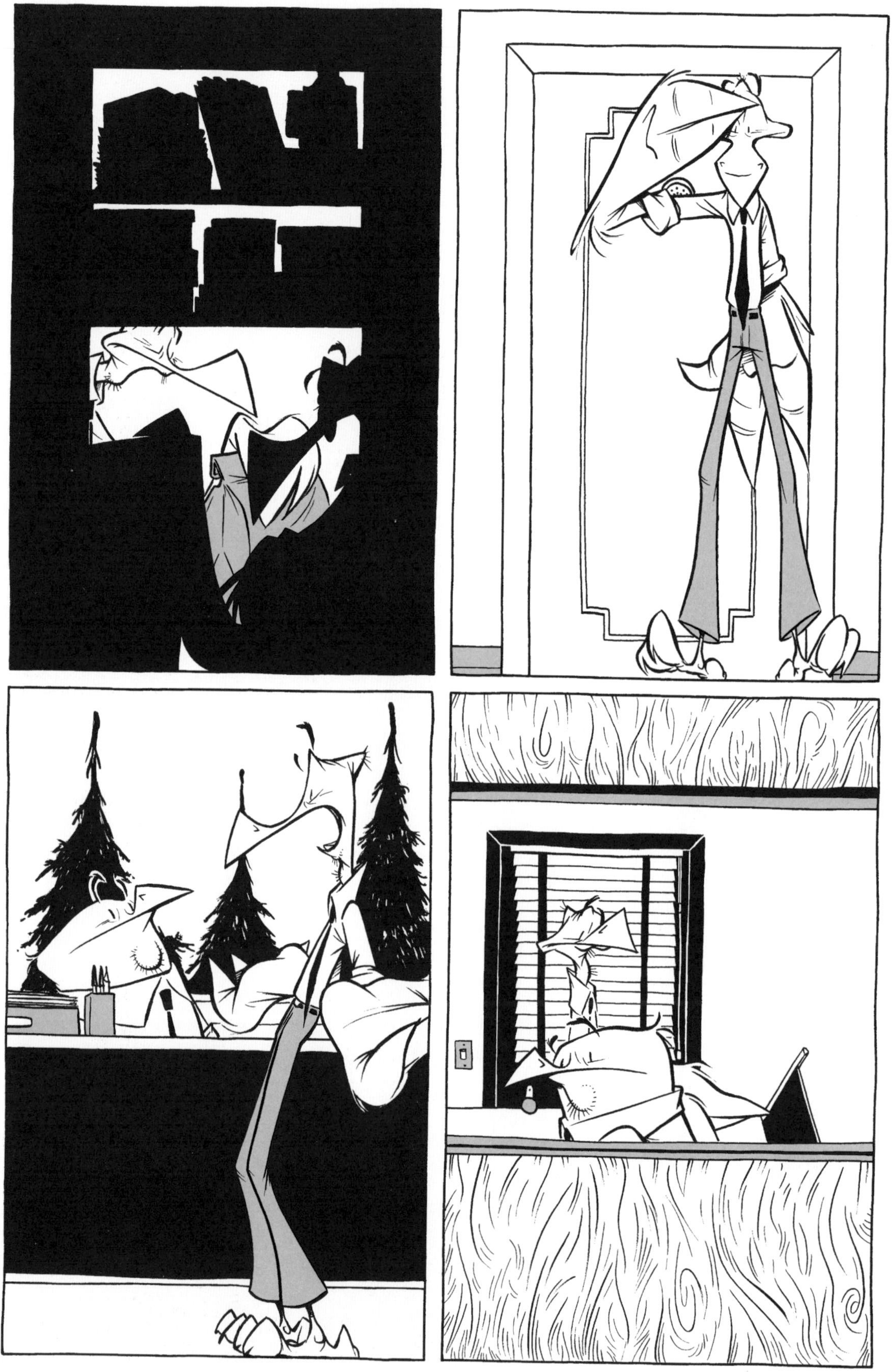

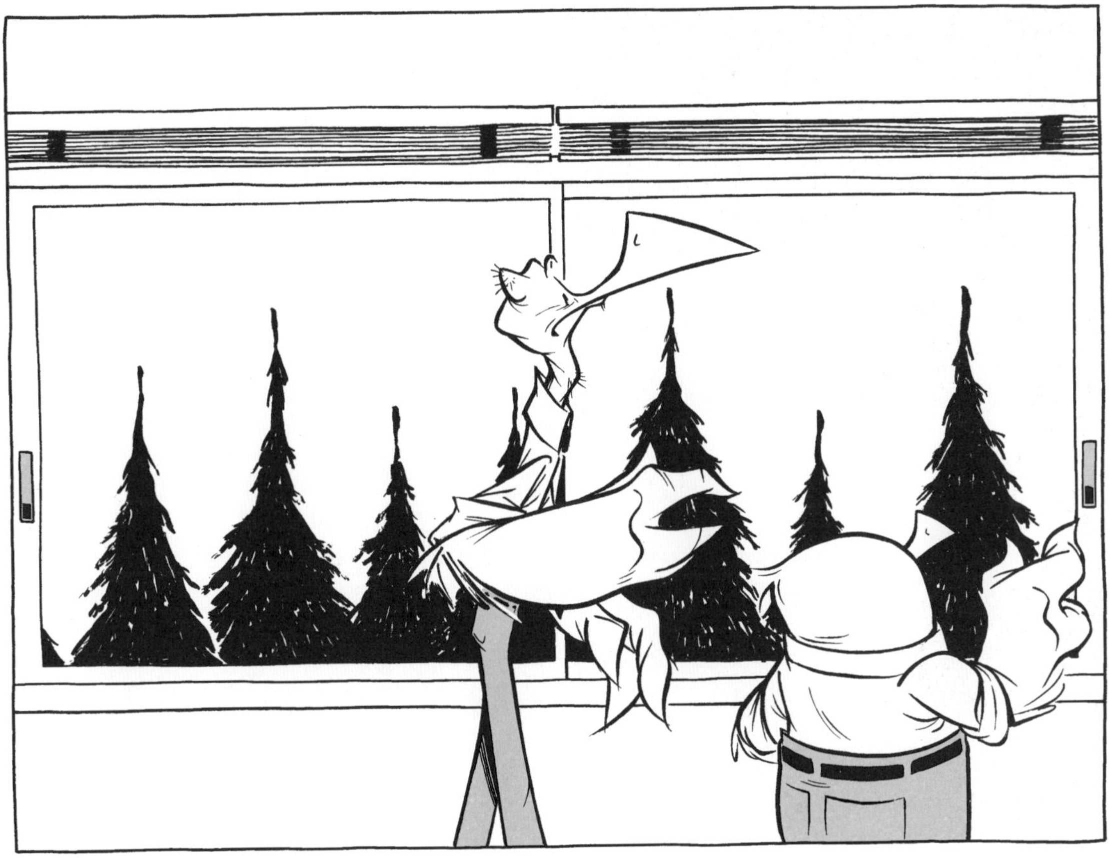
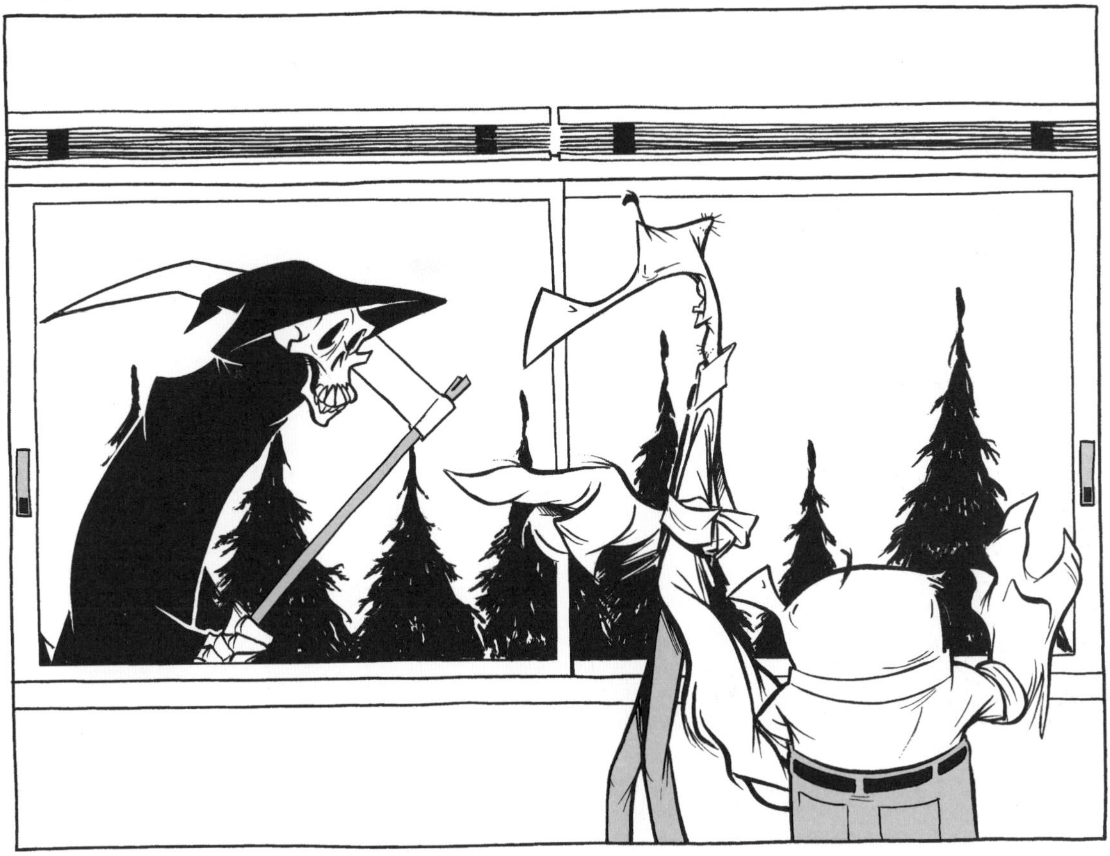

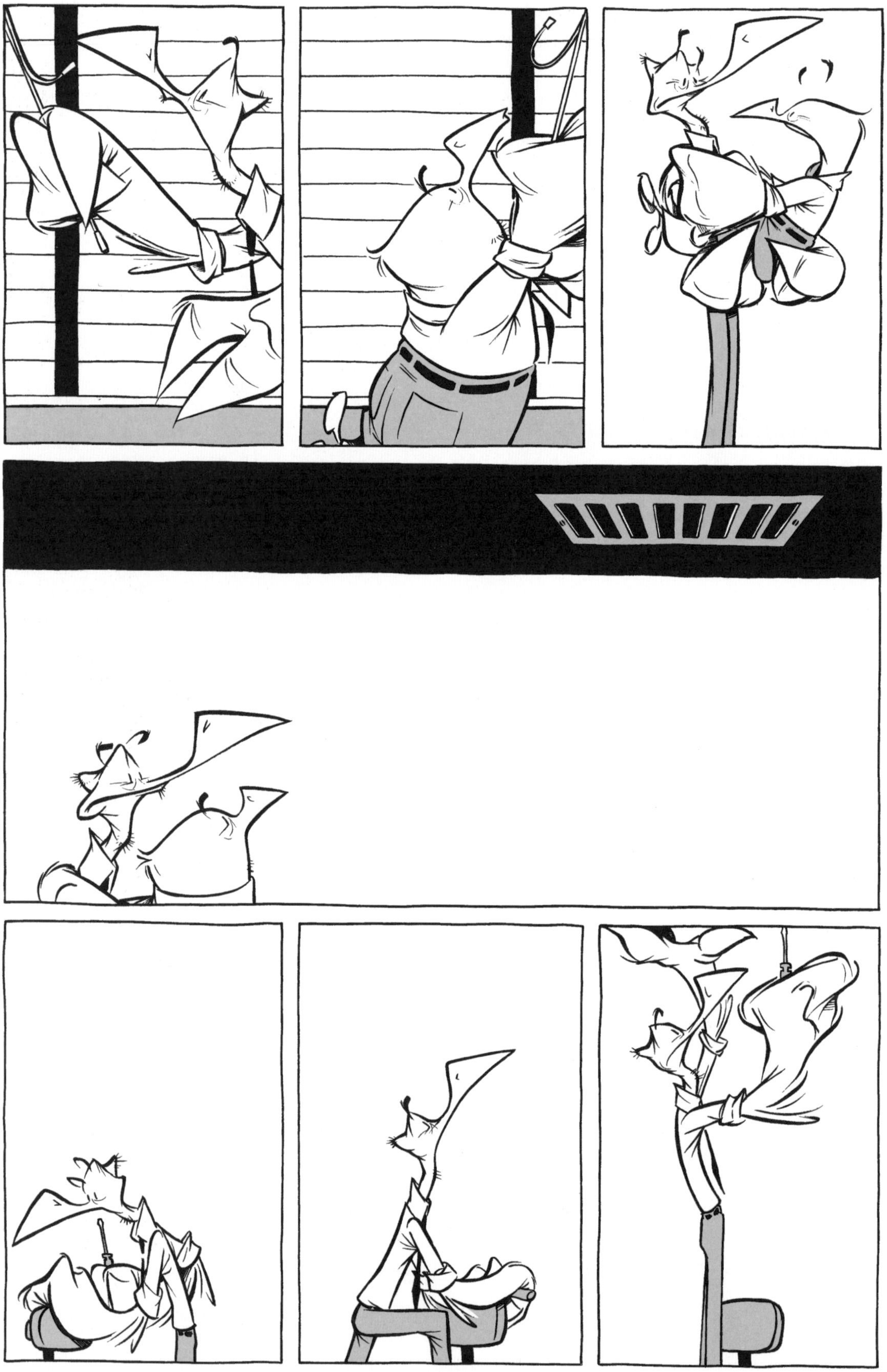

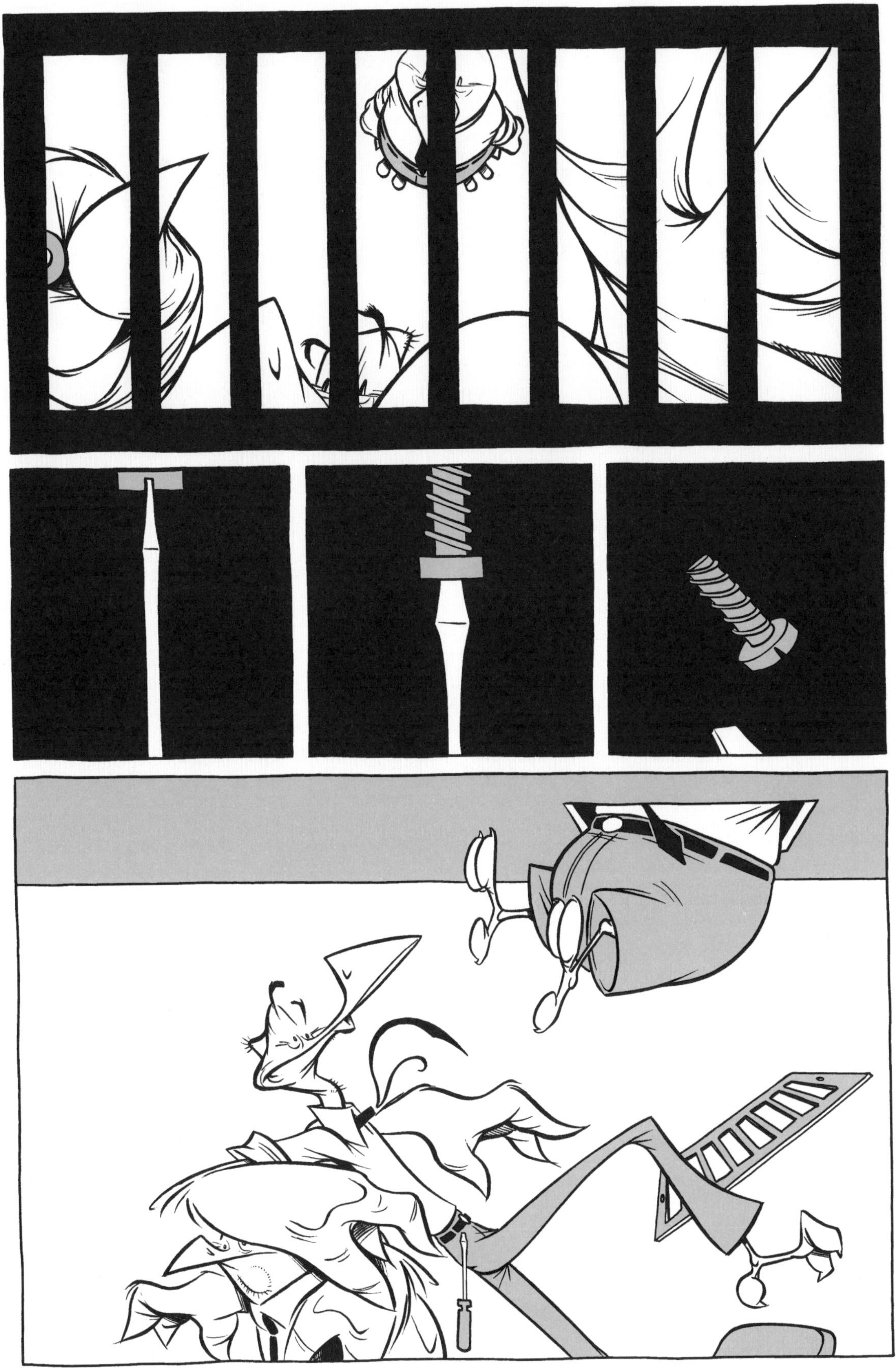

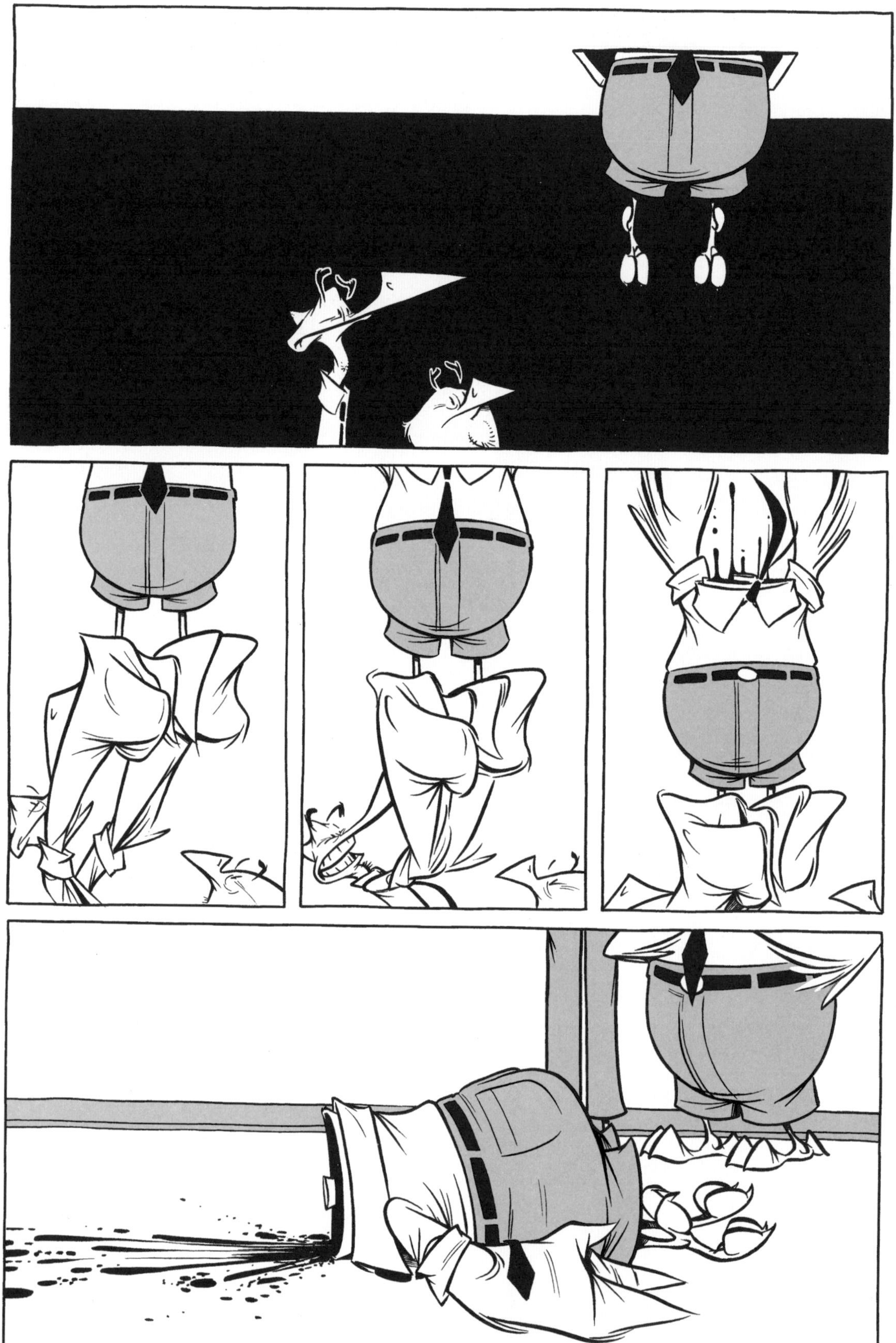

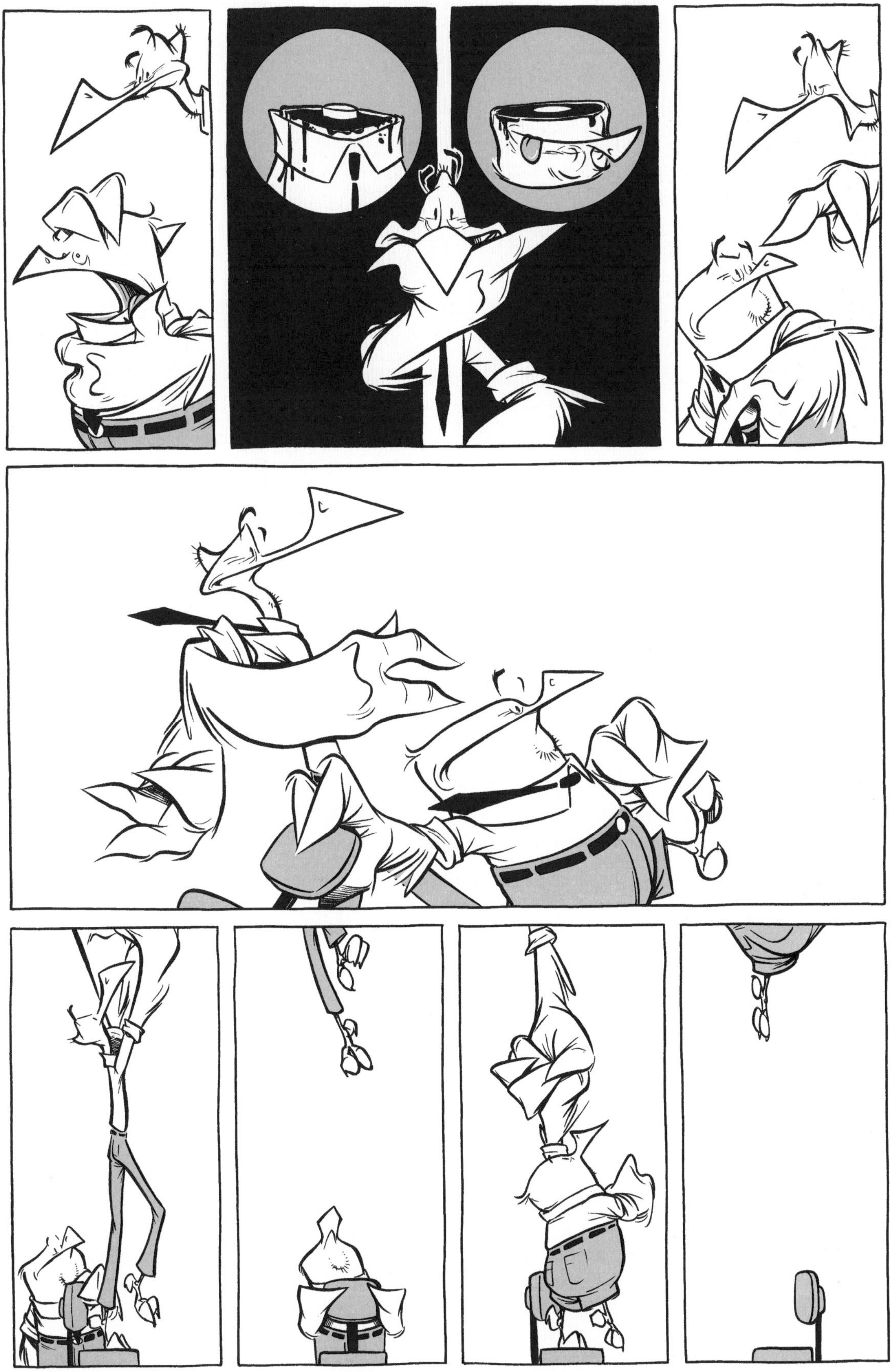

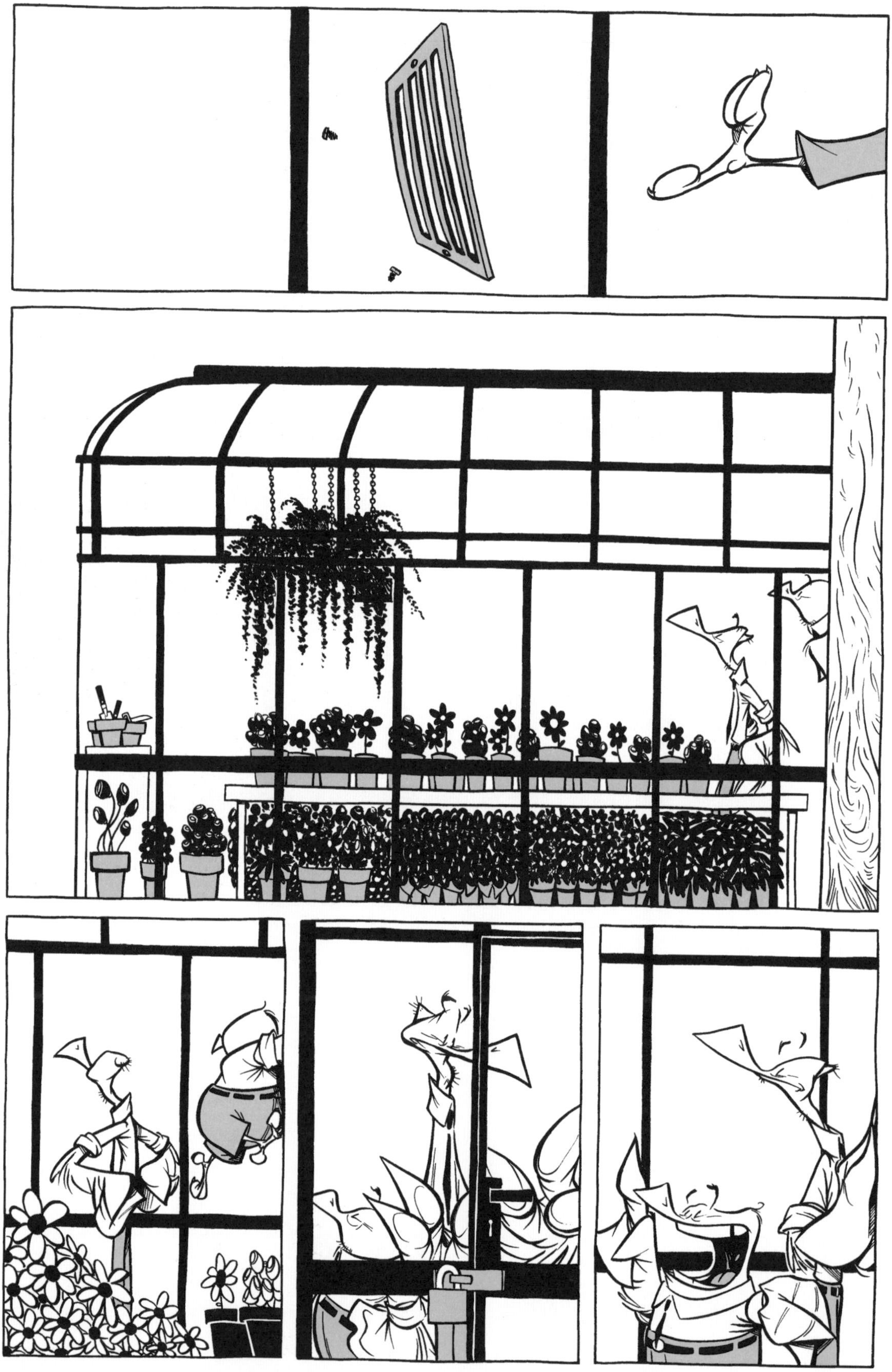

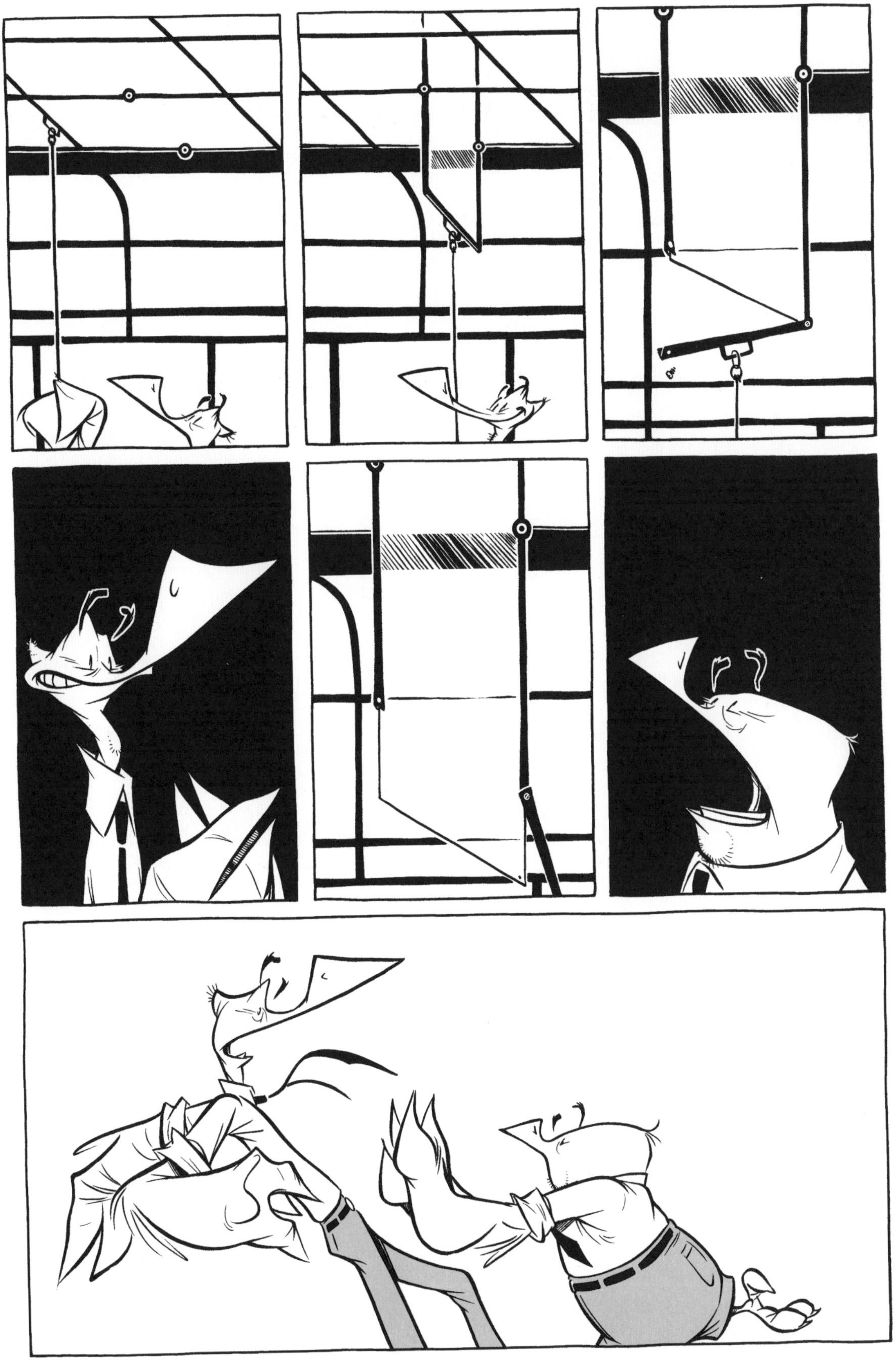

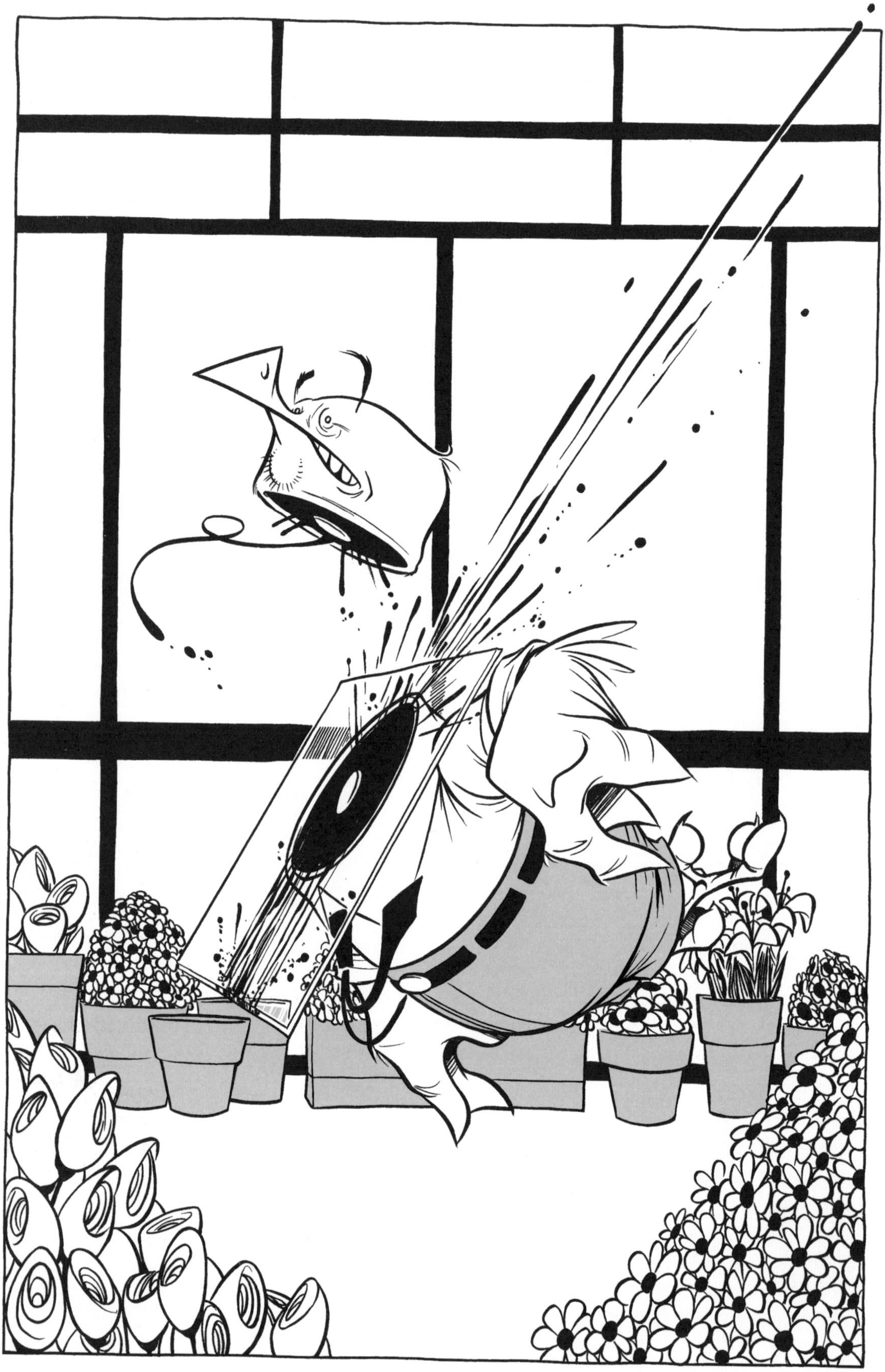

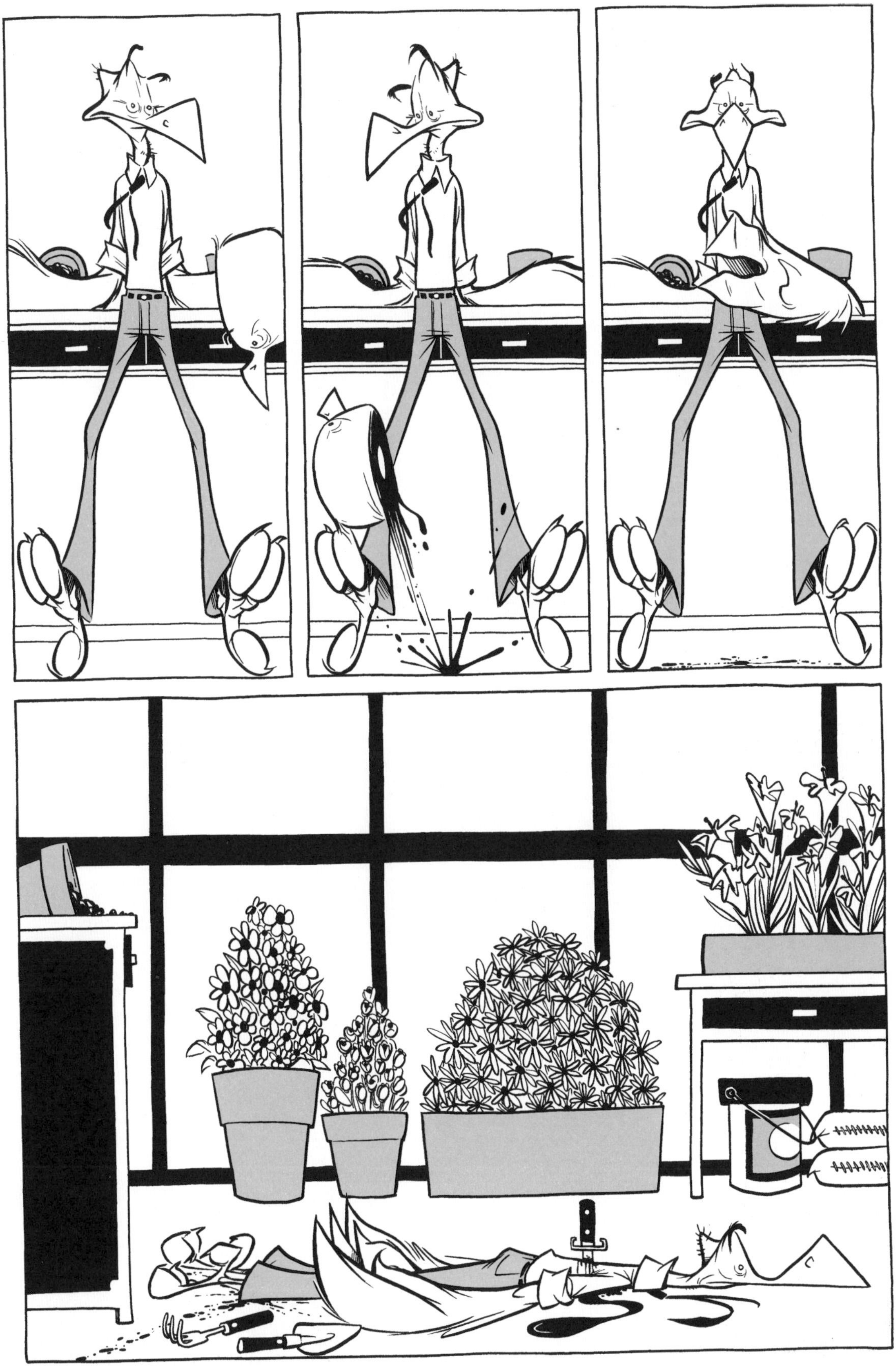

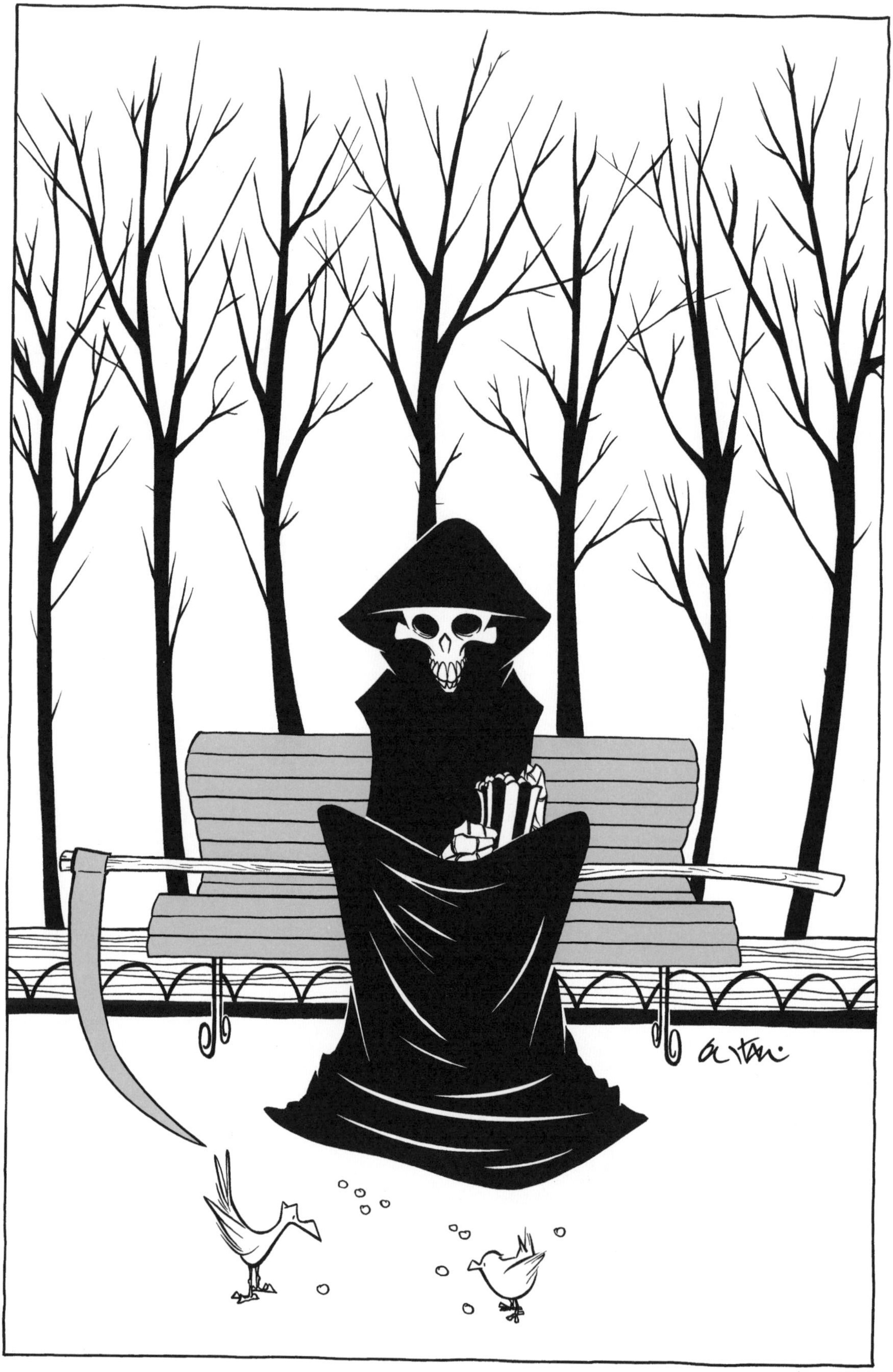

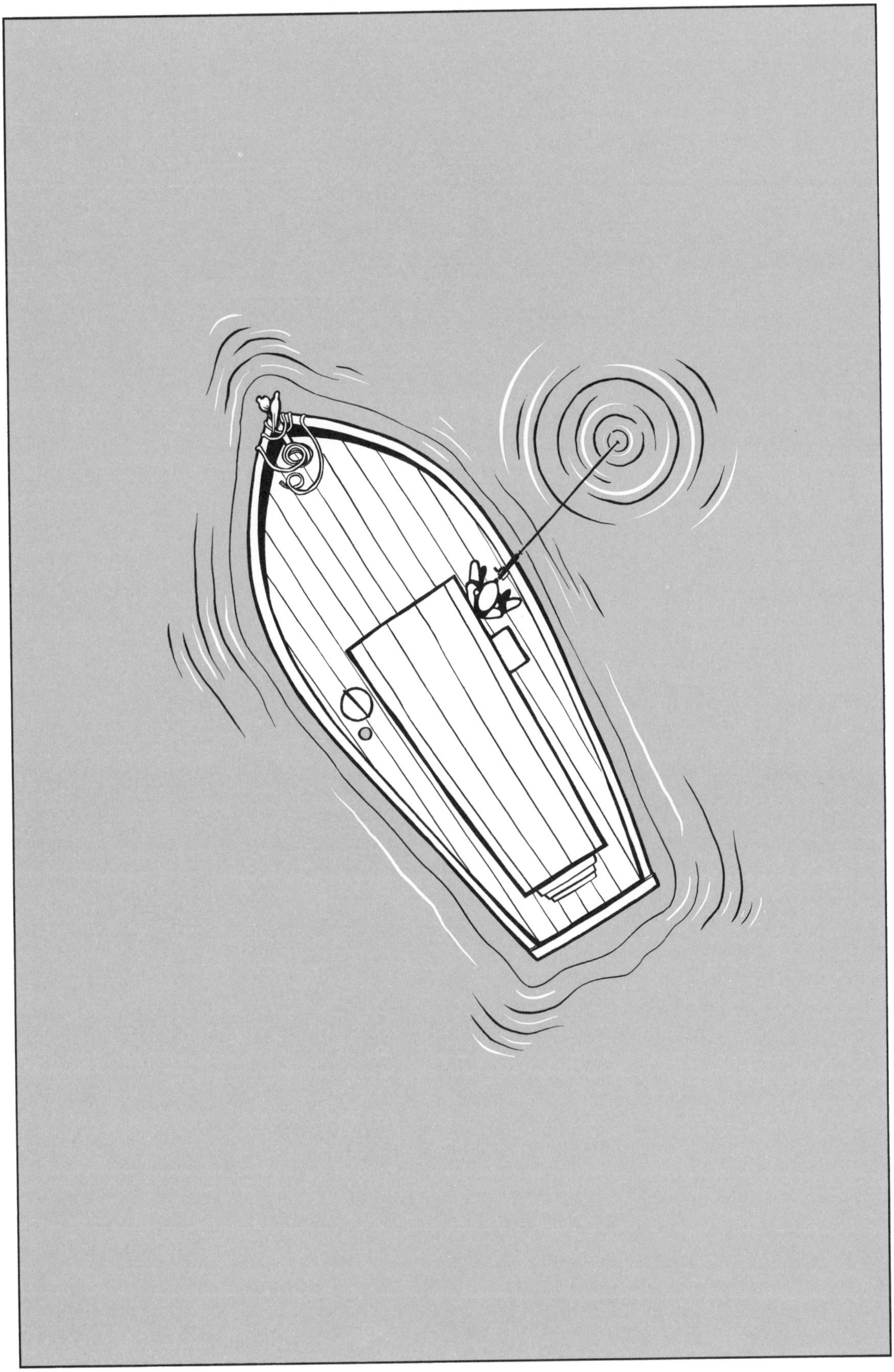

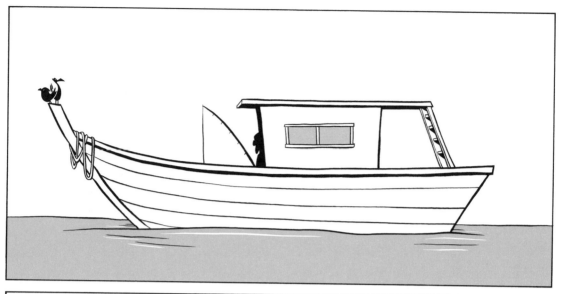

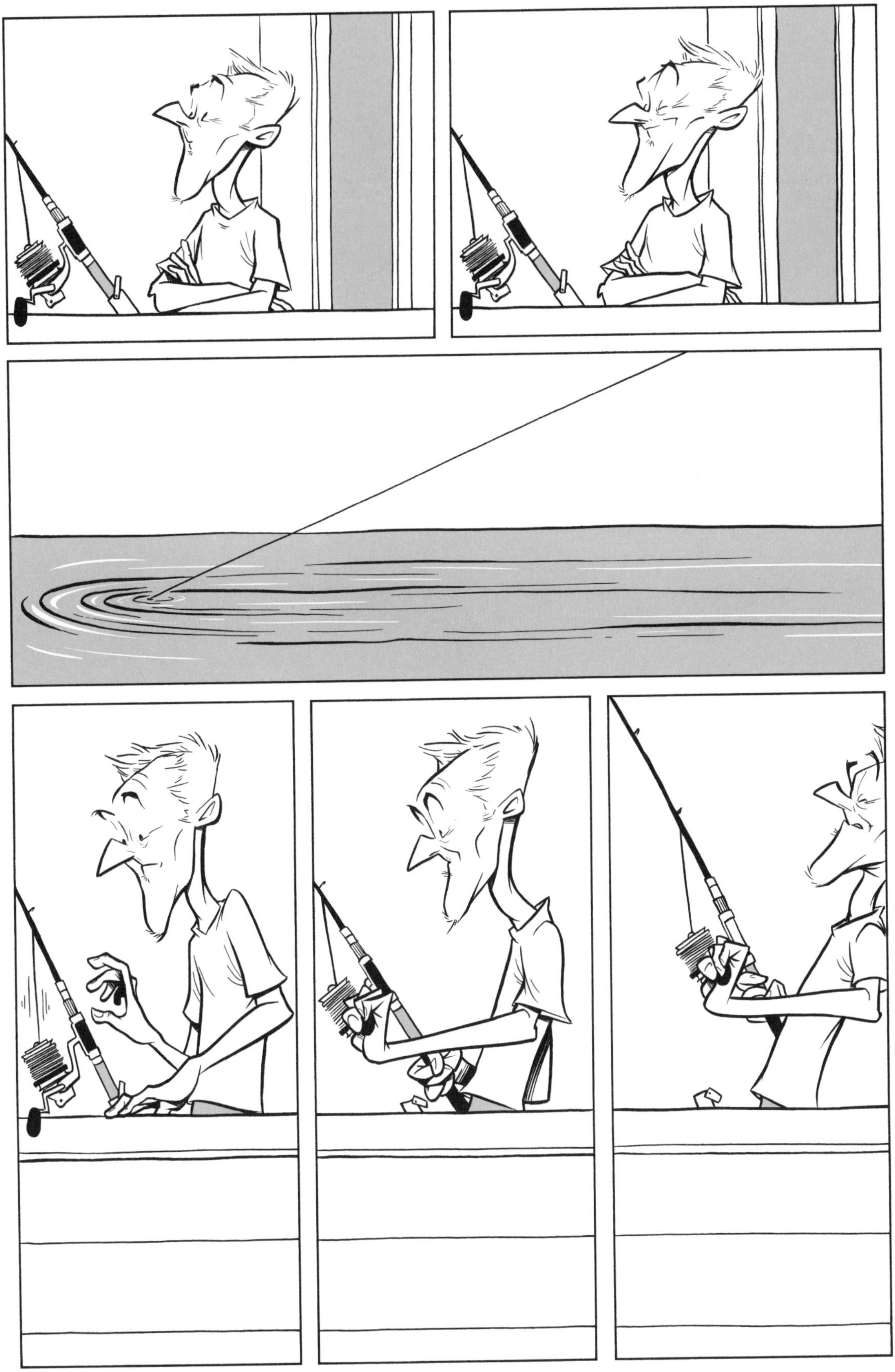

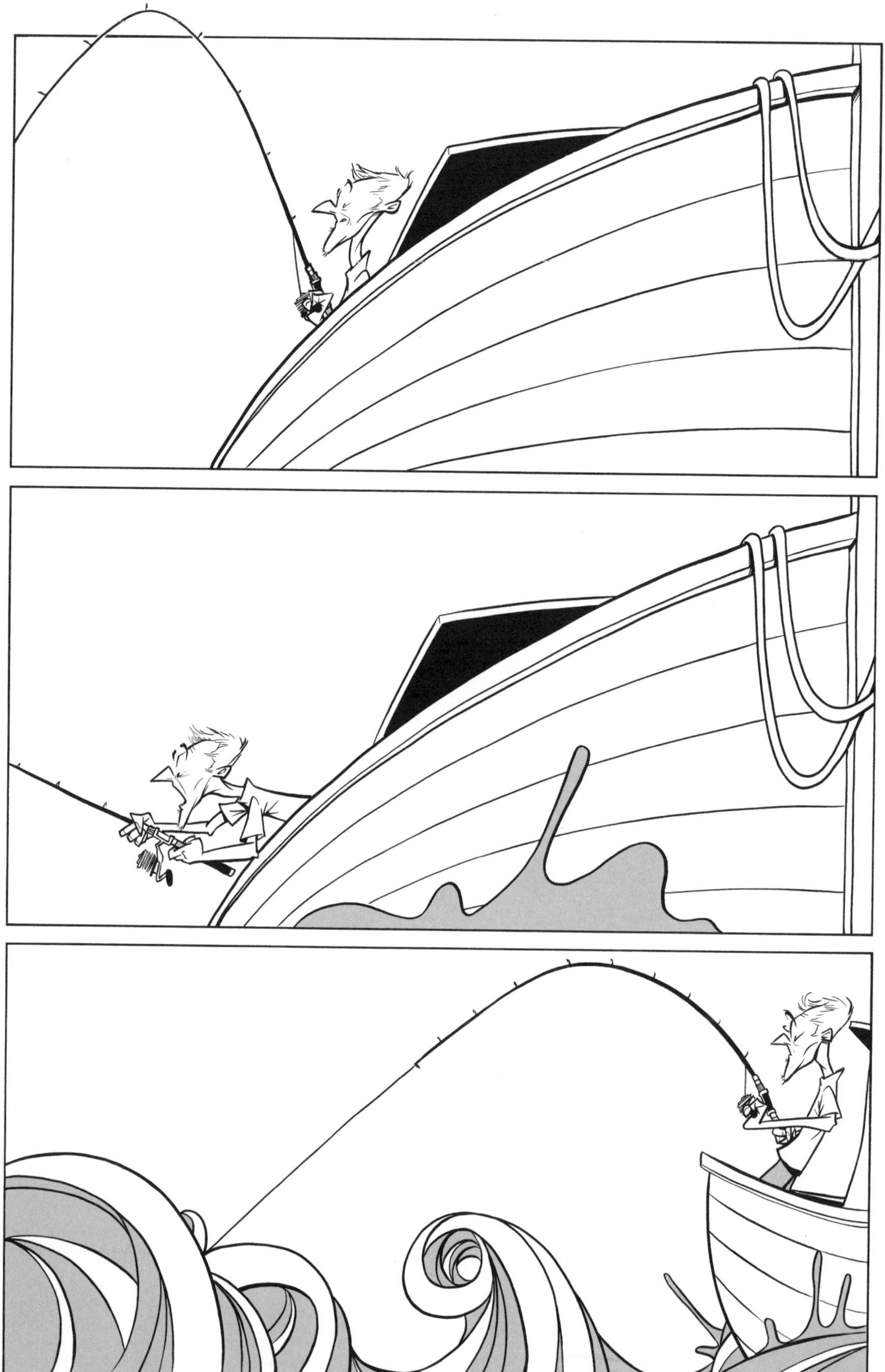

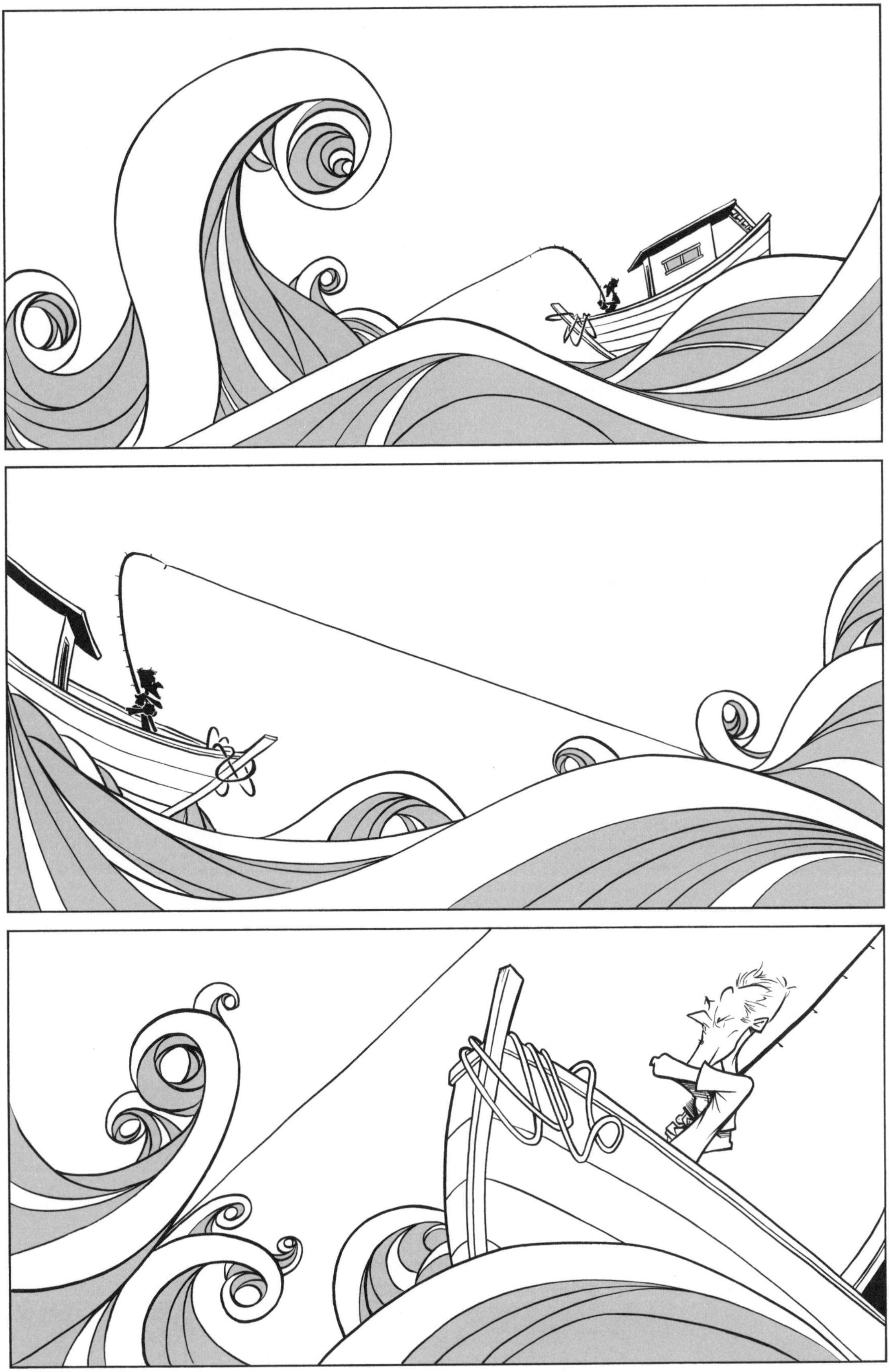

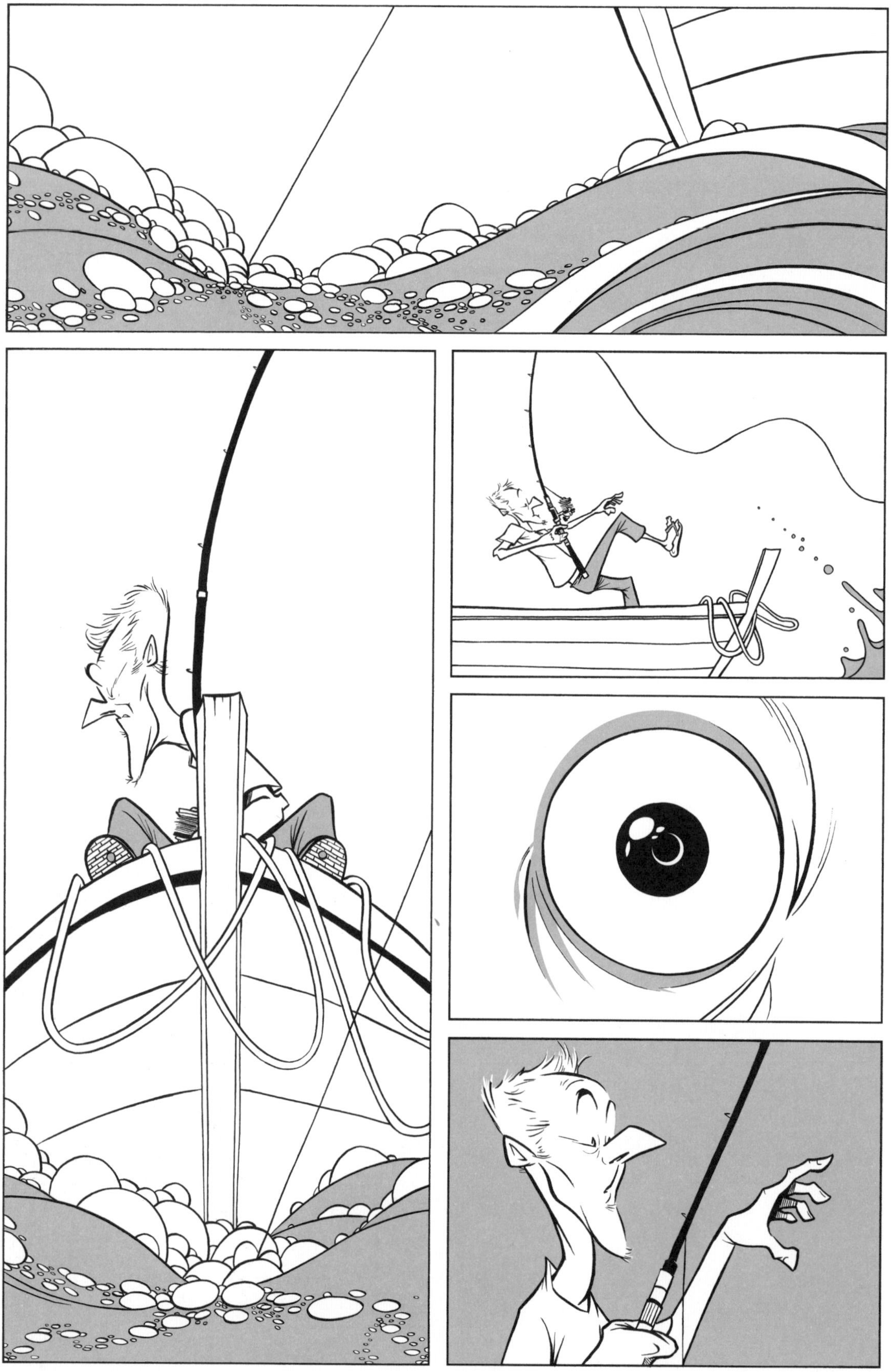

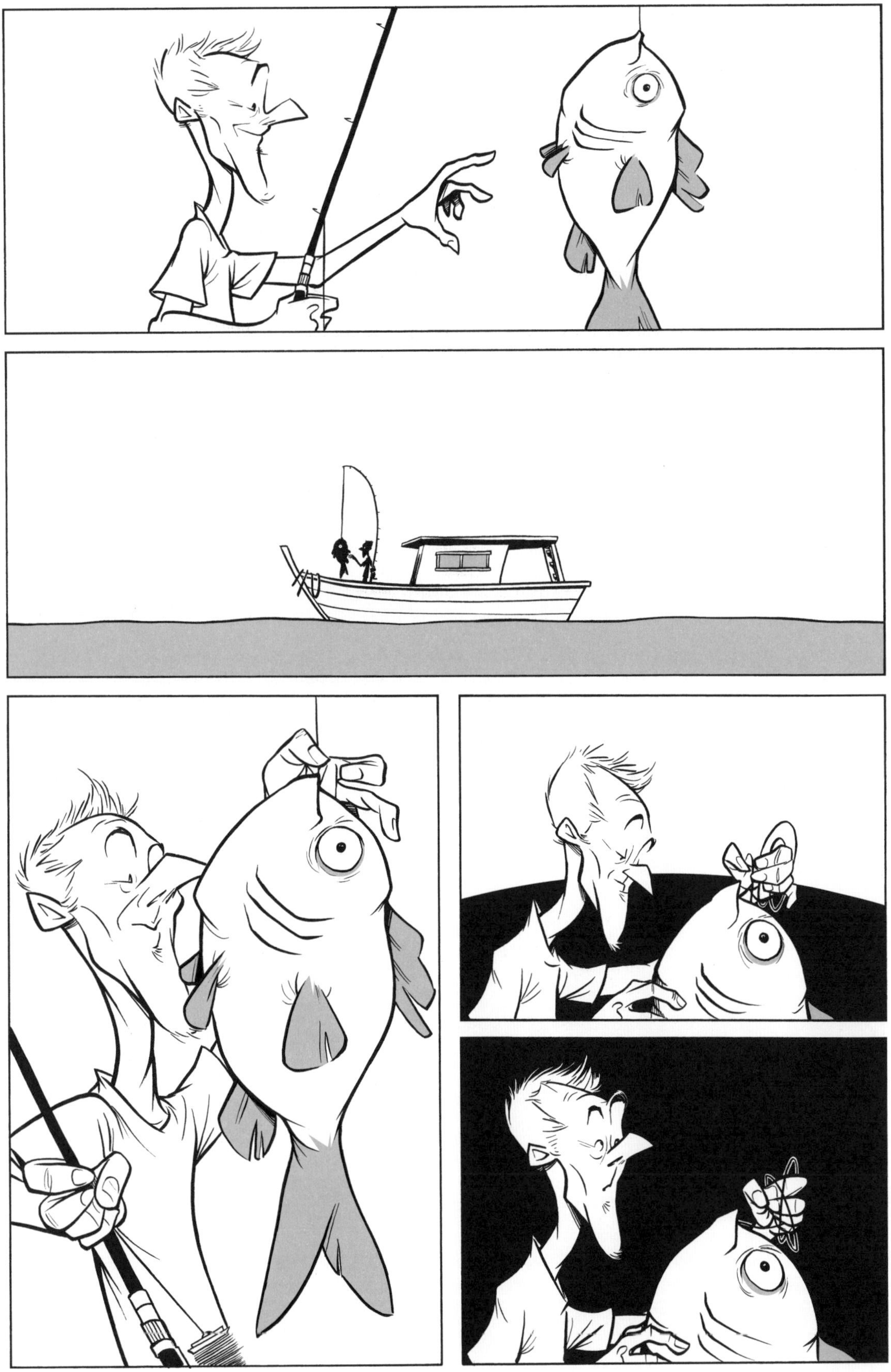

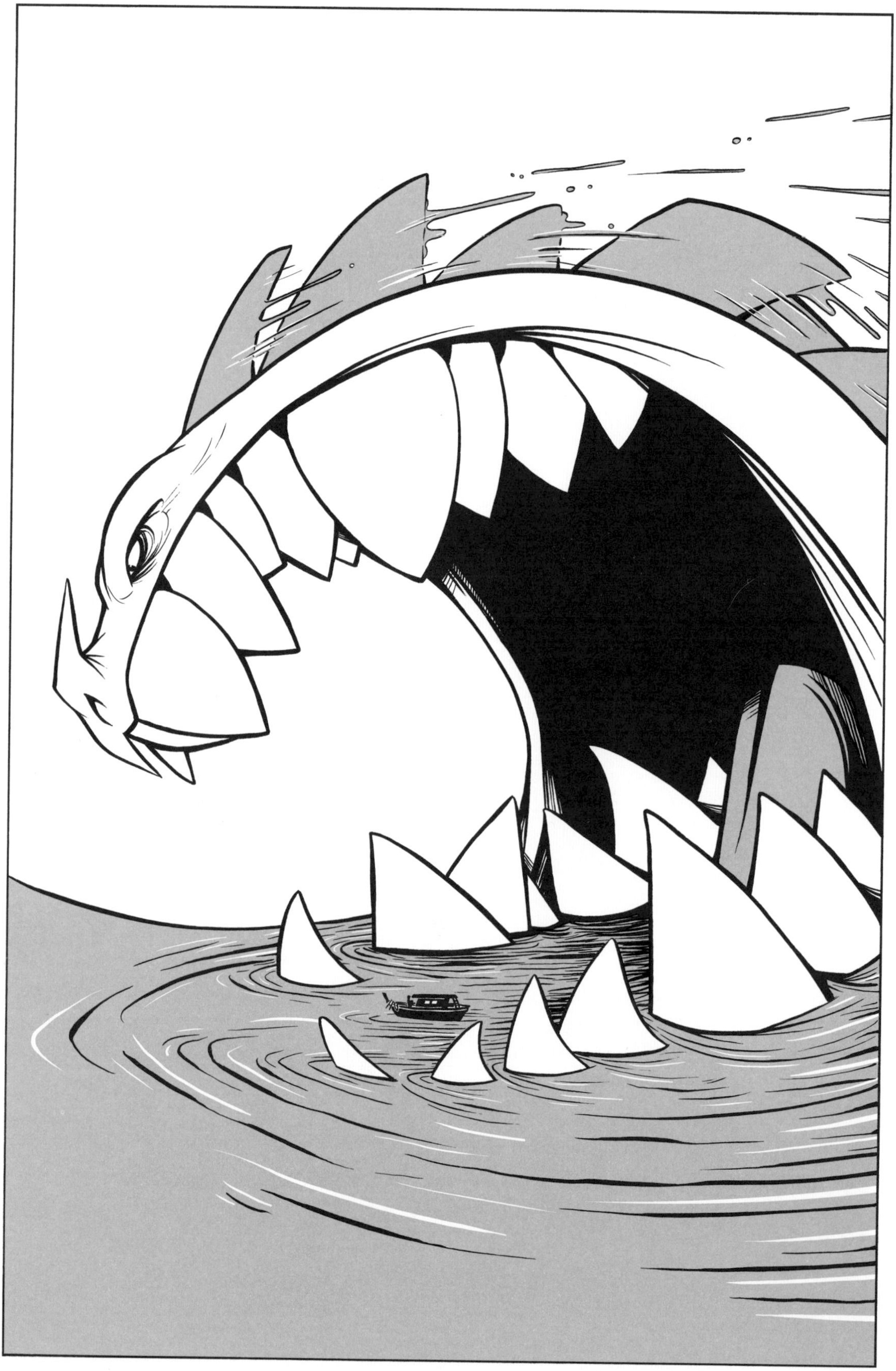

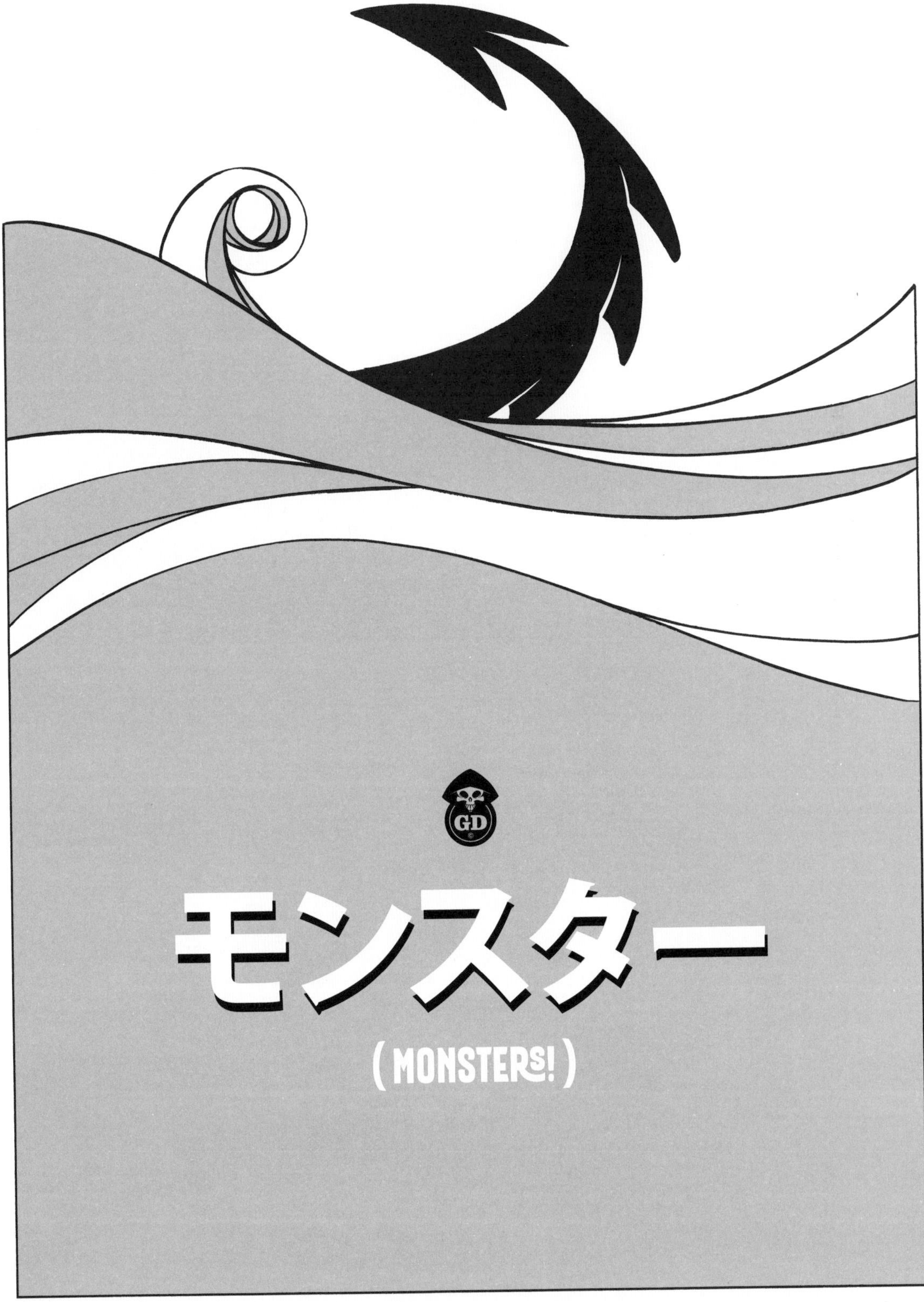

モンスター

(MONSTERS!)

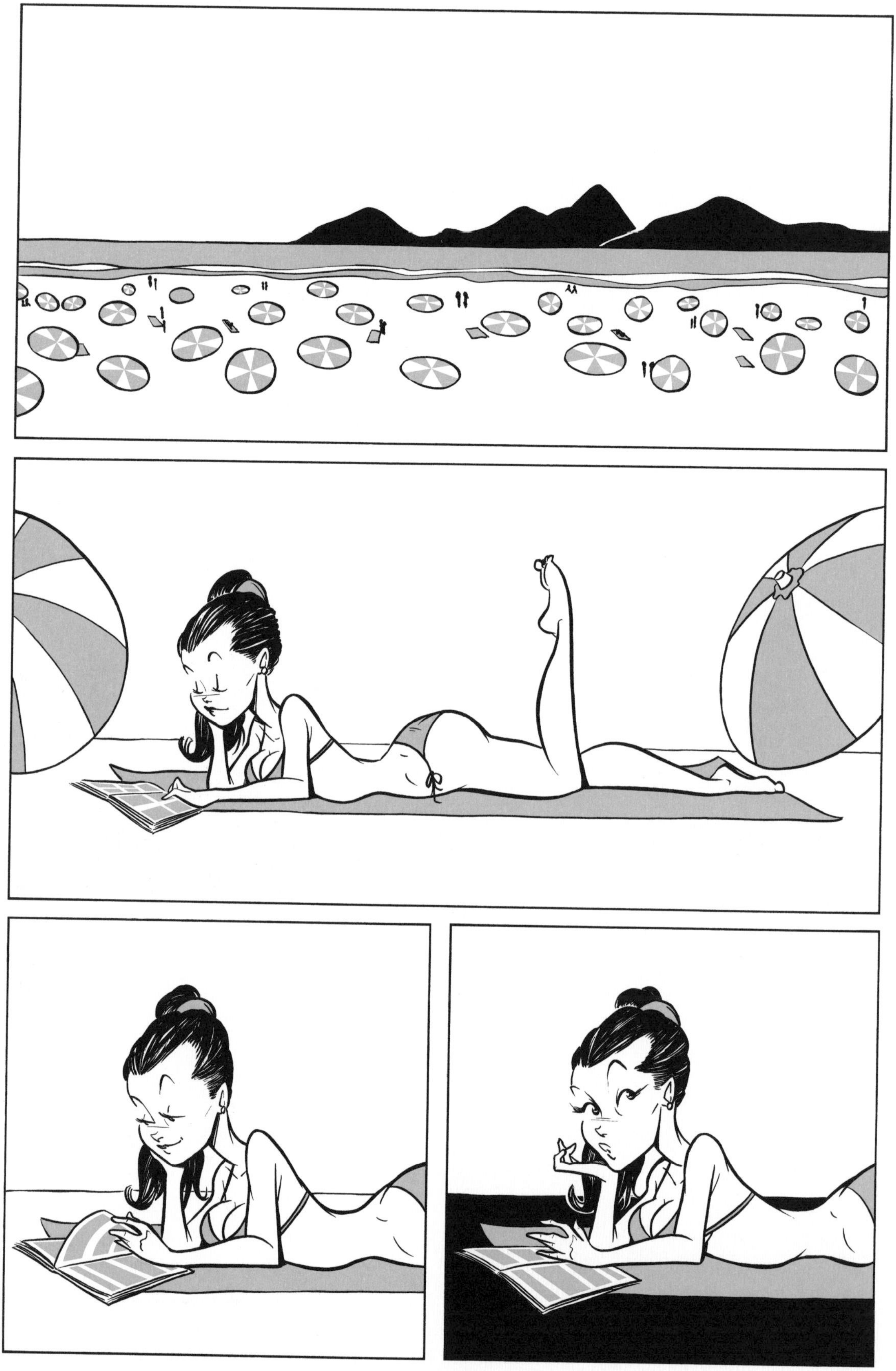

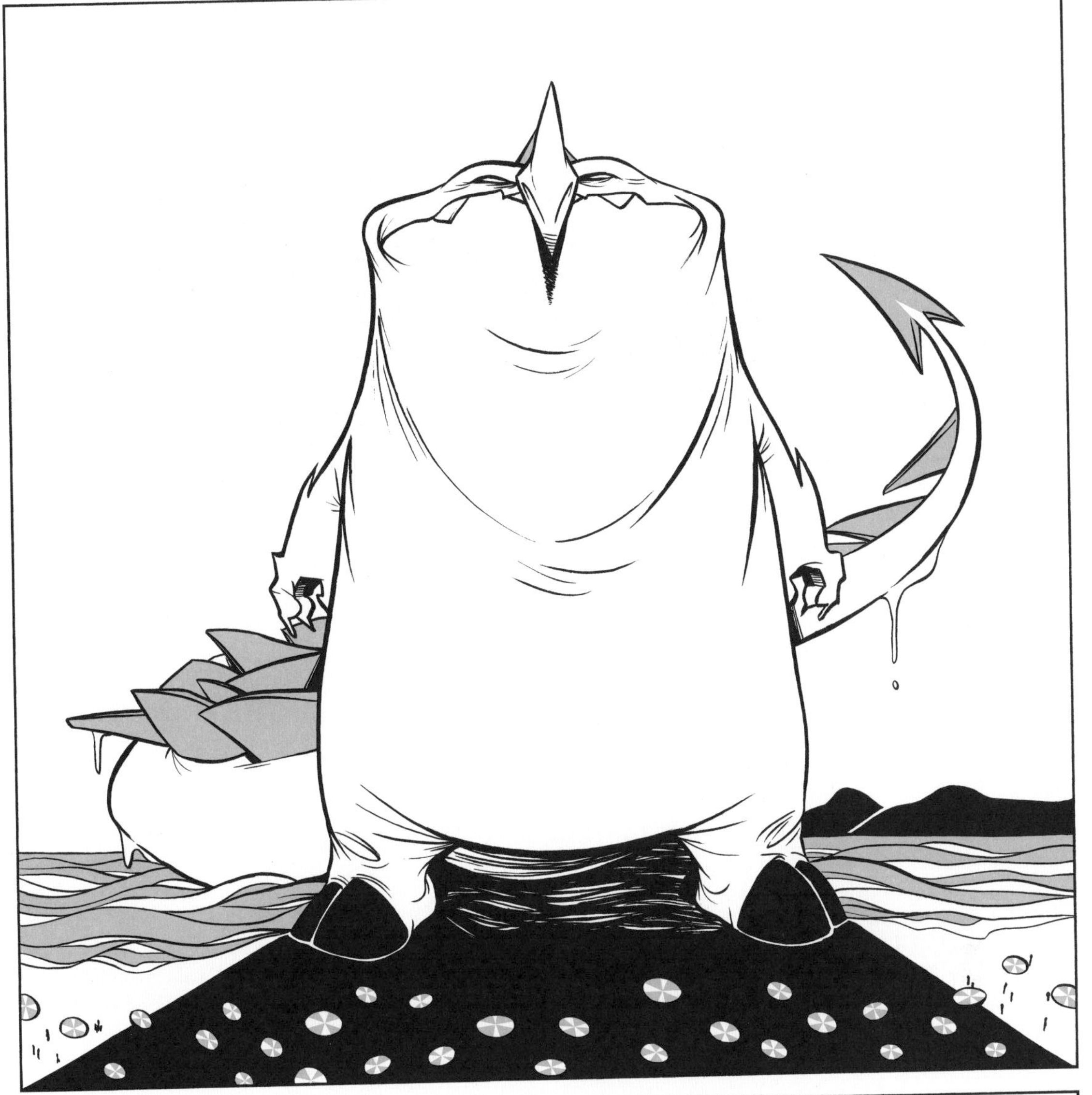
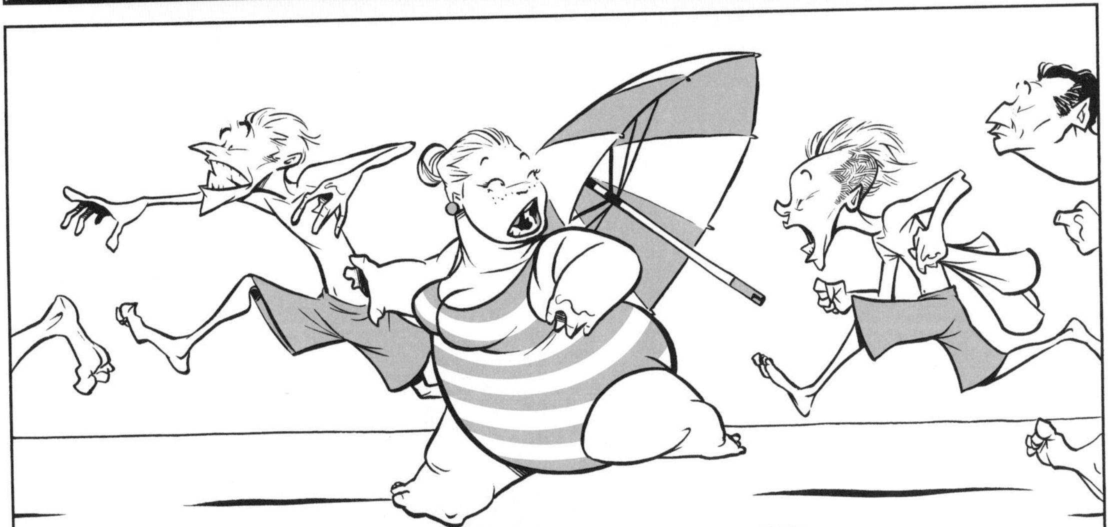

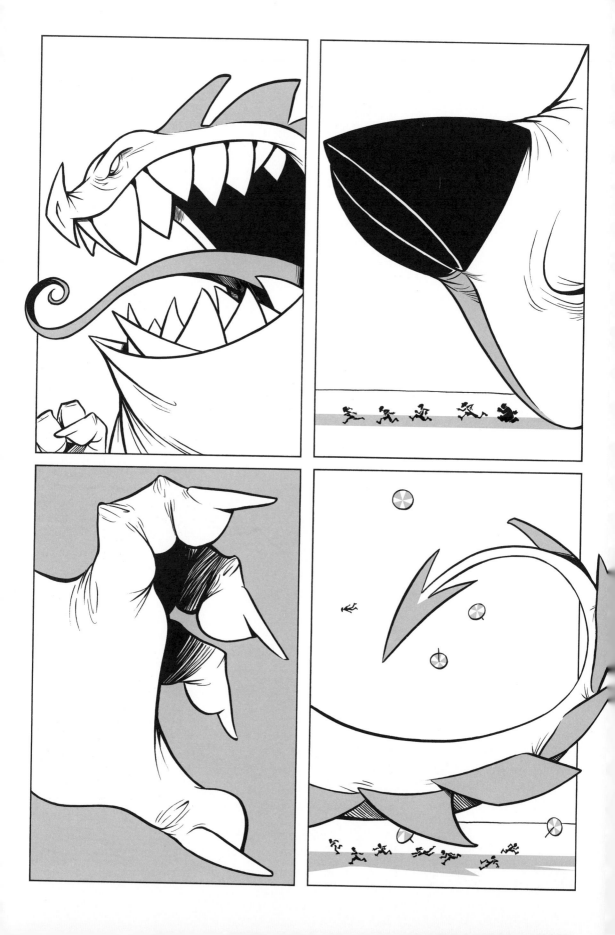

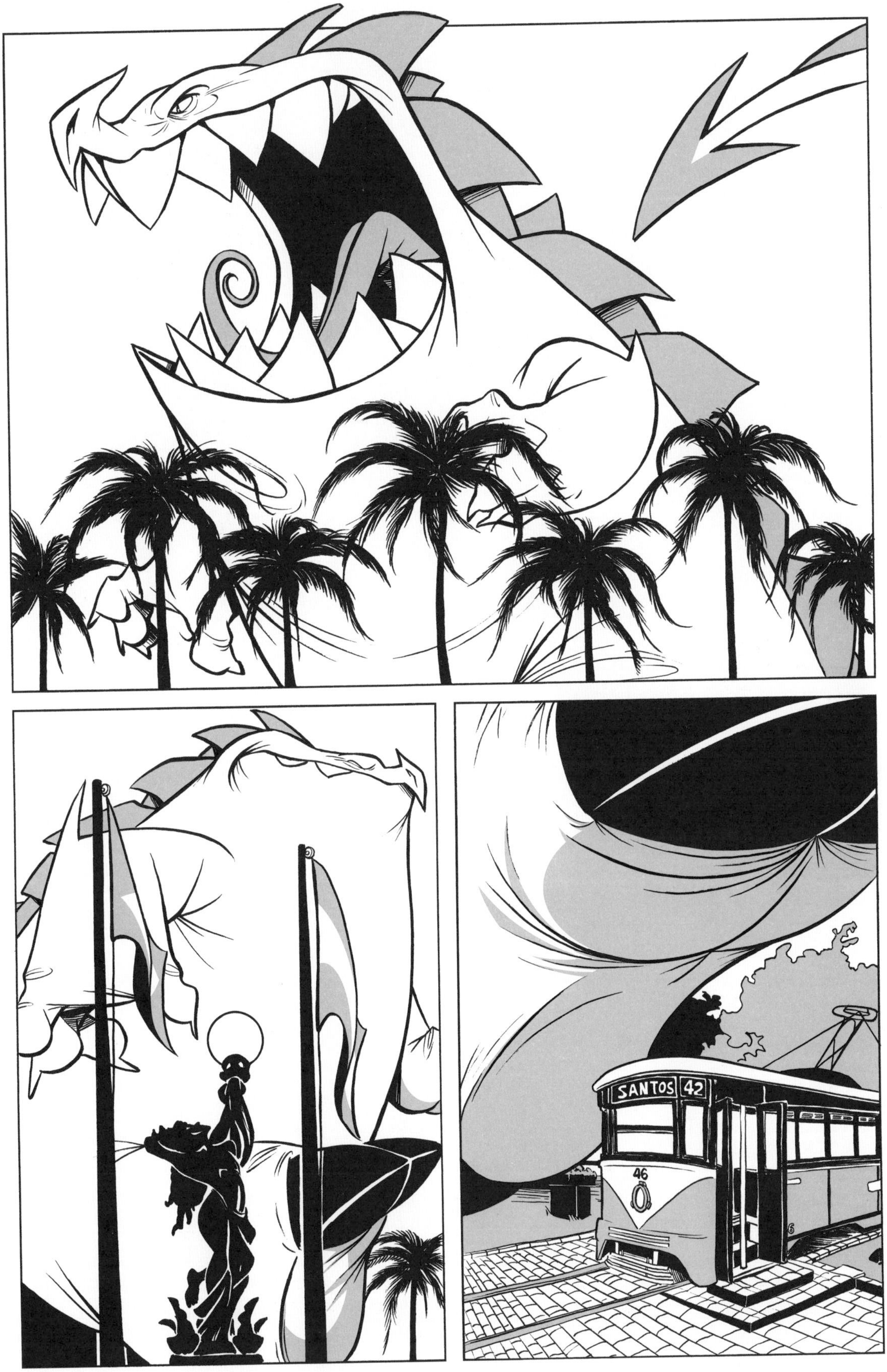
SANTOS 42
46

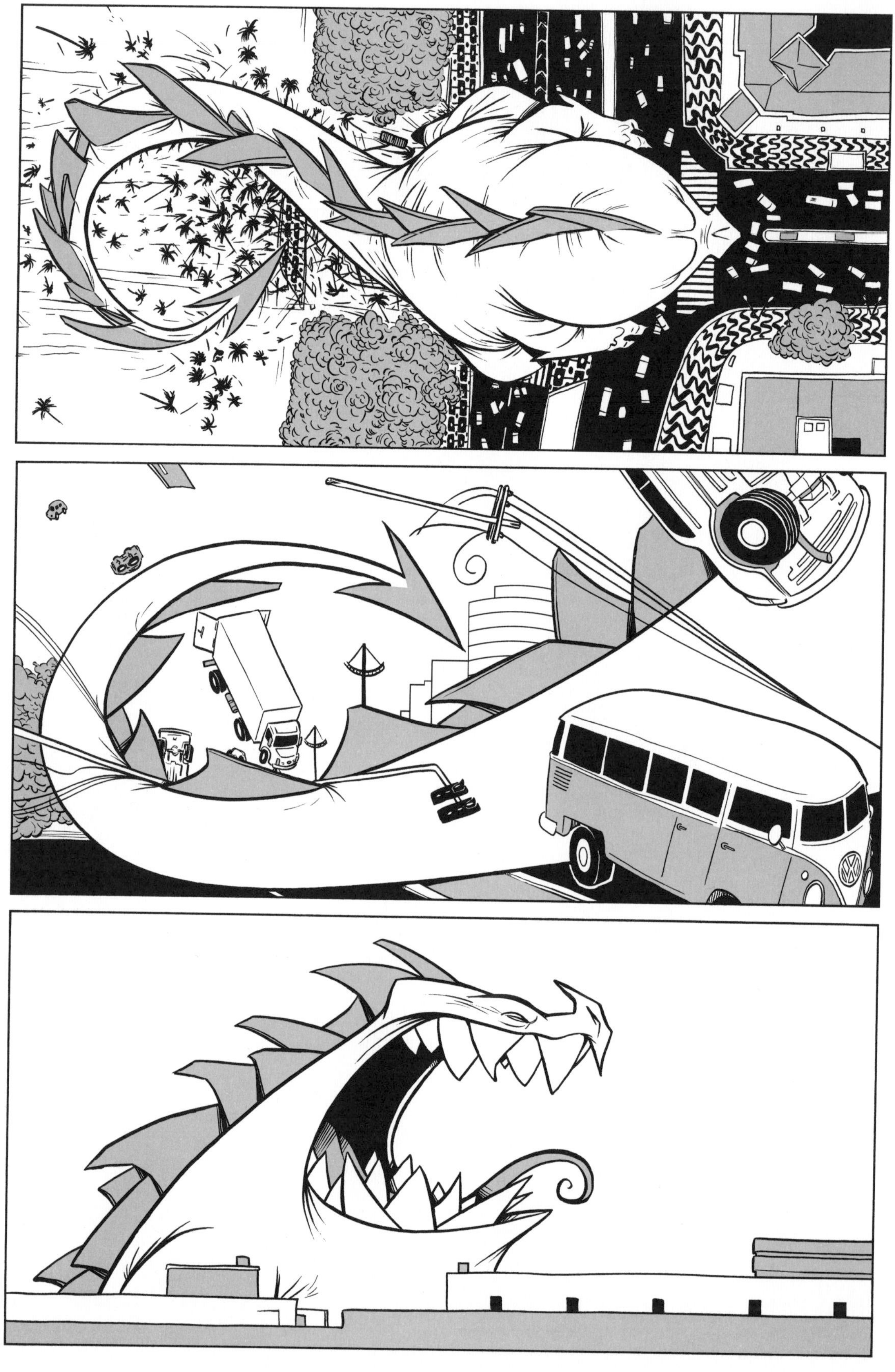

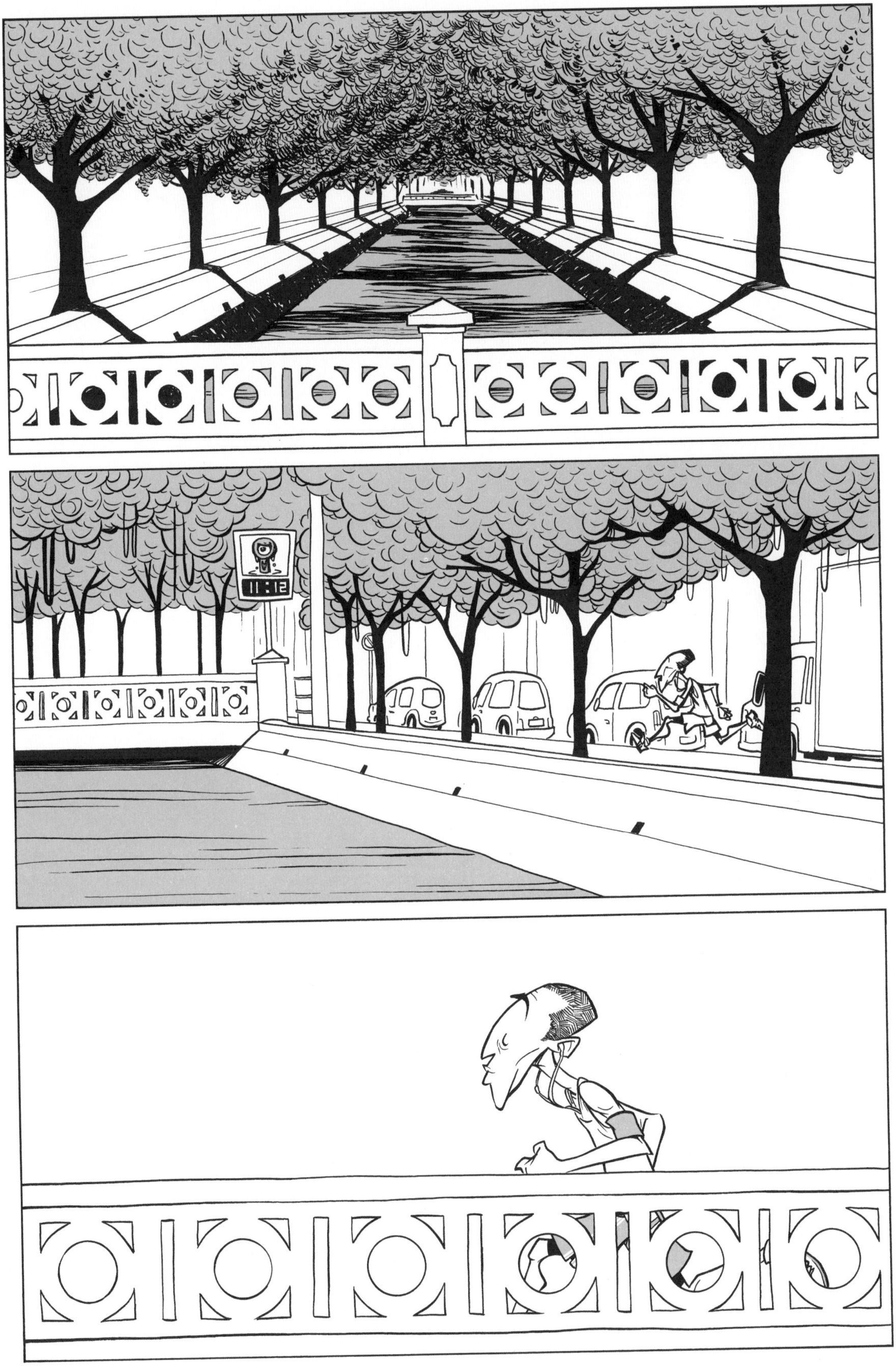
11:12

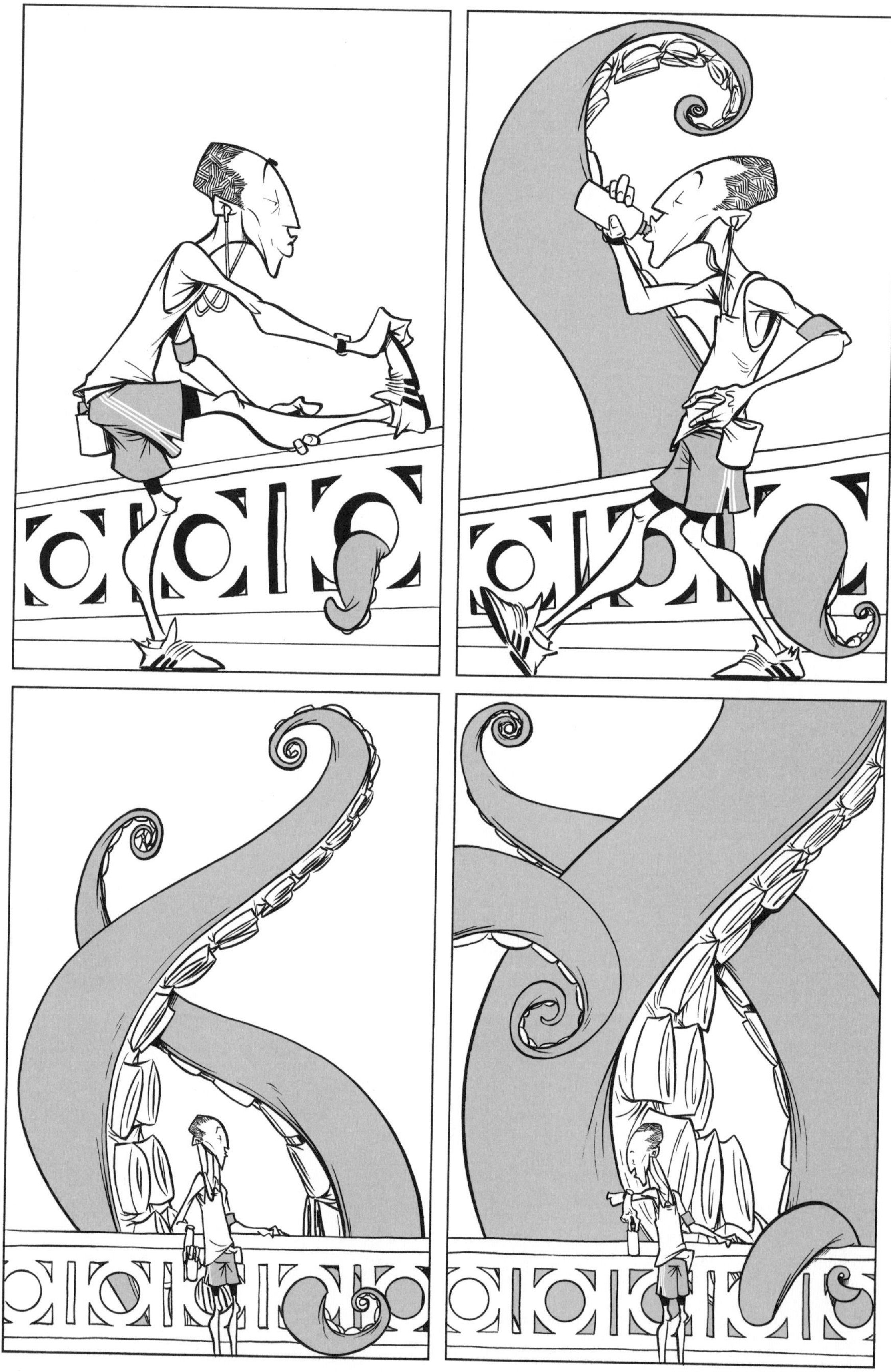

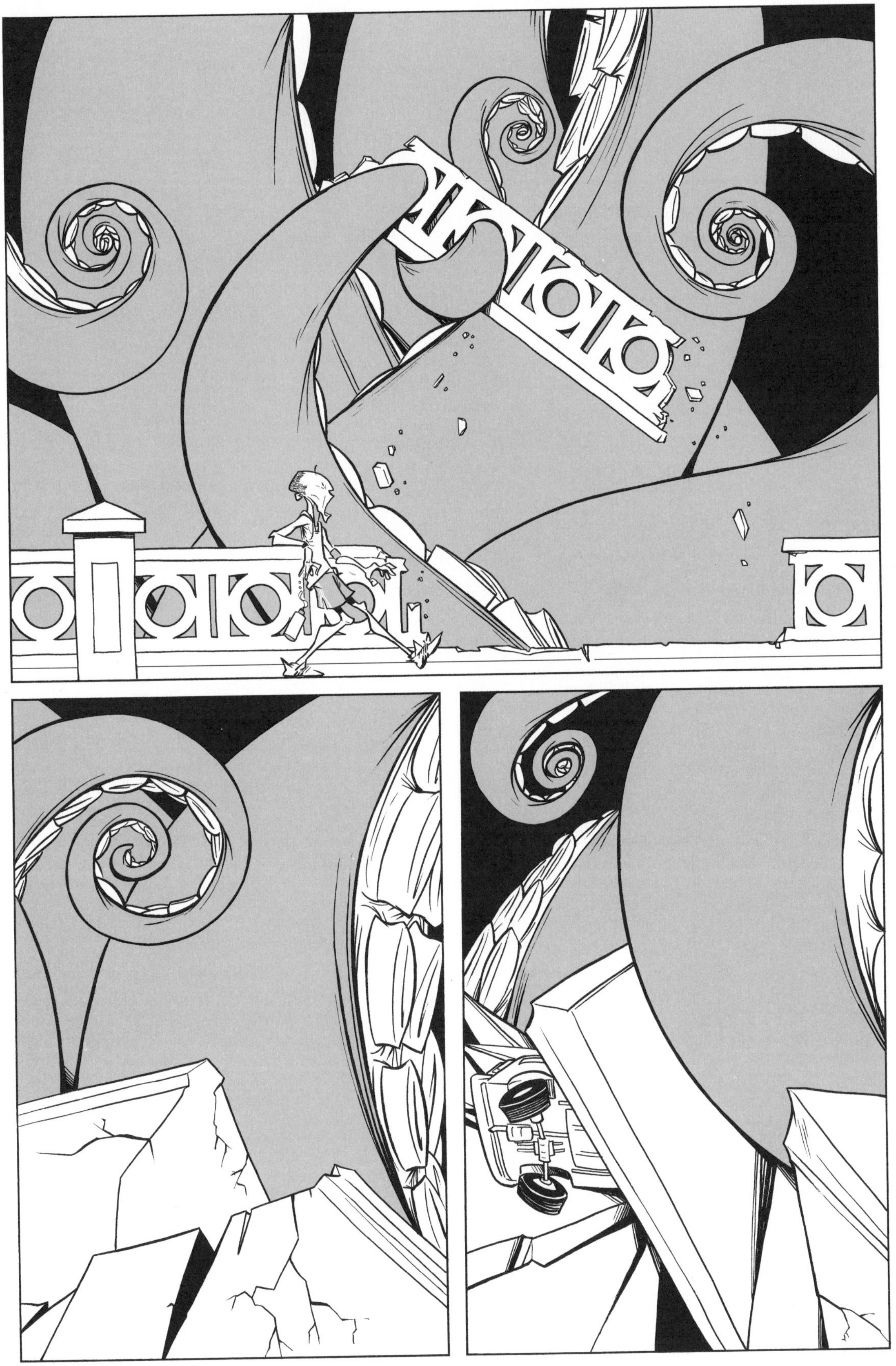

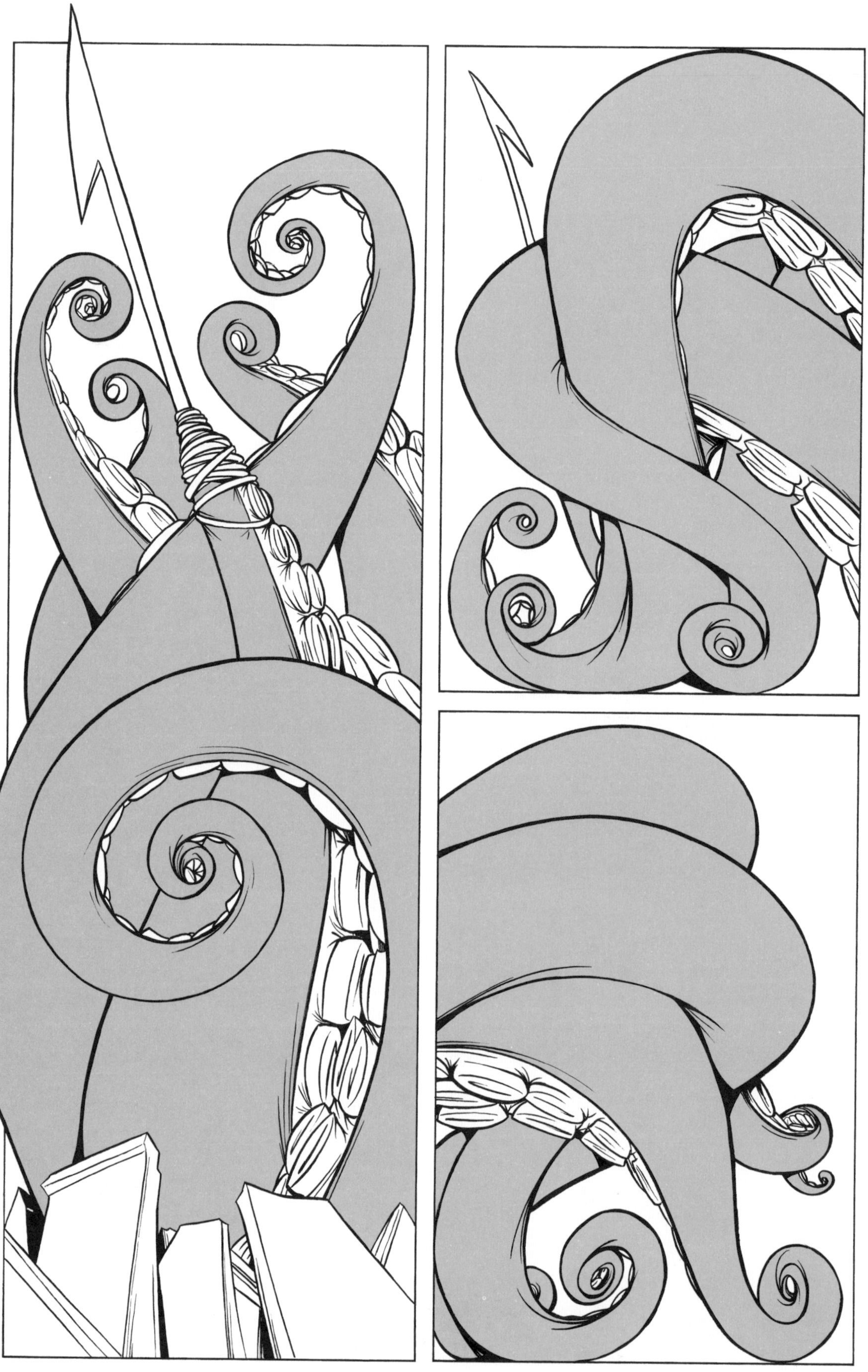

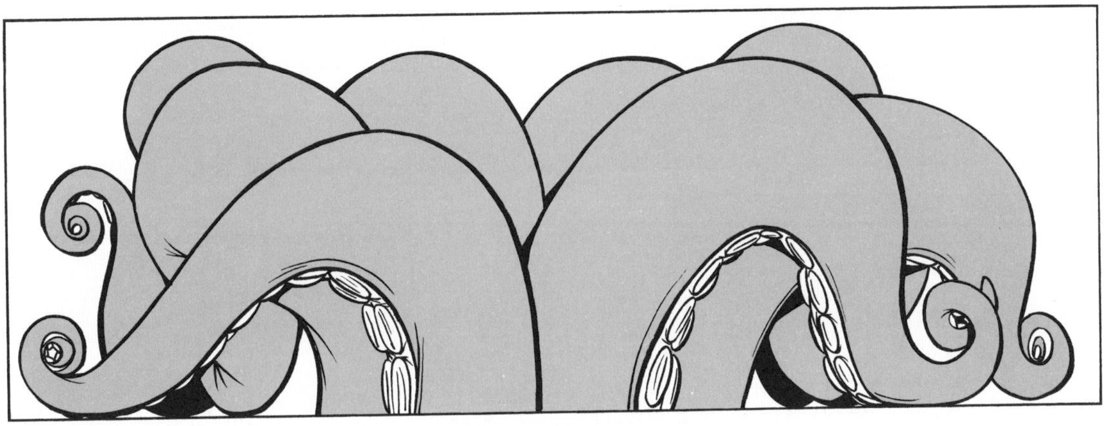
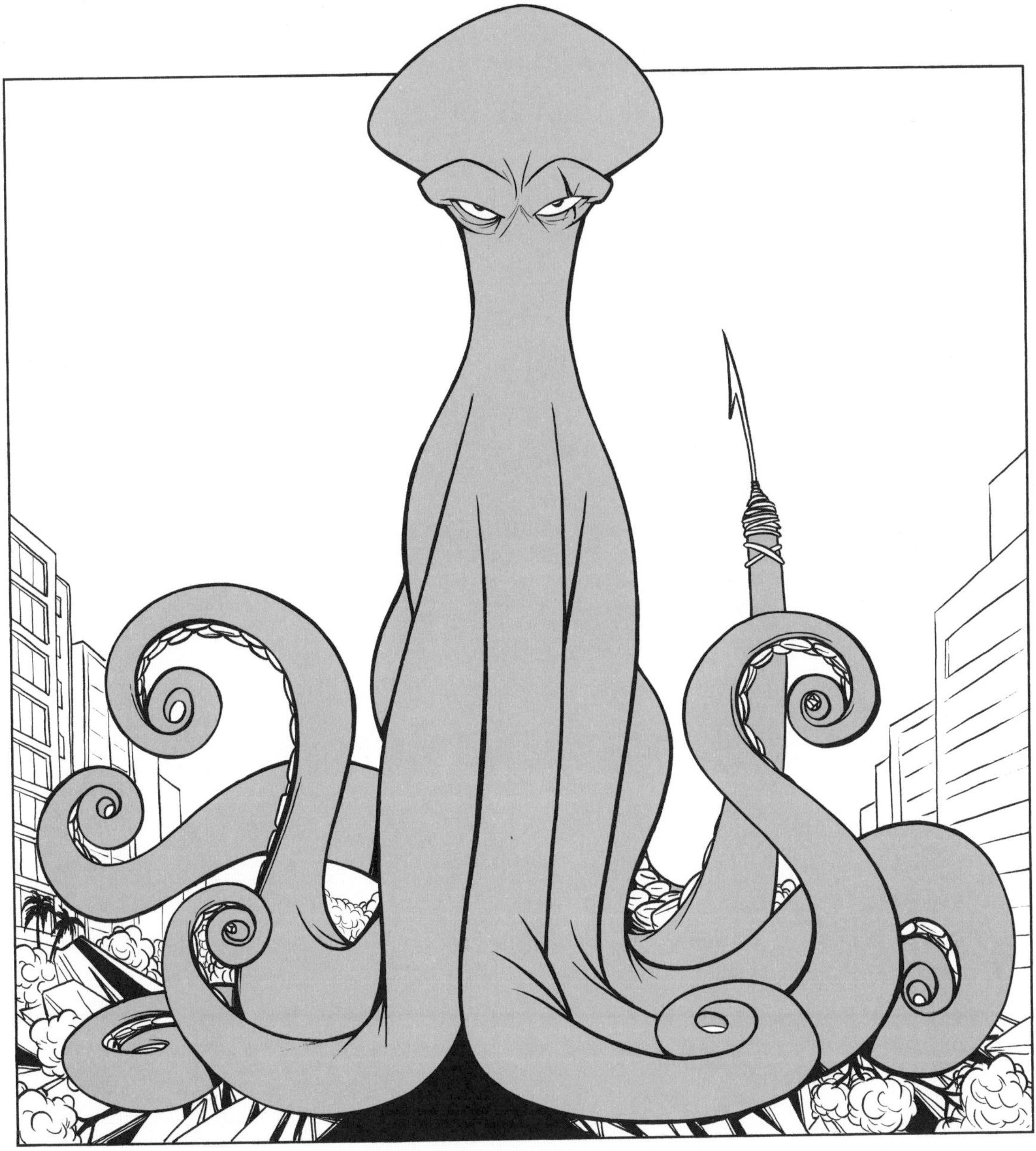

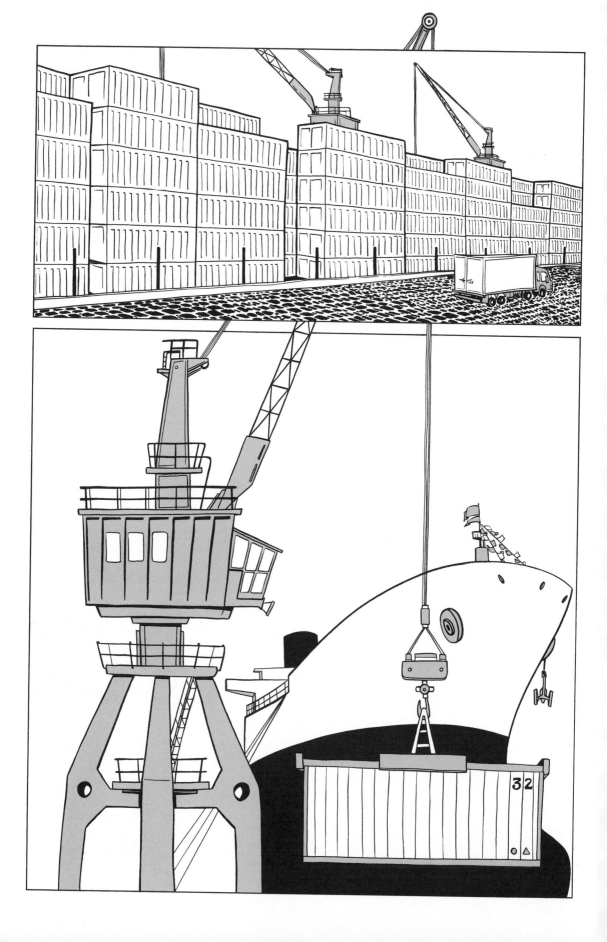

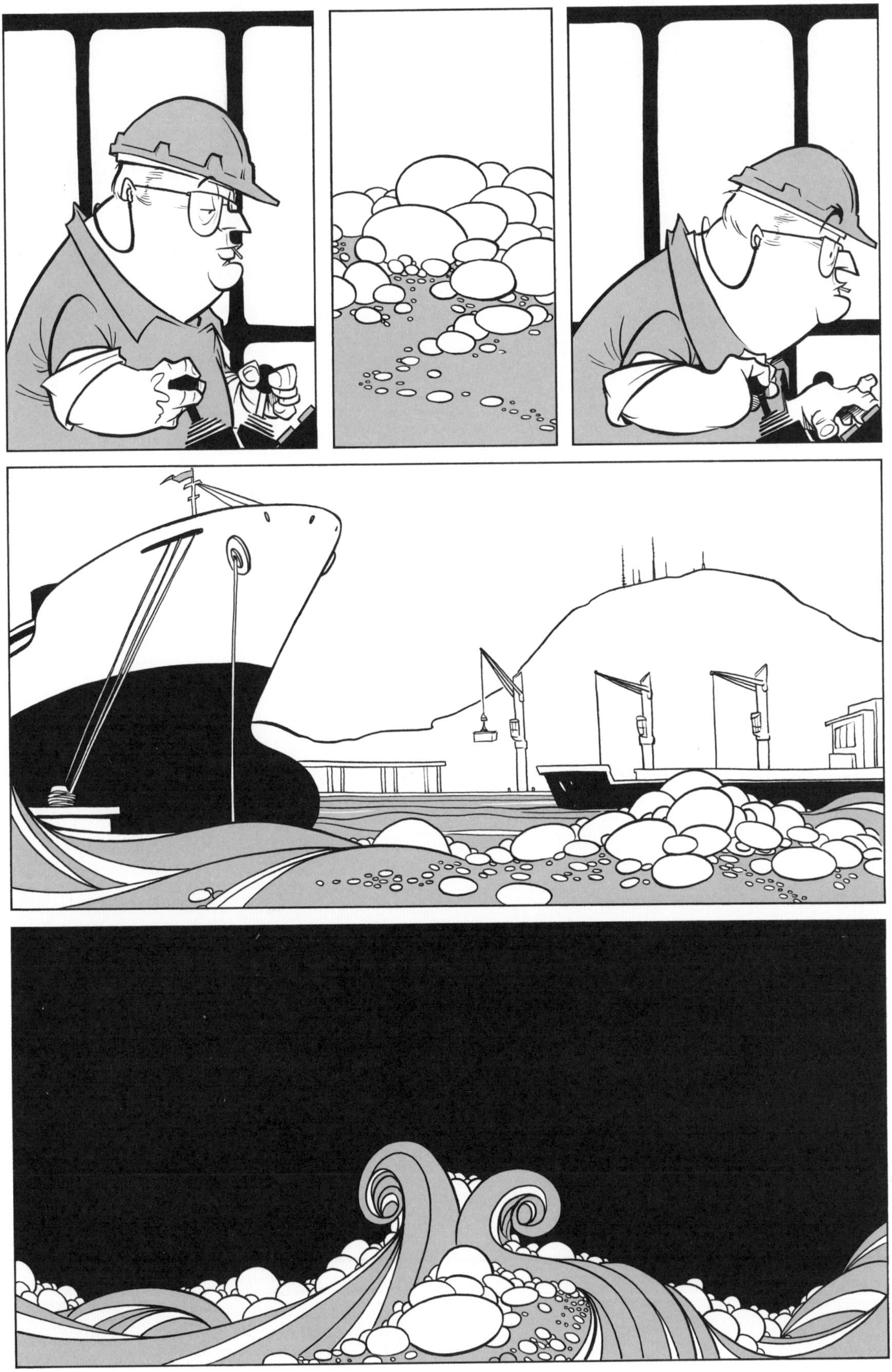

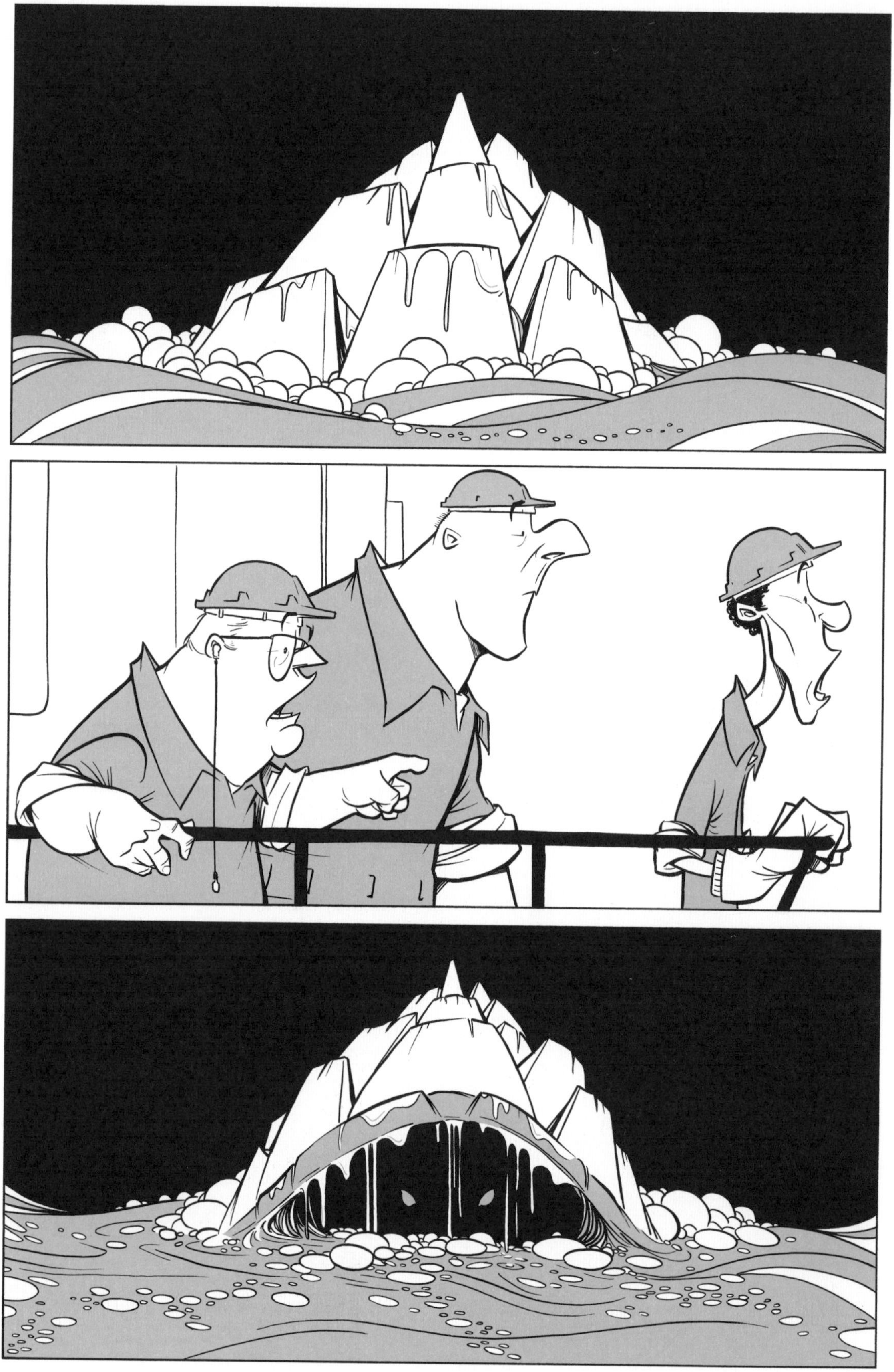

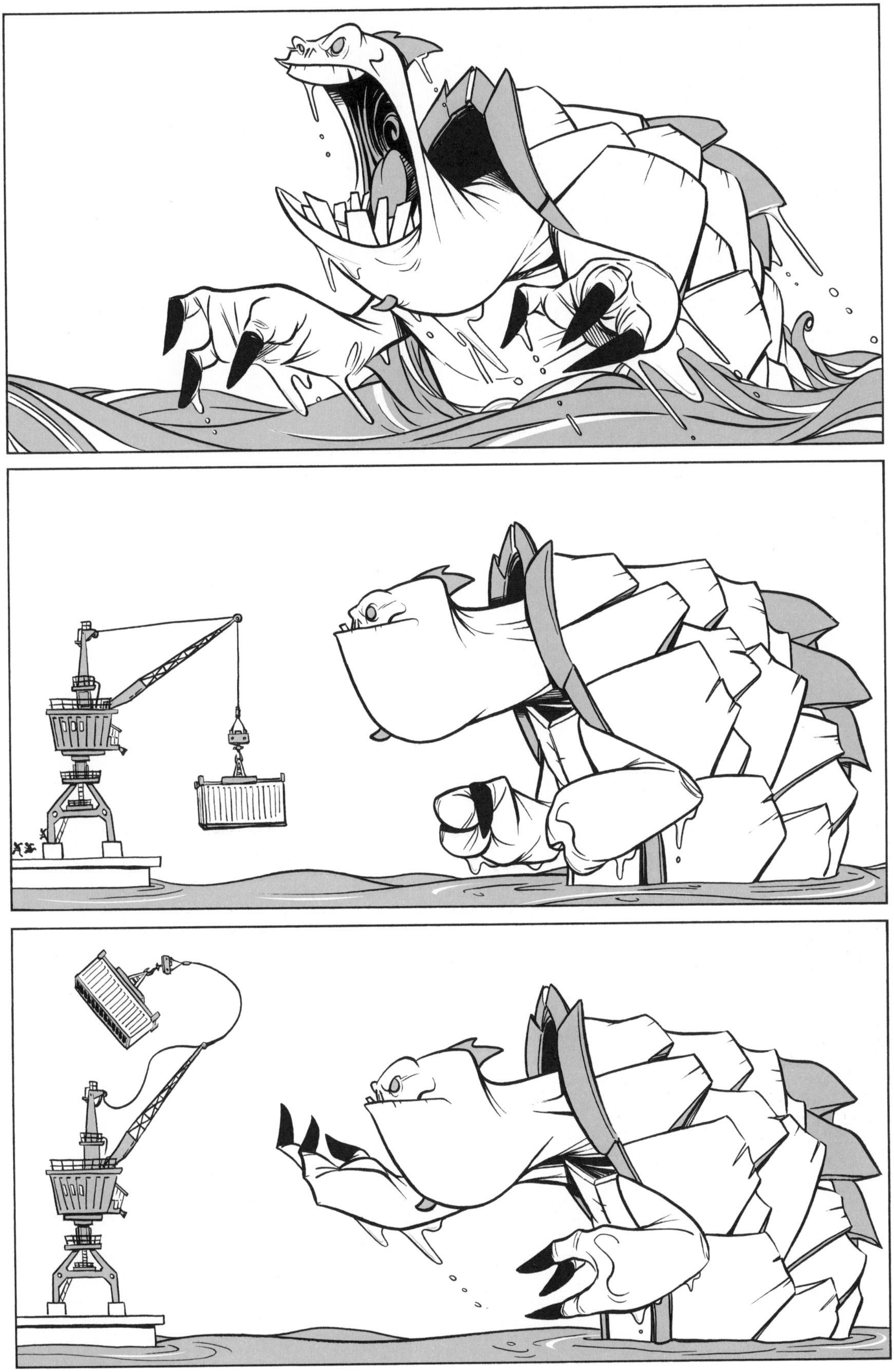

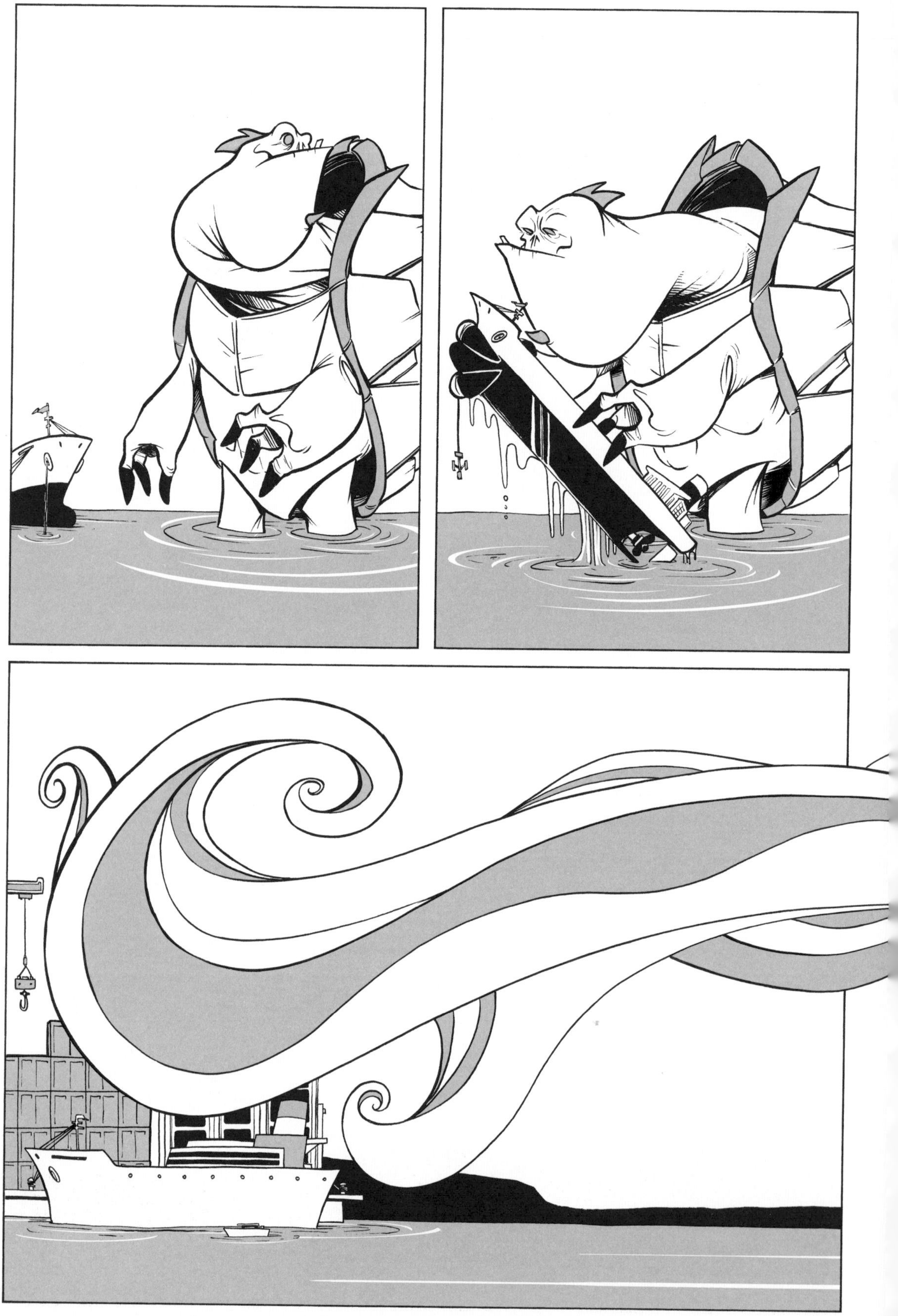

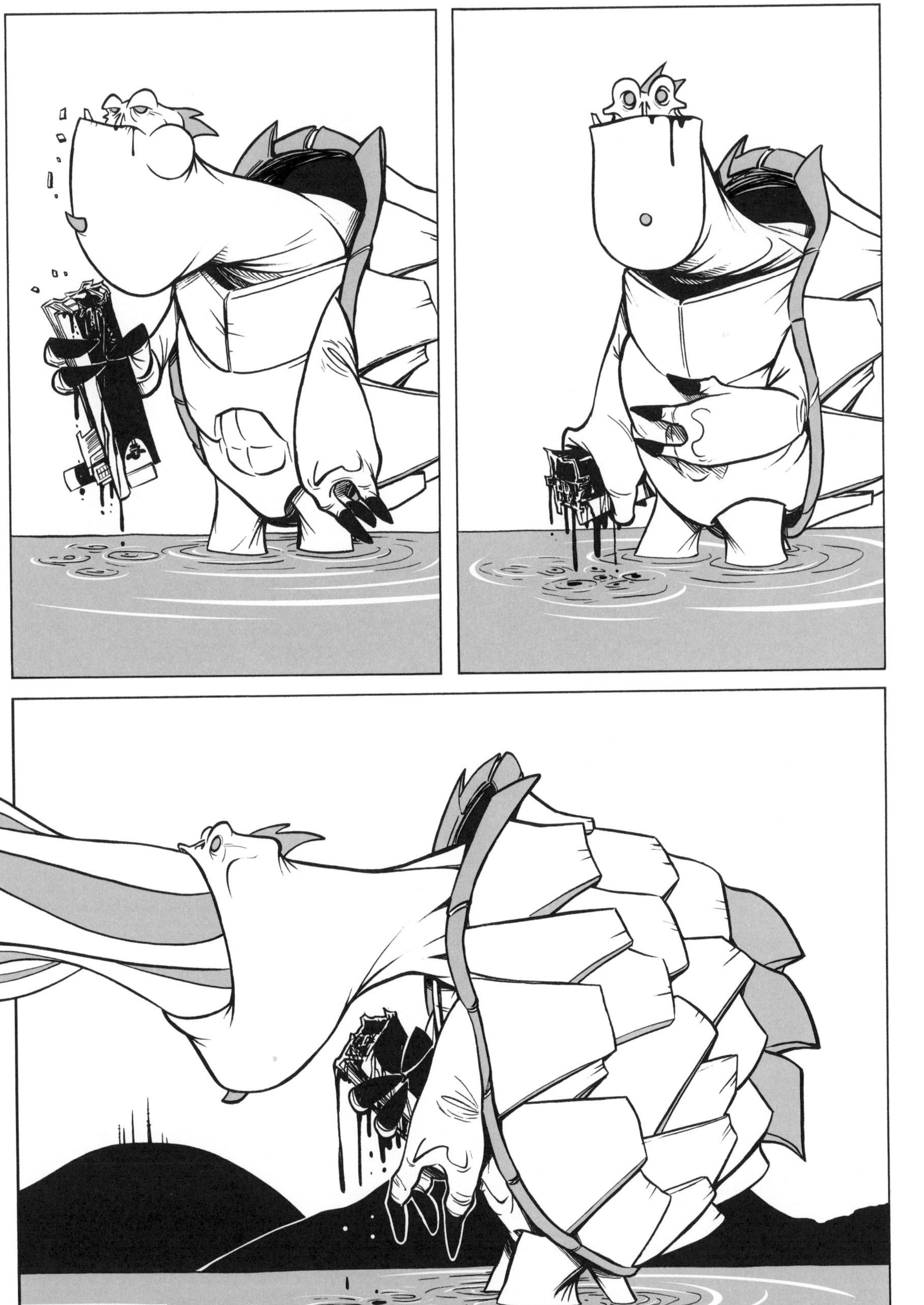

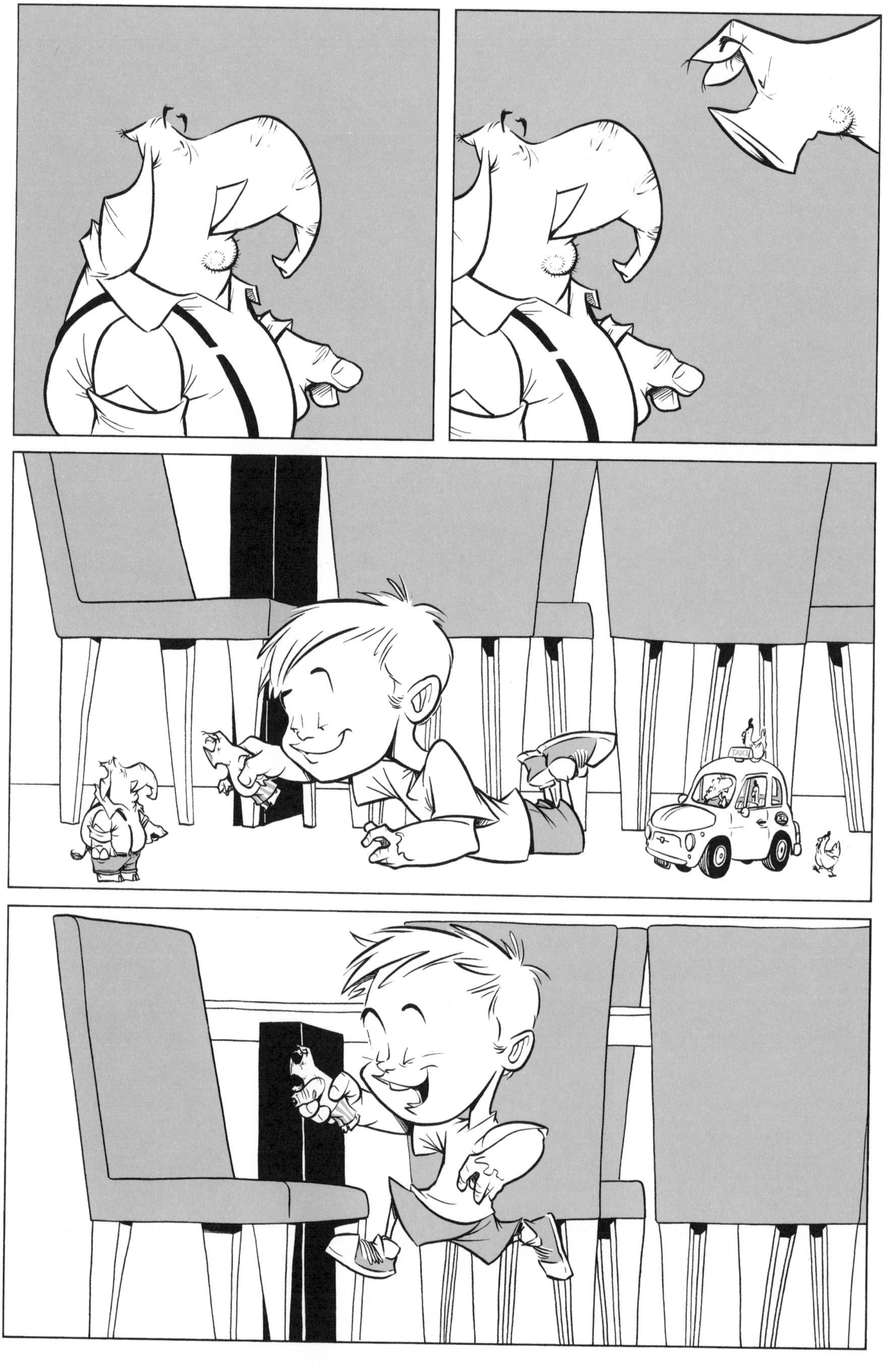
TAXI

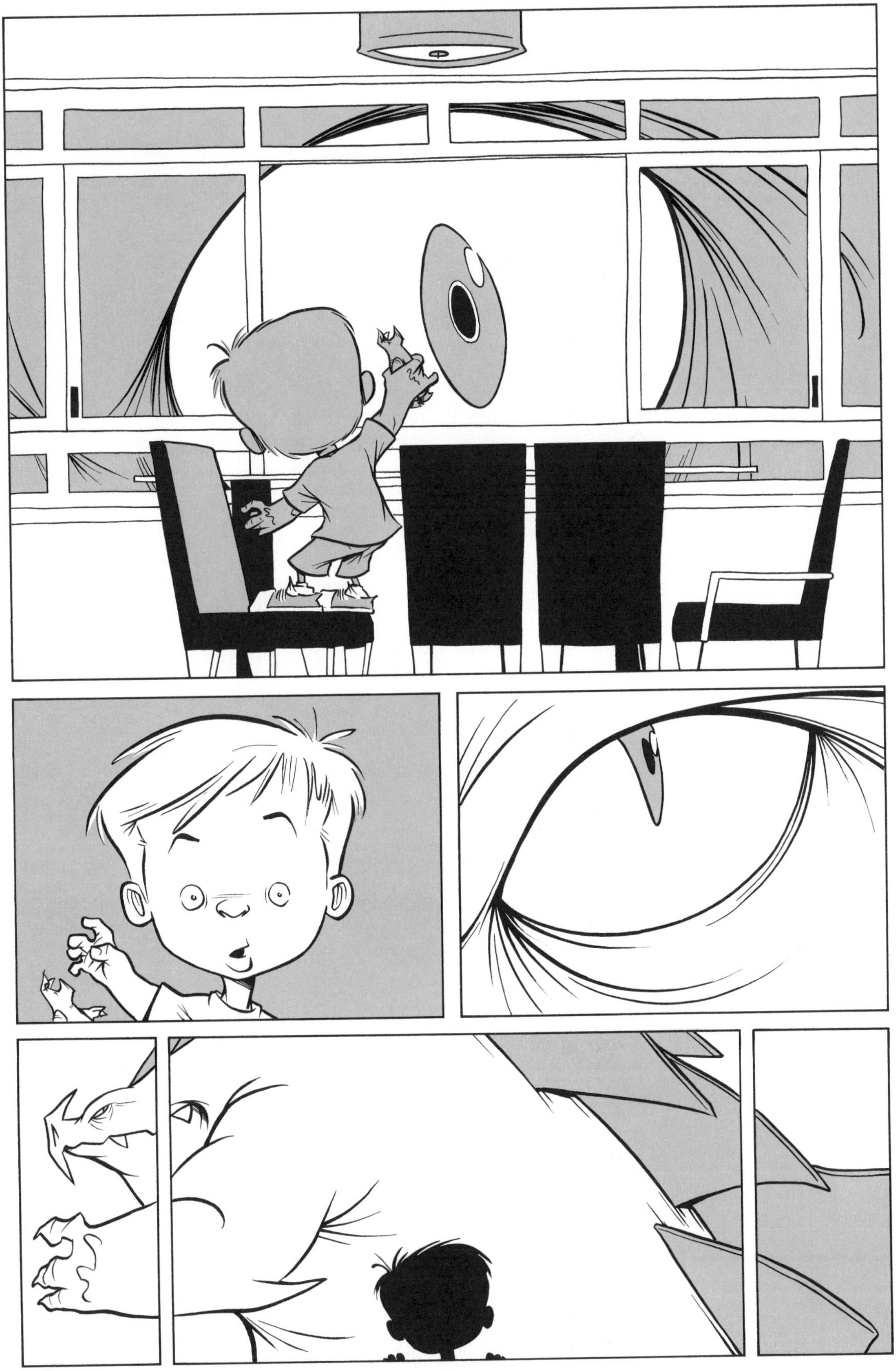

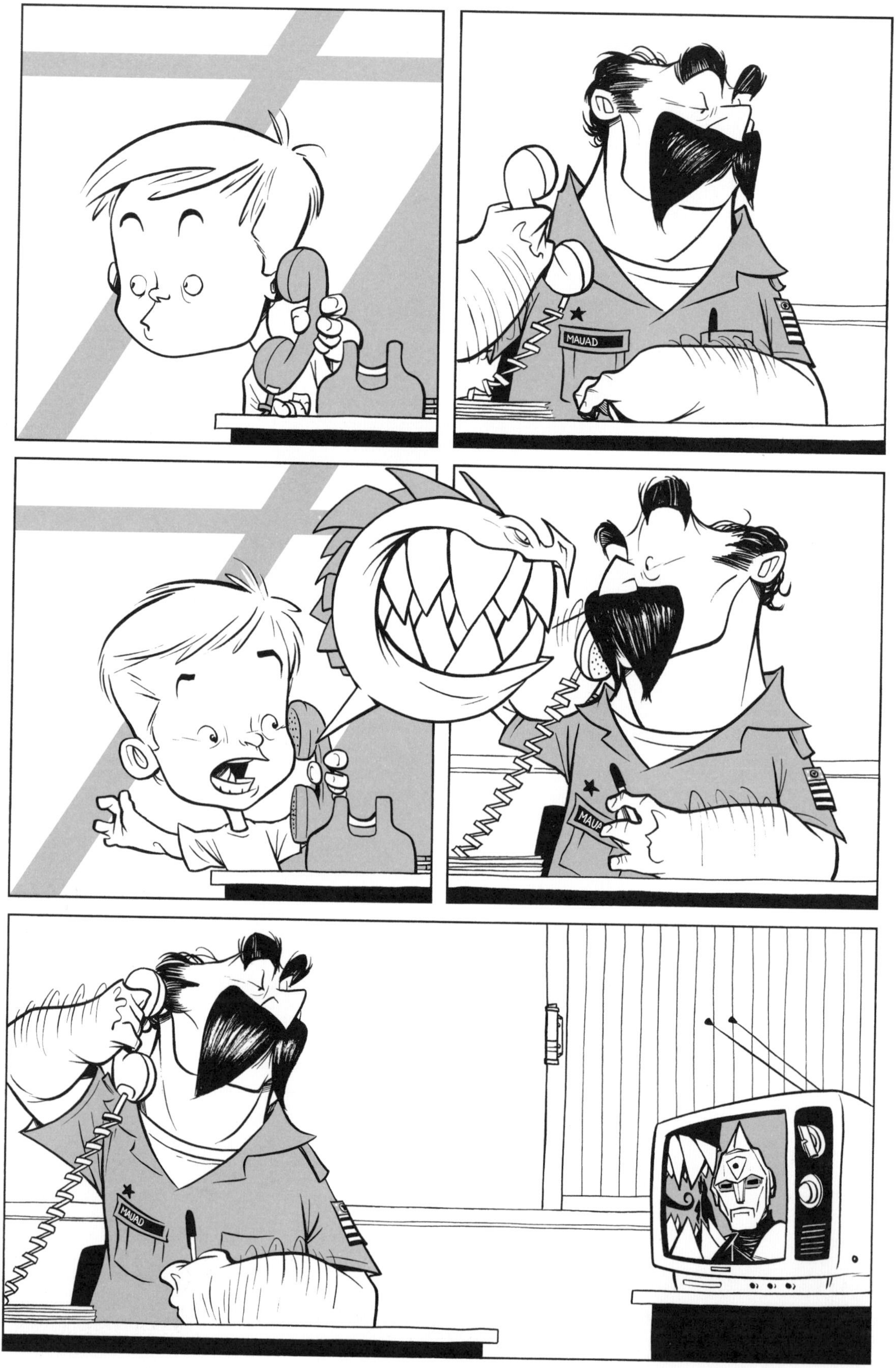
MAUAD
MAUAD

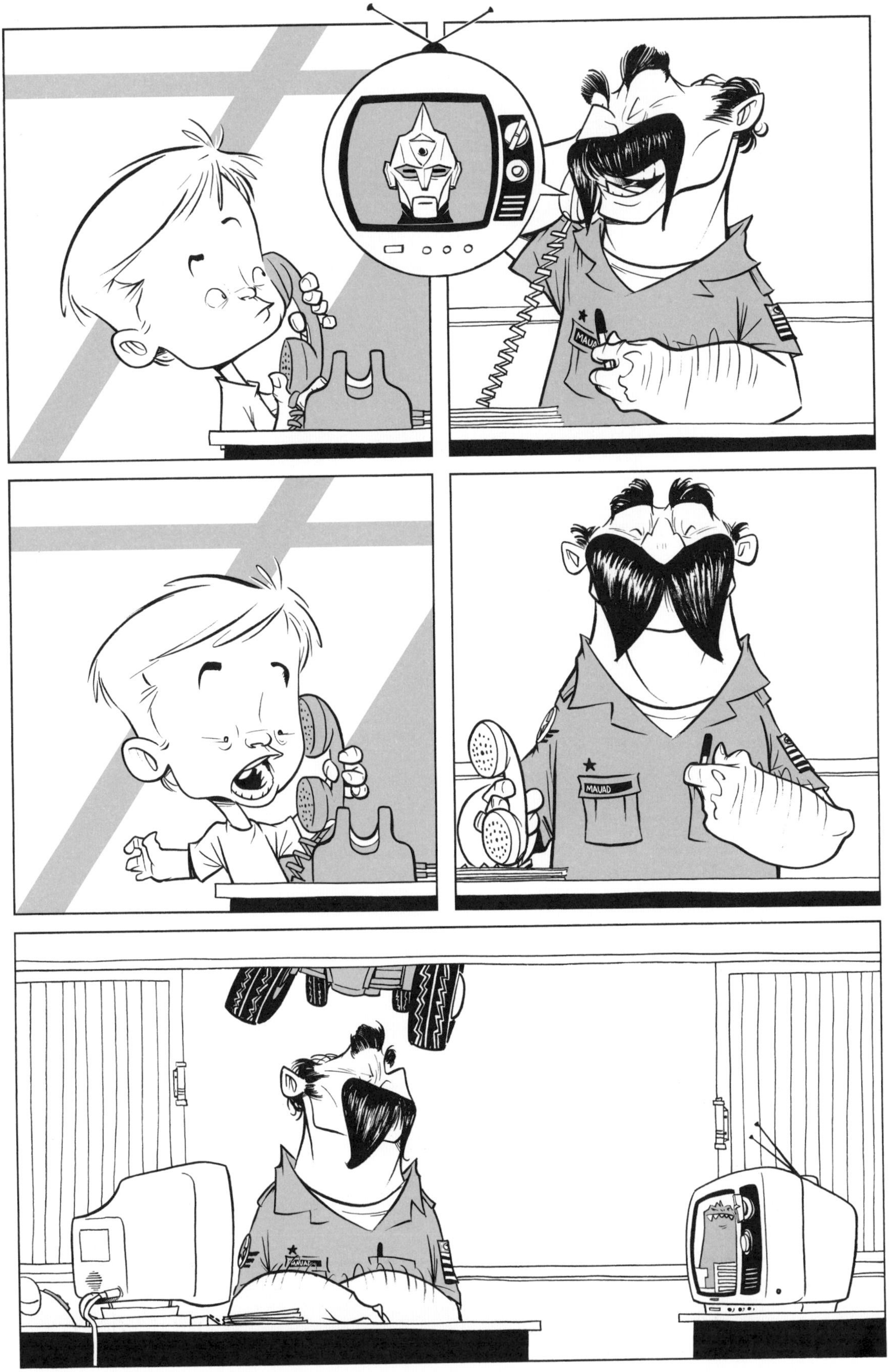
MAUAD
MAUAD
MAUAD

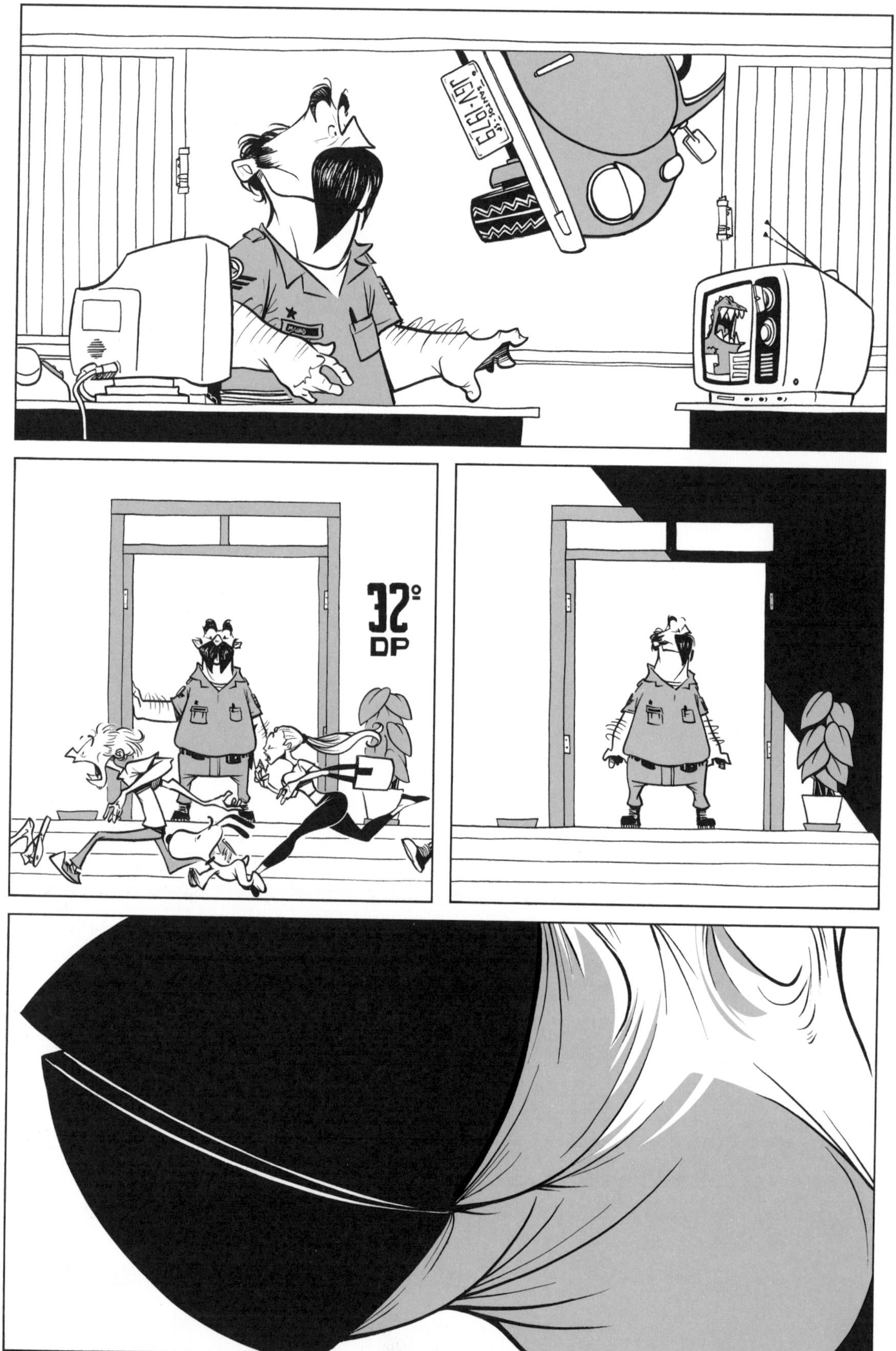
JGV-1979
32º
DP

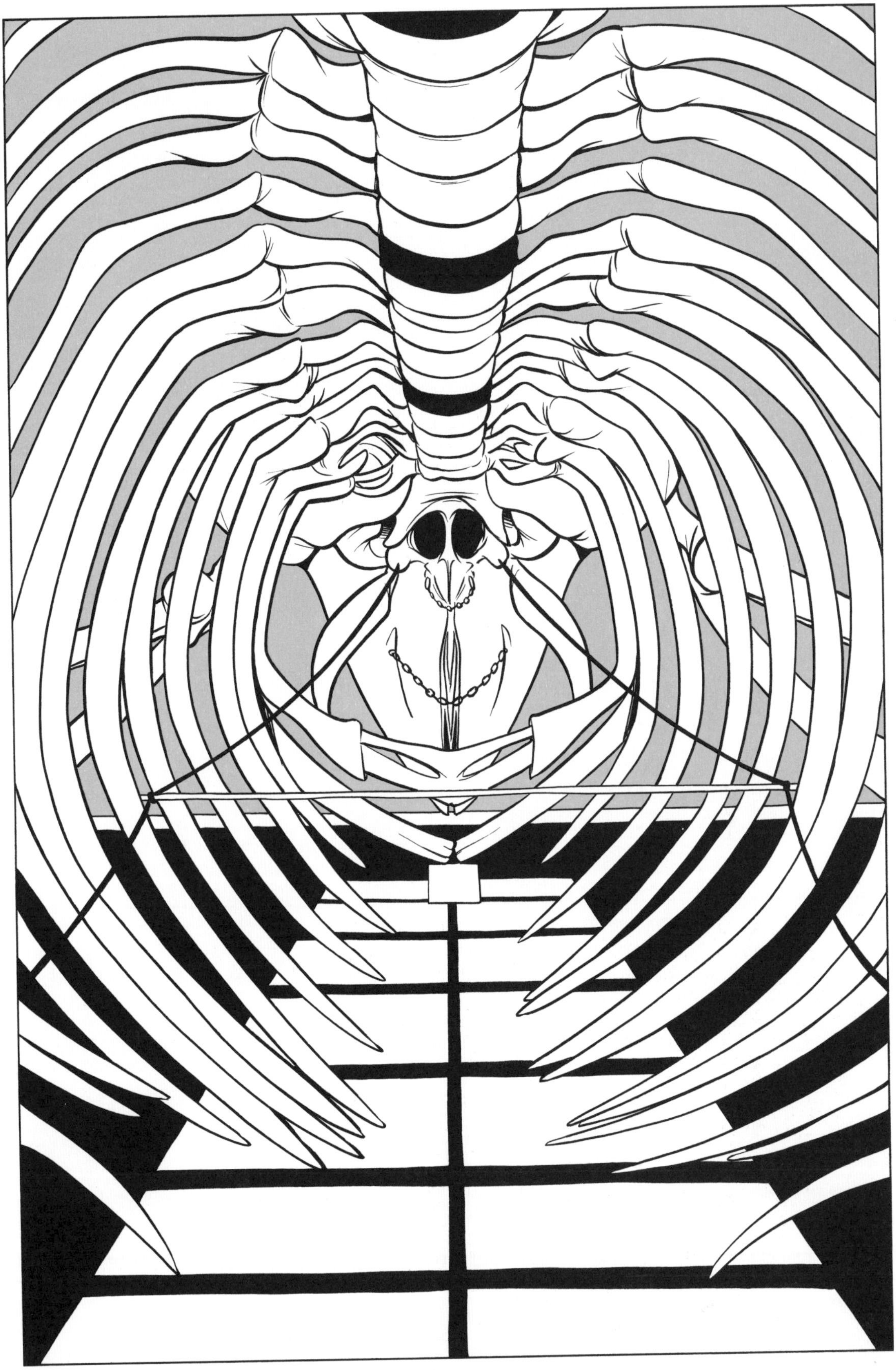

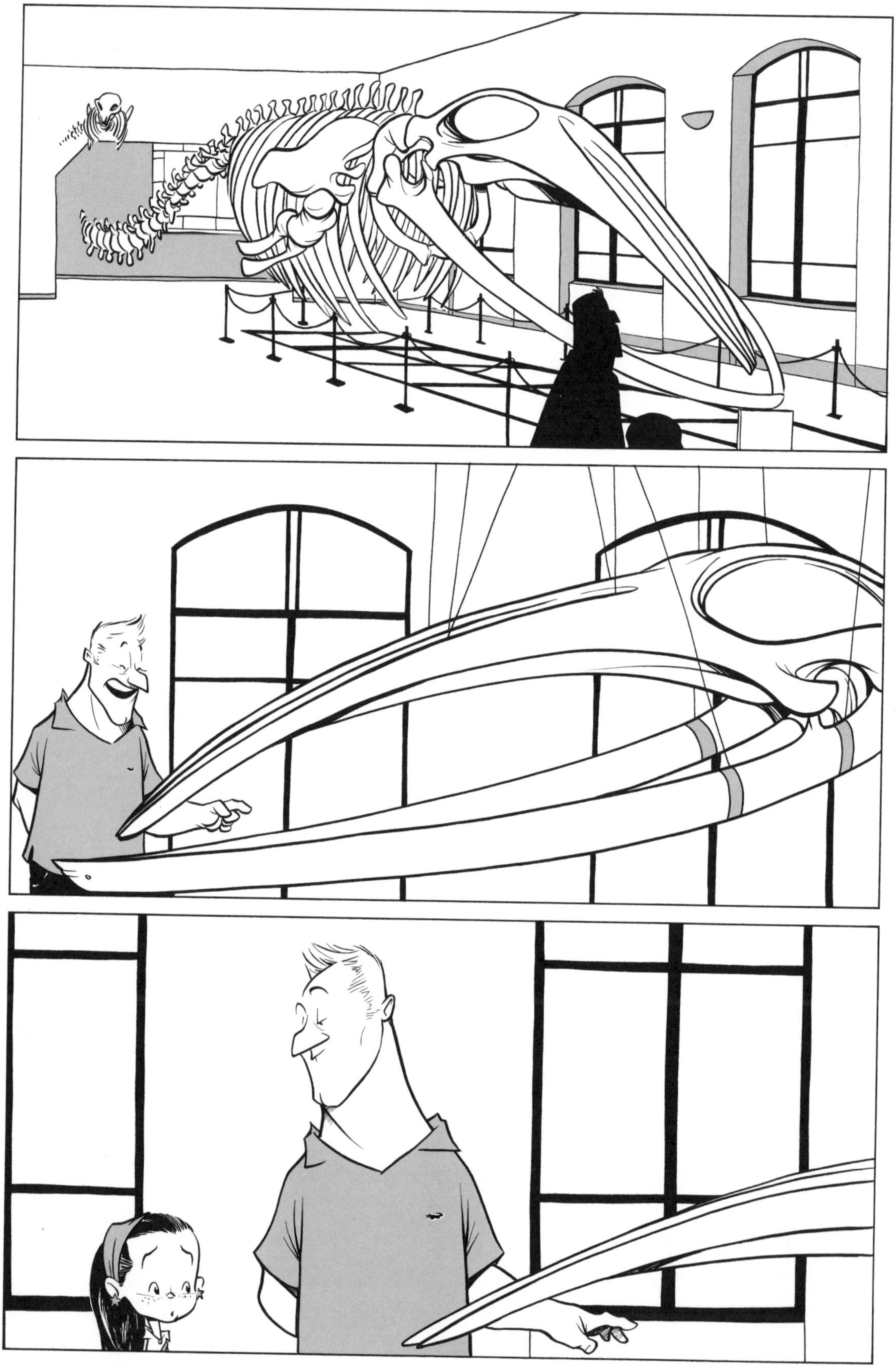

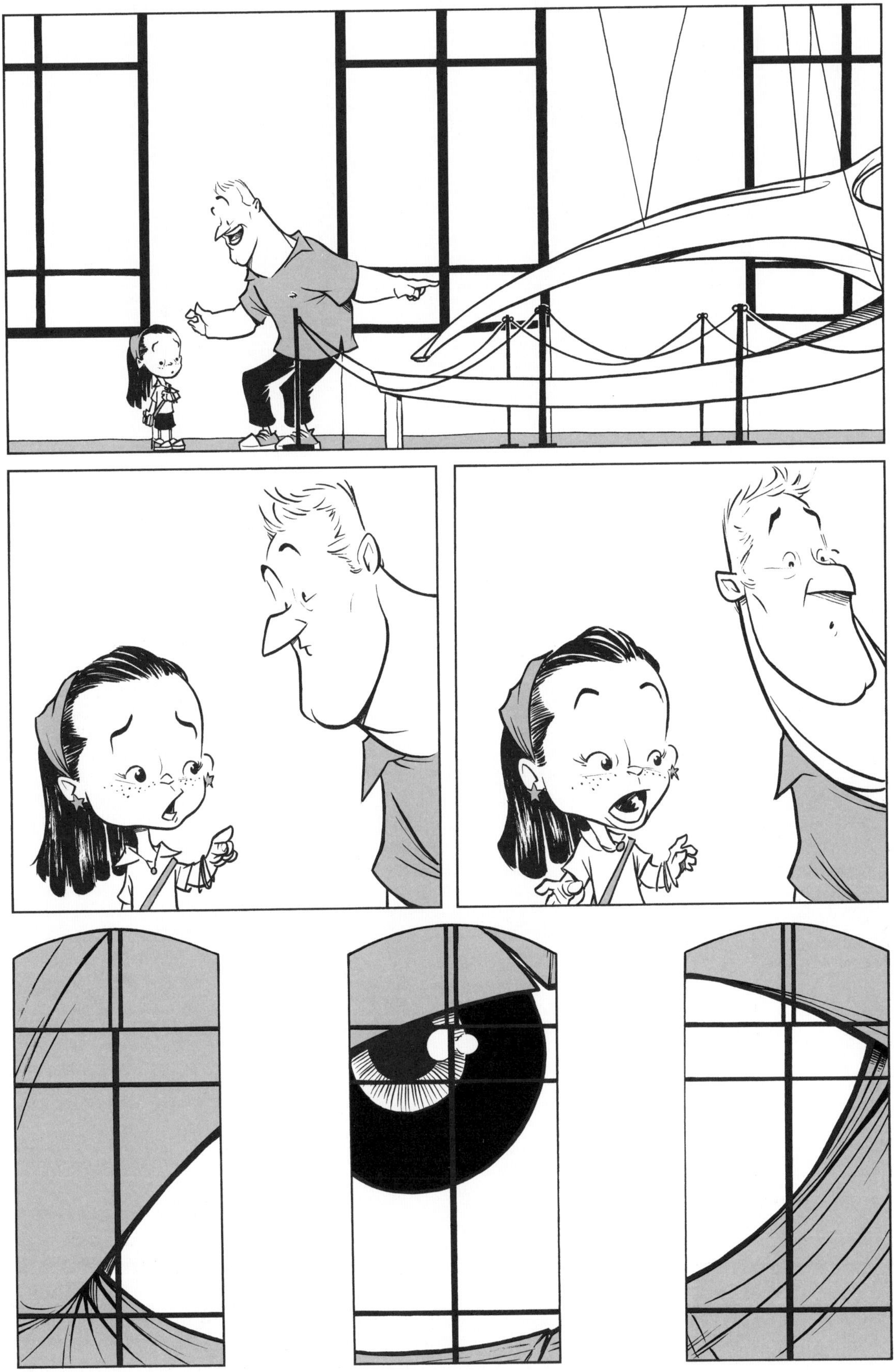

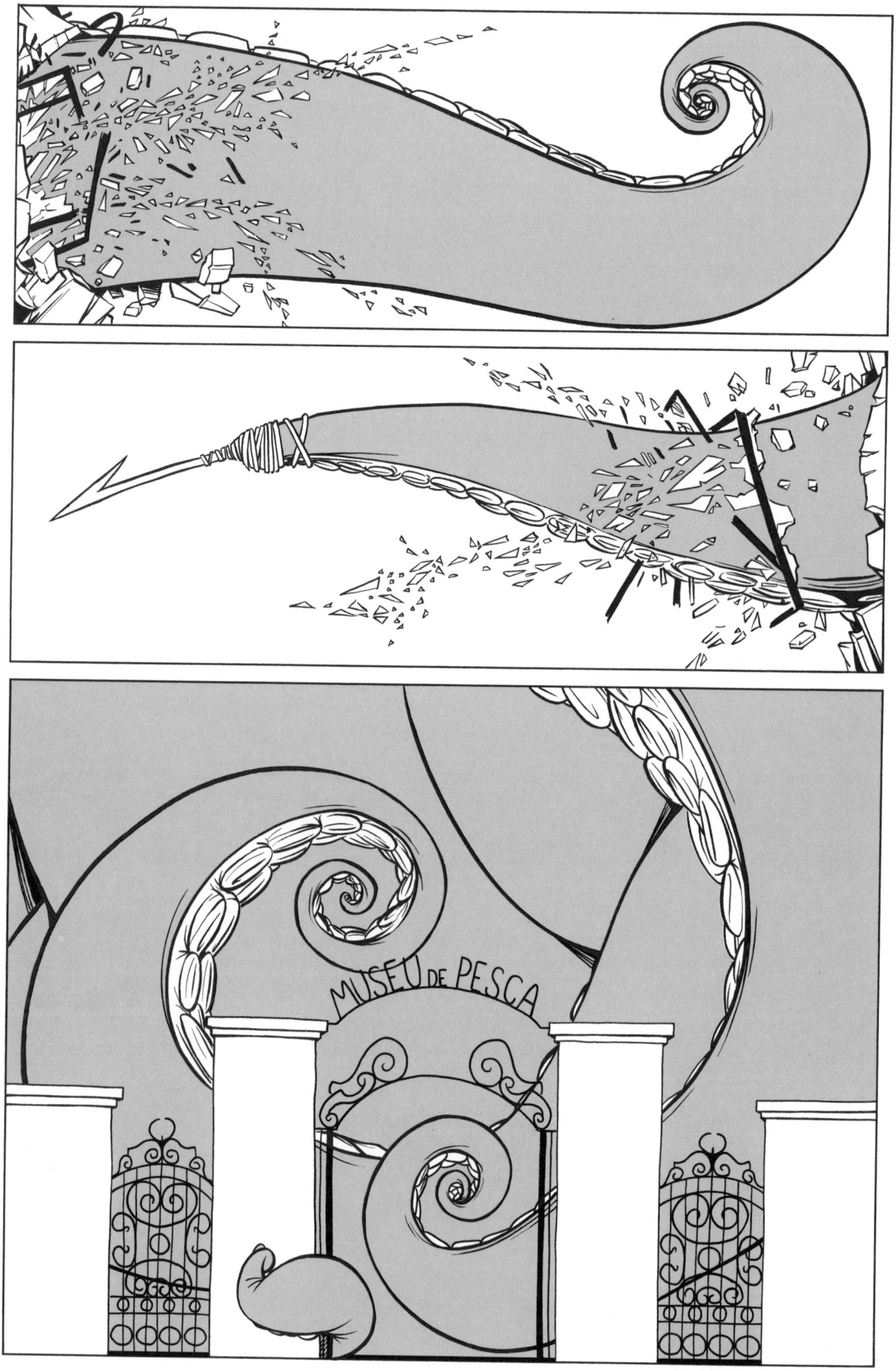
MUSEU DE PESCA

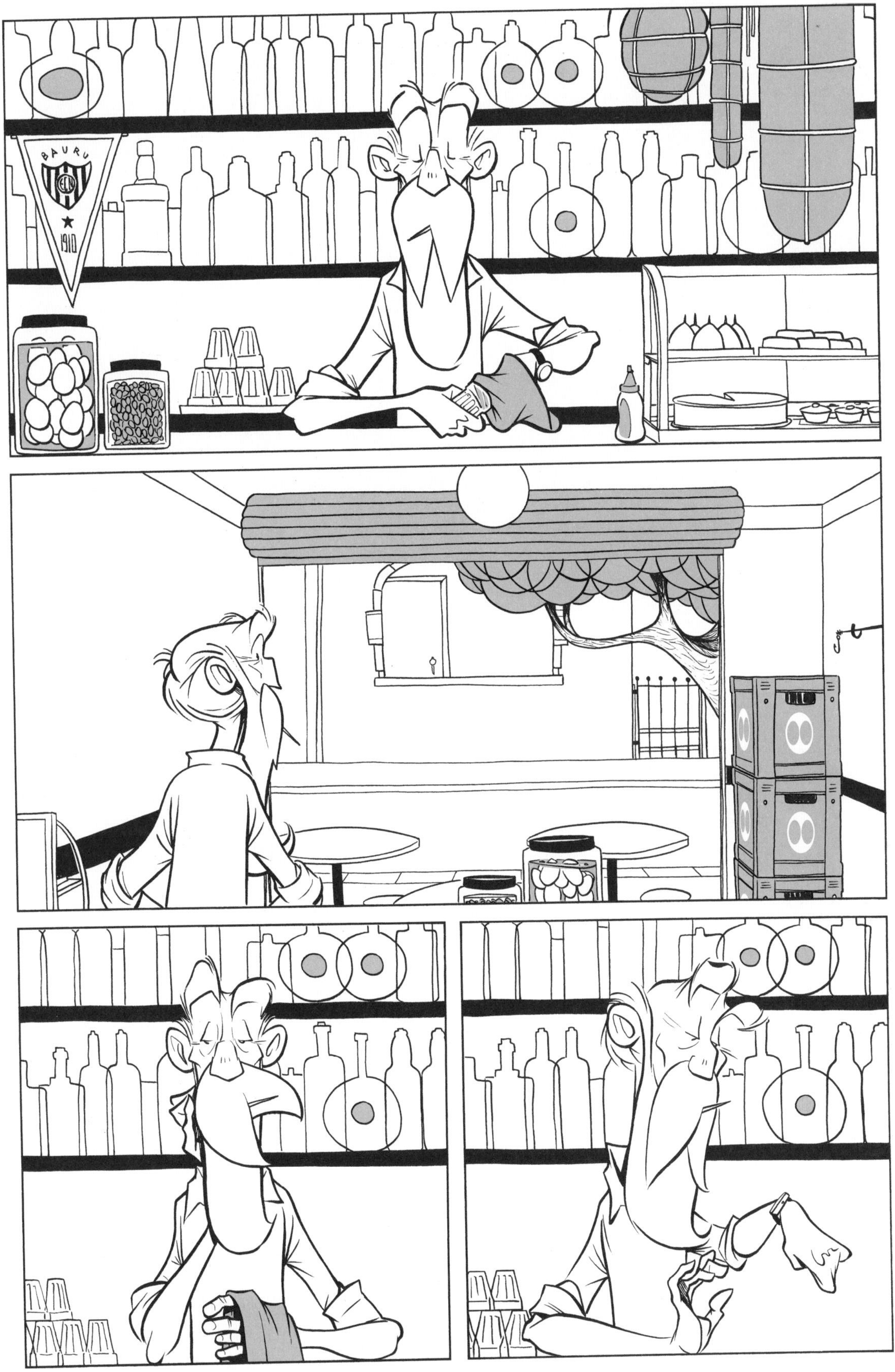
BAURU
1910

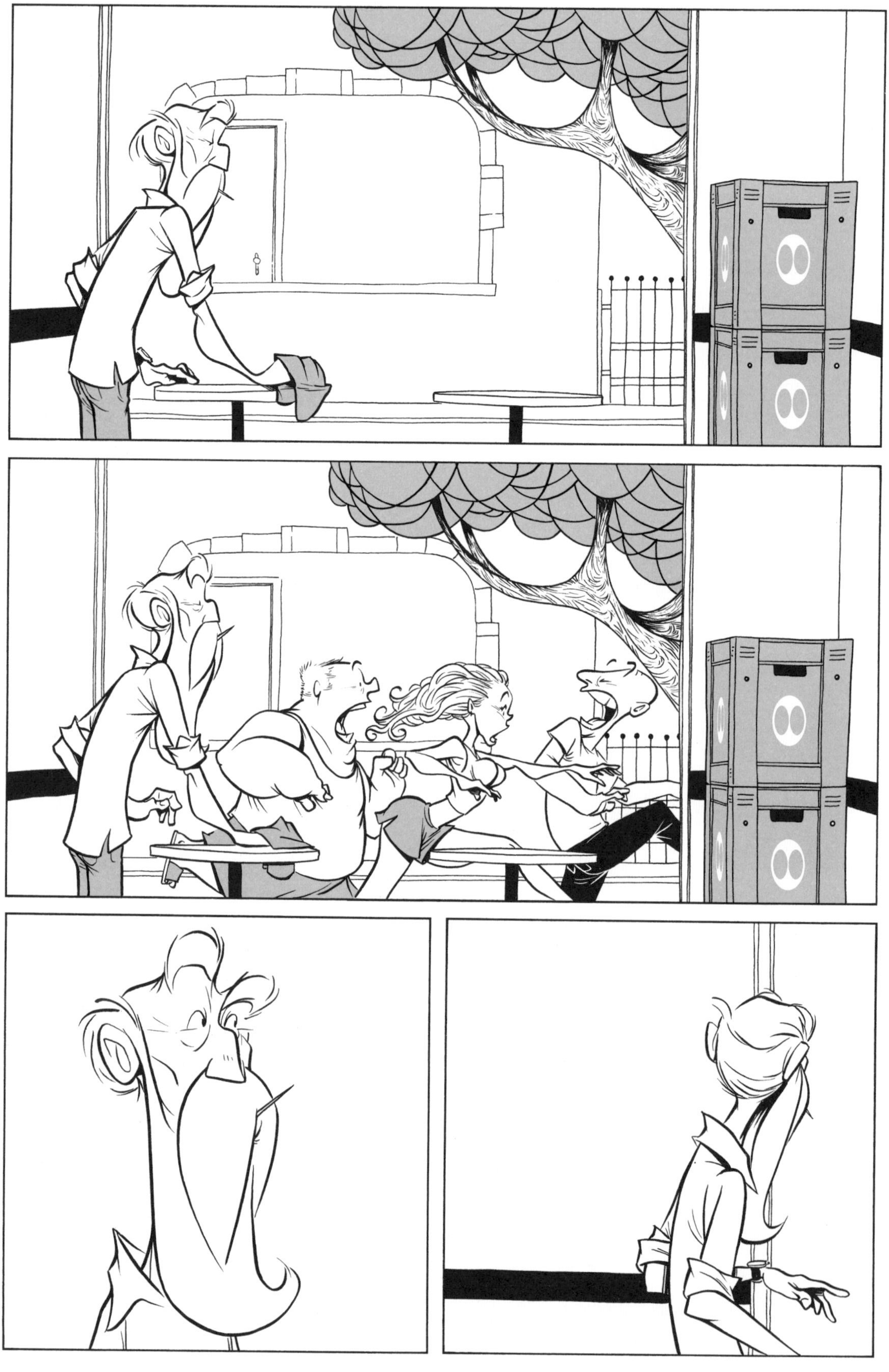

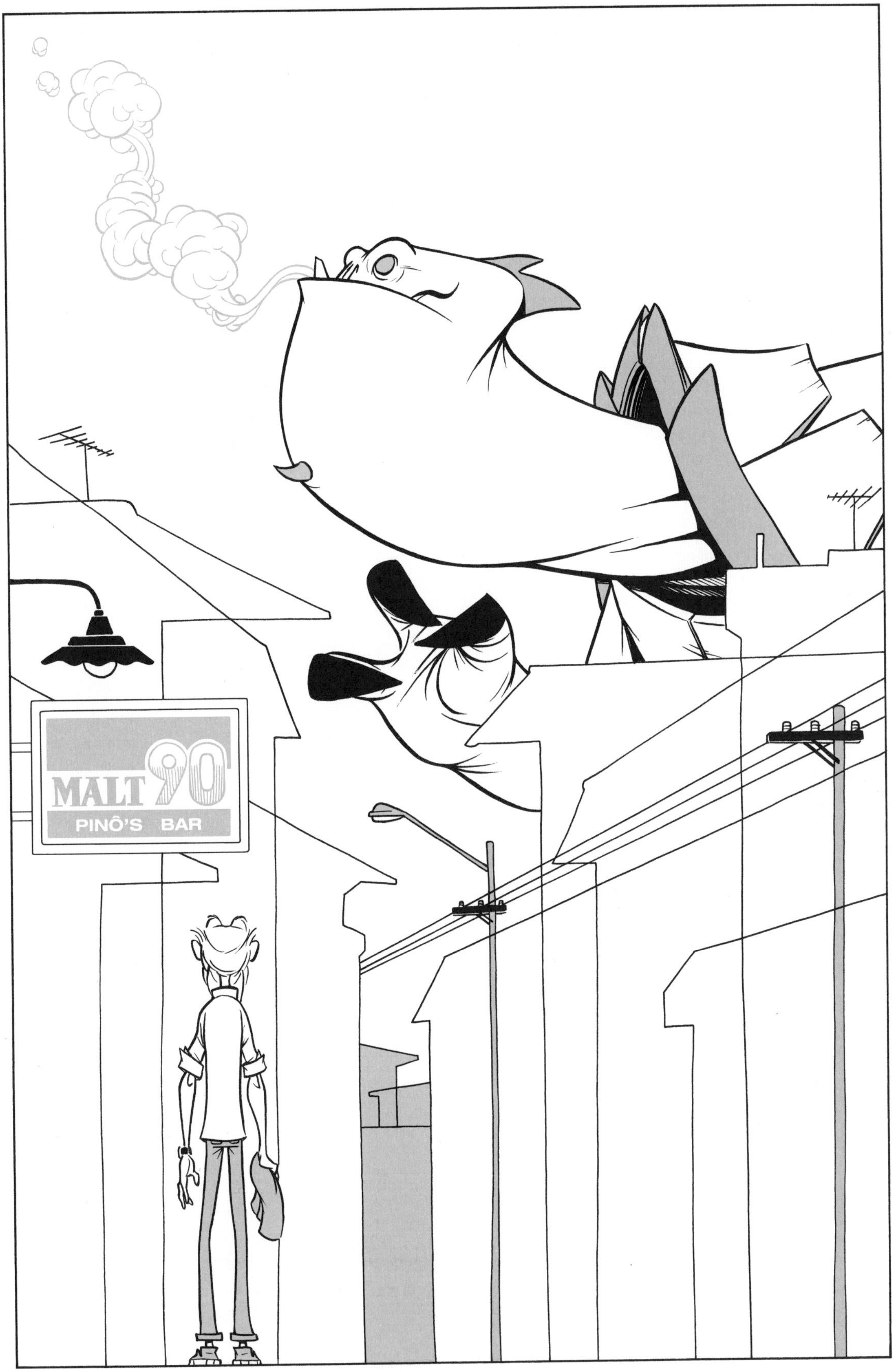
MALT 90
PINÔ'S BAR

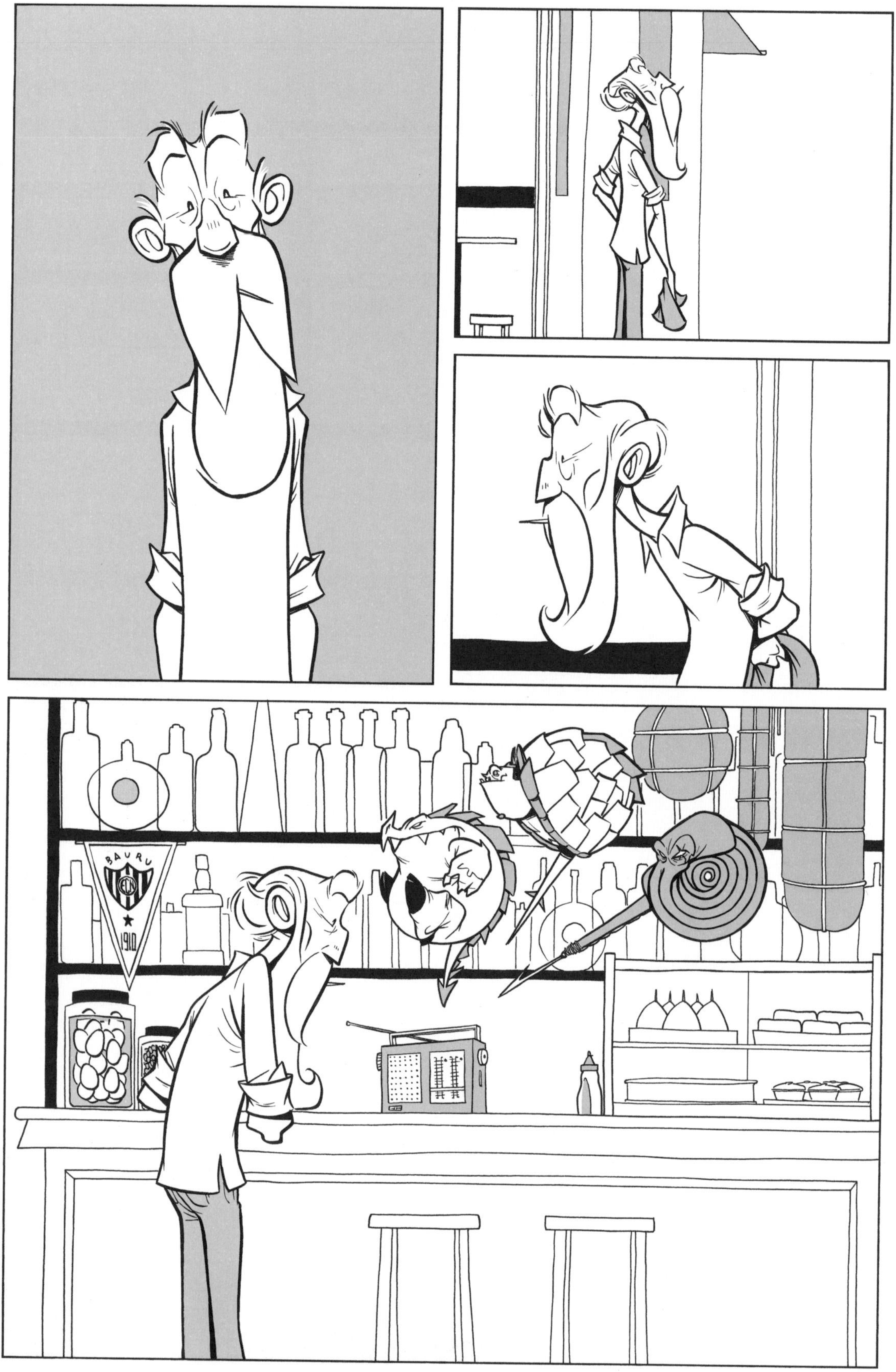
BAURU
ECN
1910

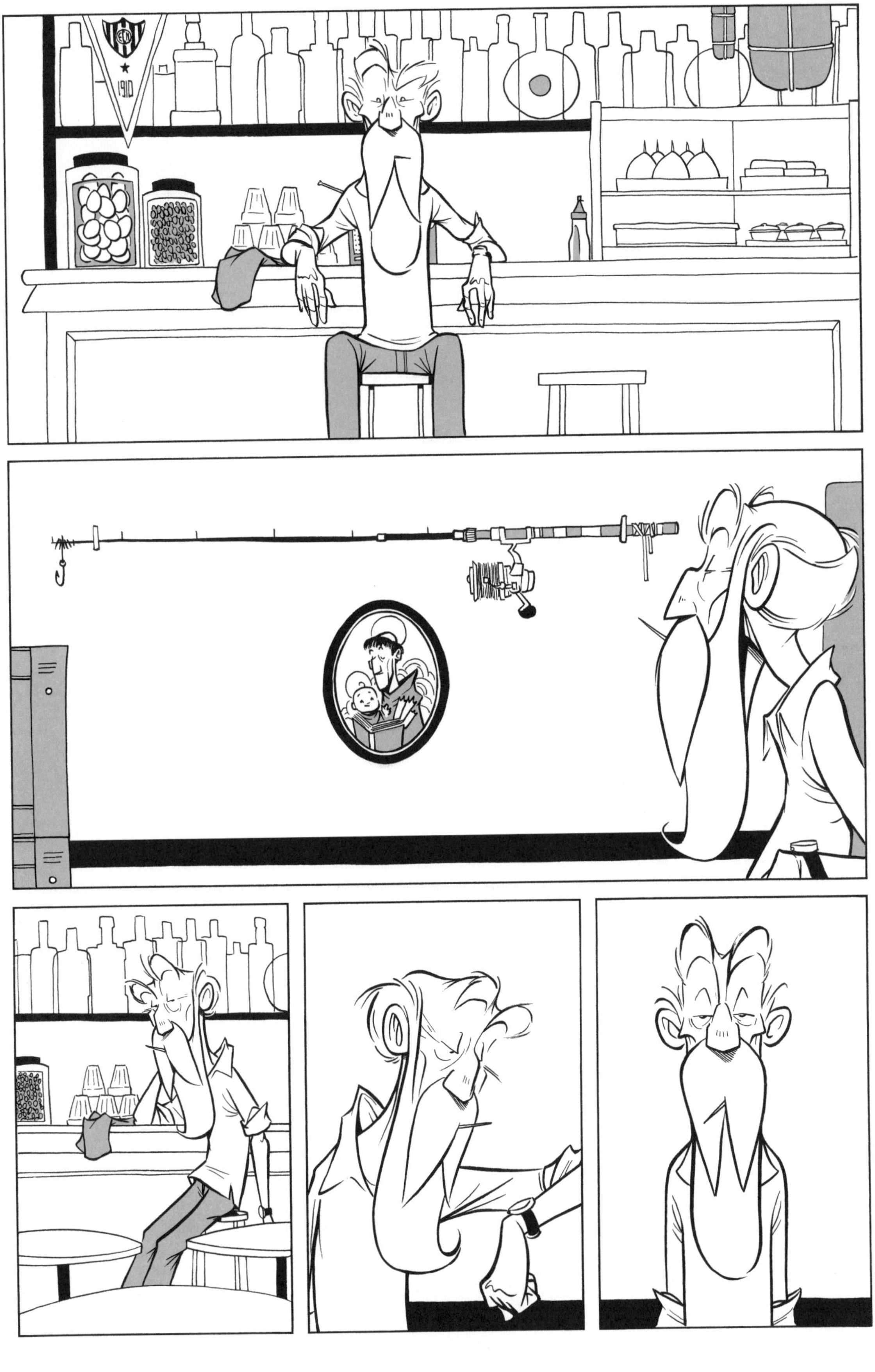
1910

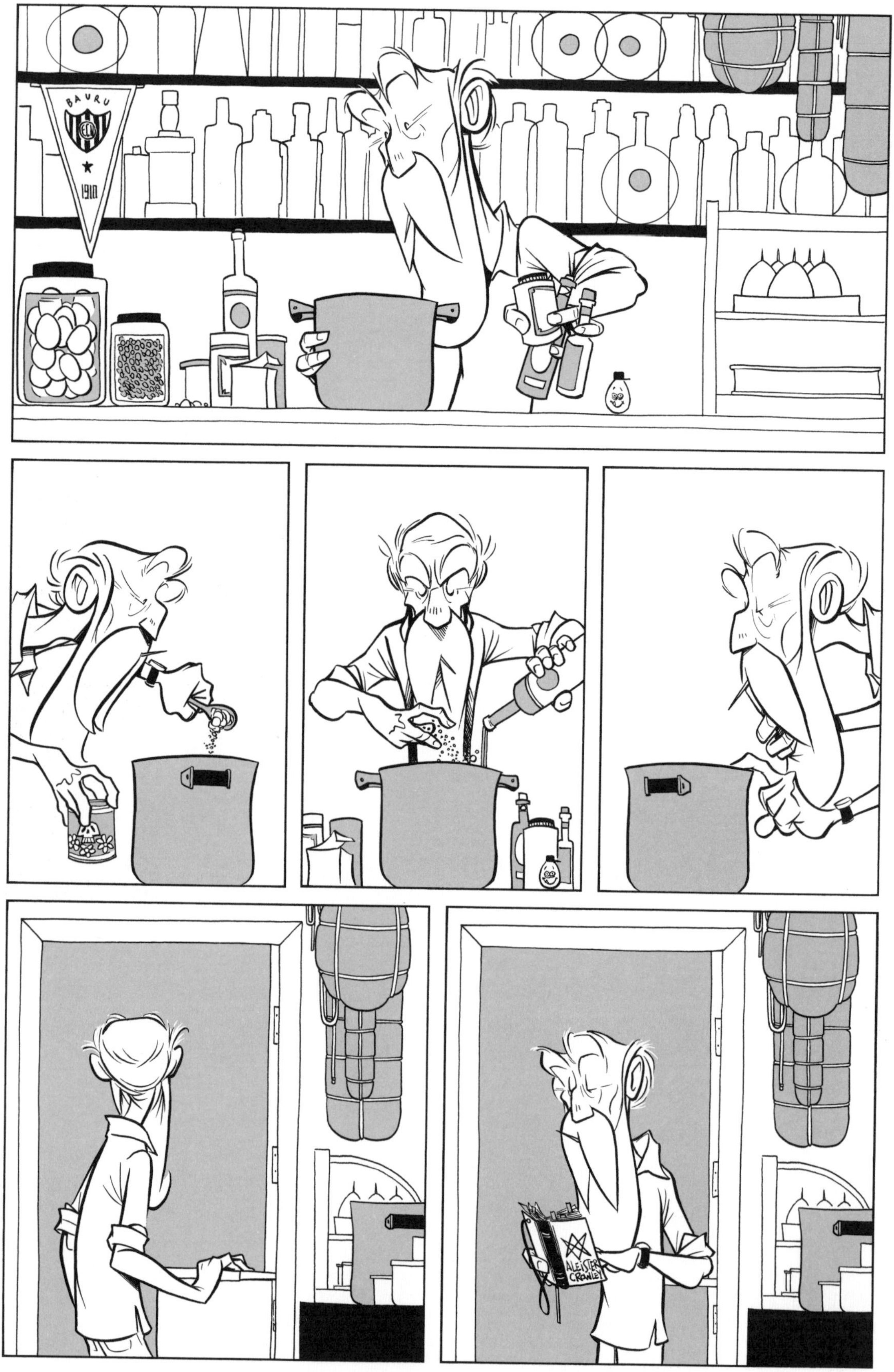
BAURU
1910
ALEISTER CROWLEY

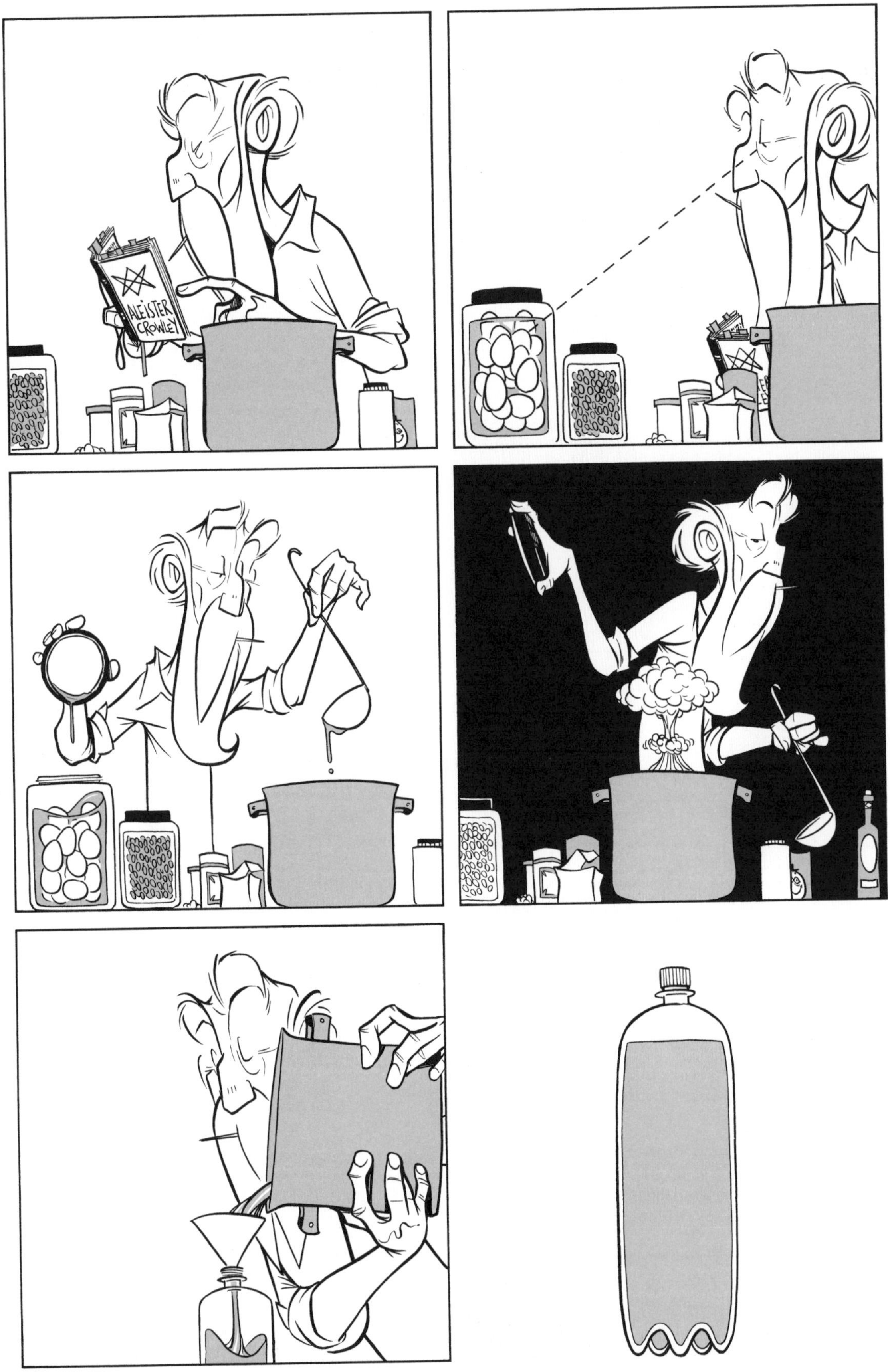
ALEISTER
CROWLEY

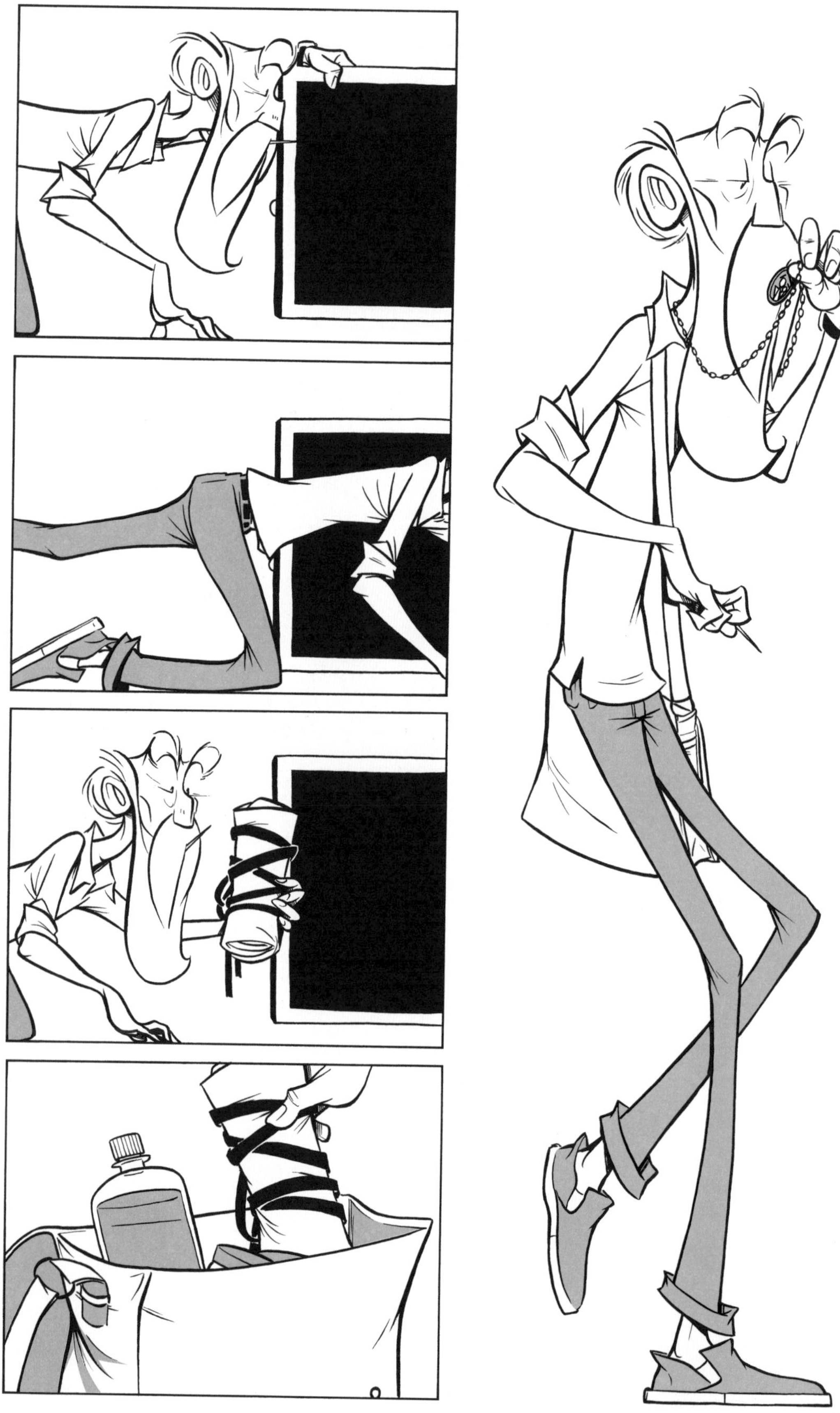

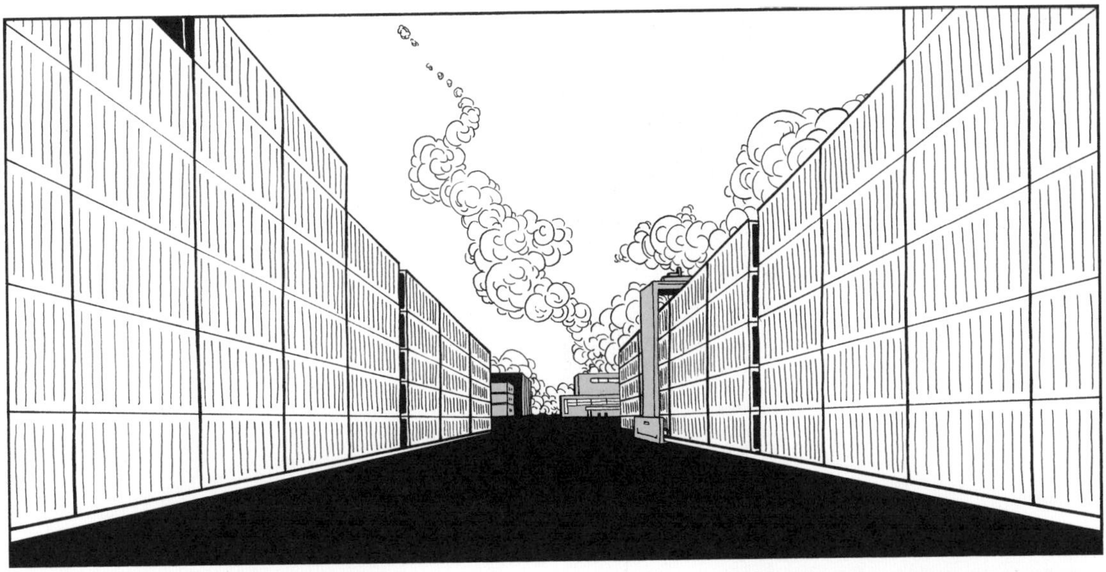
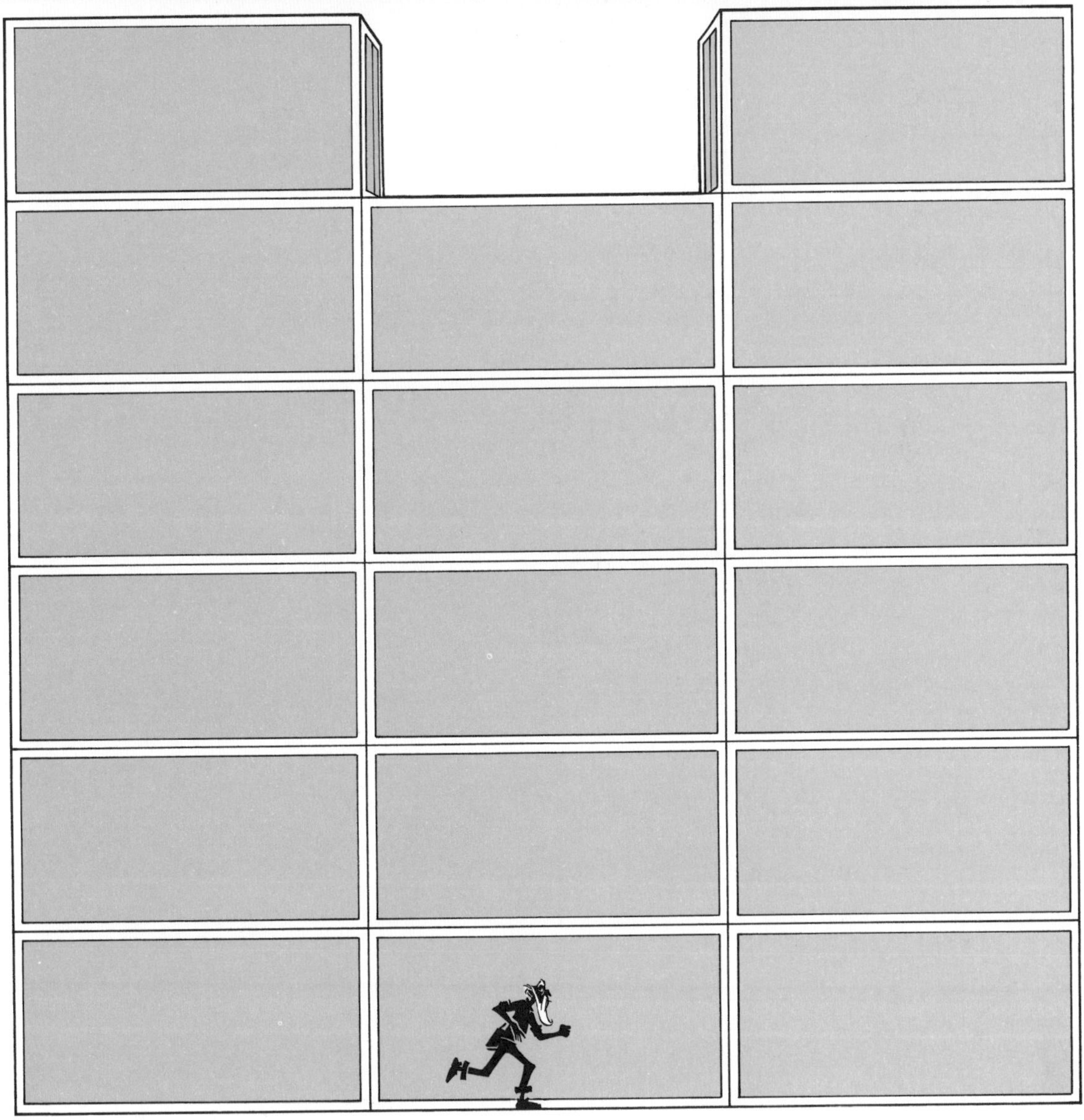

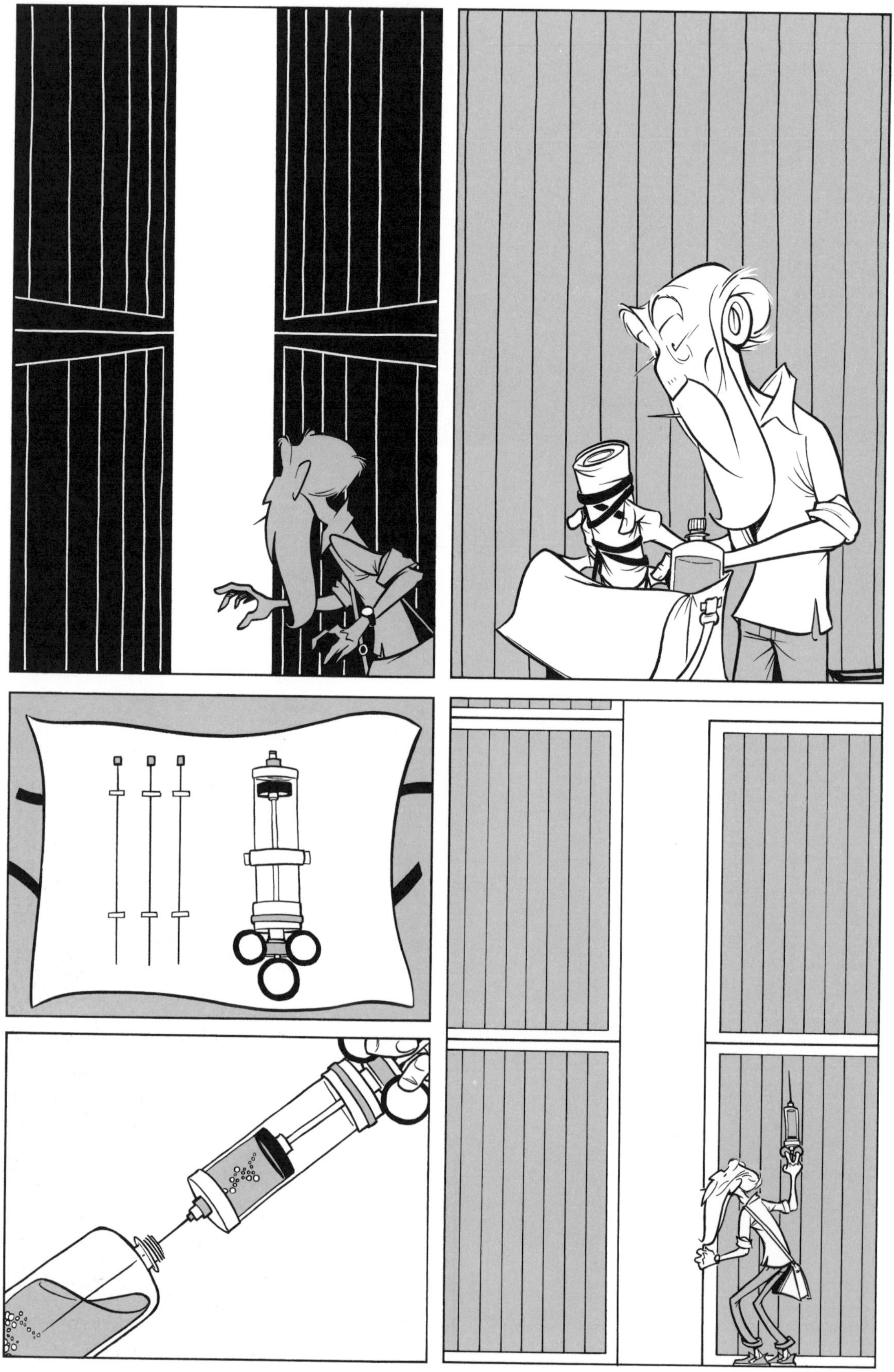

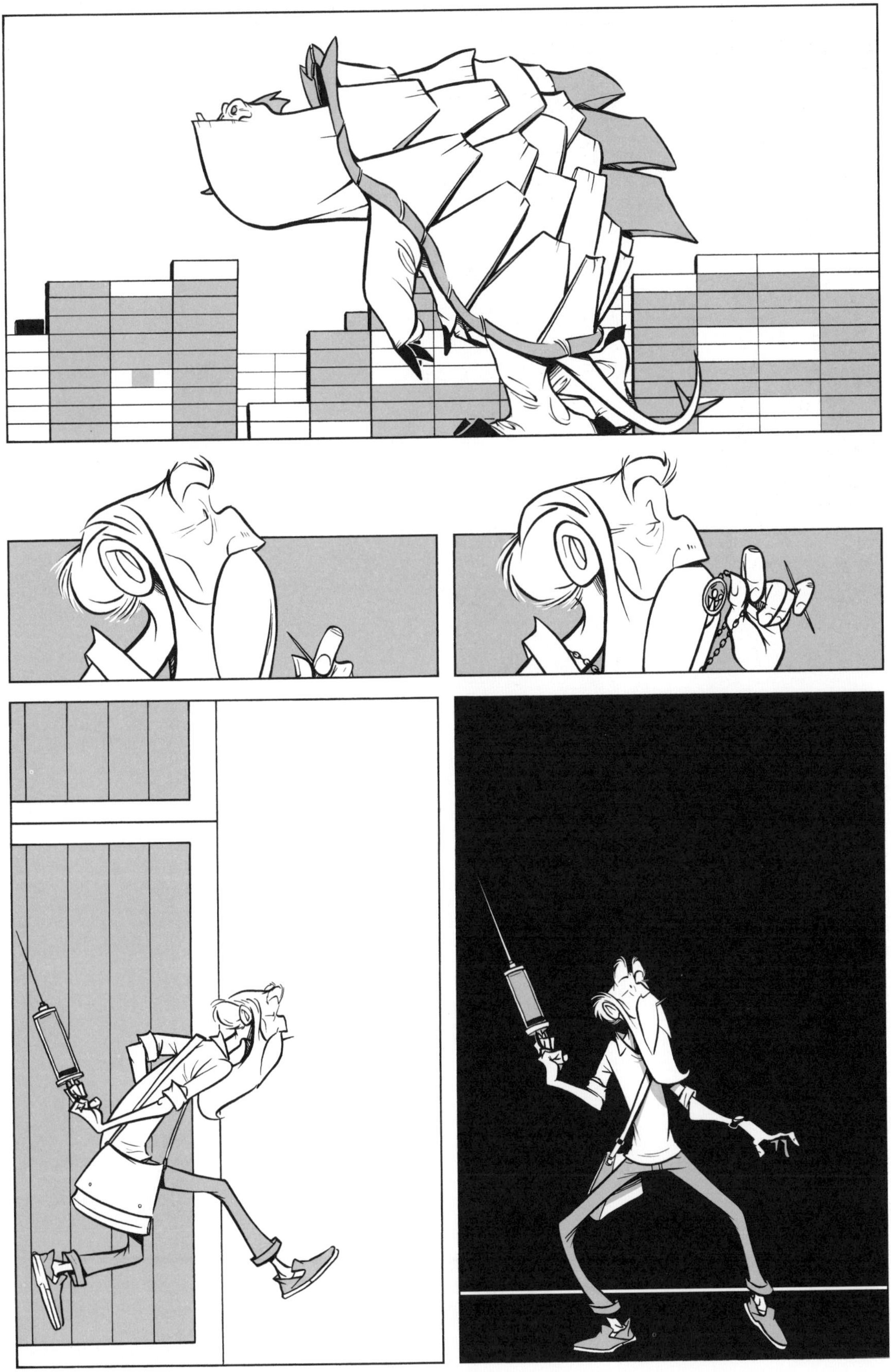

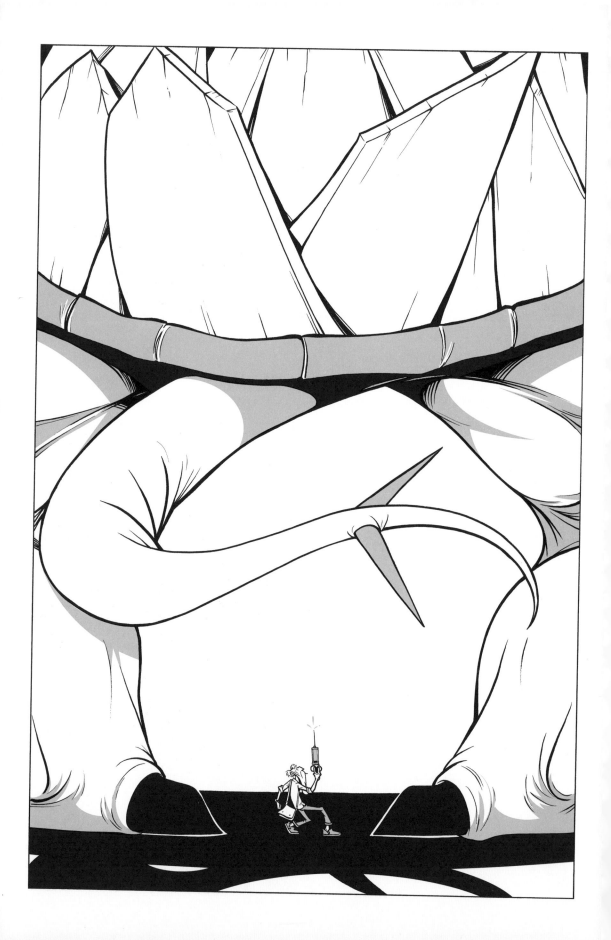

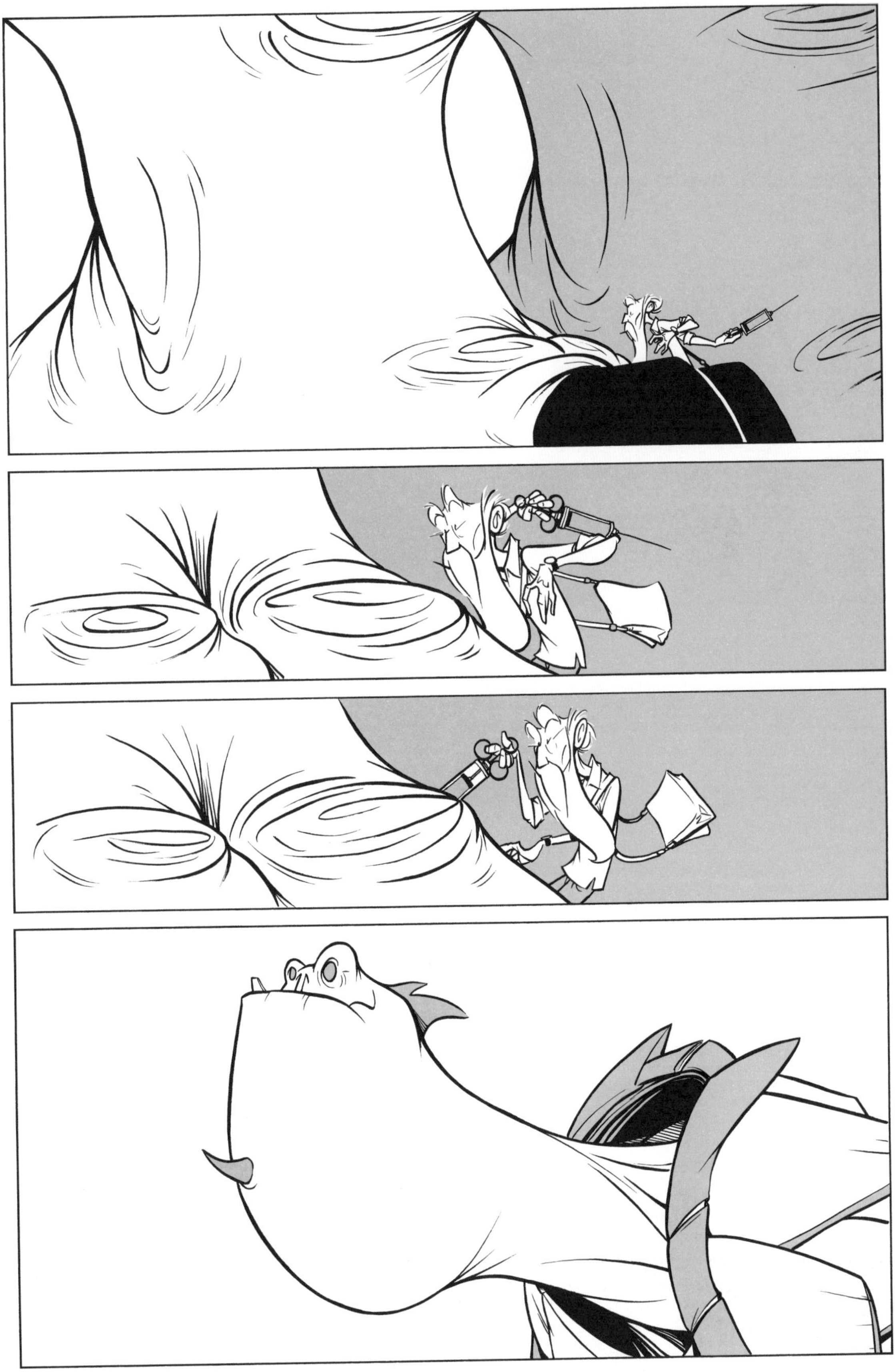

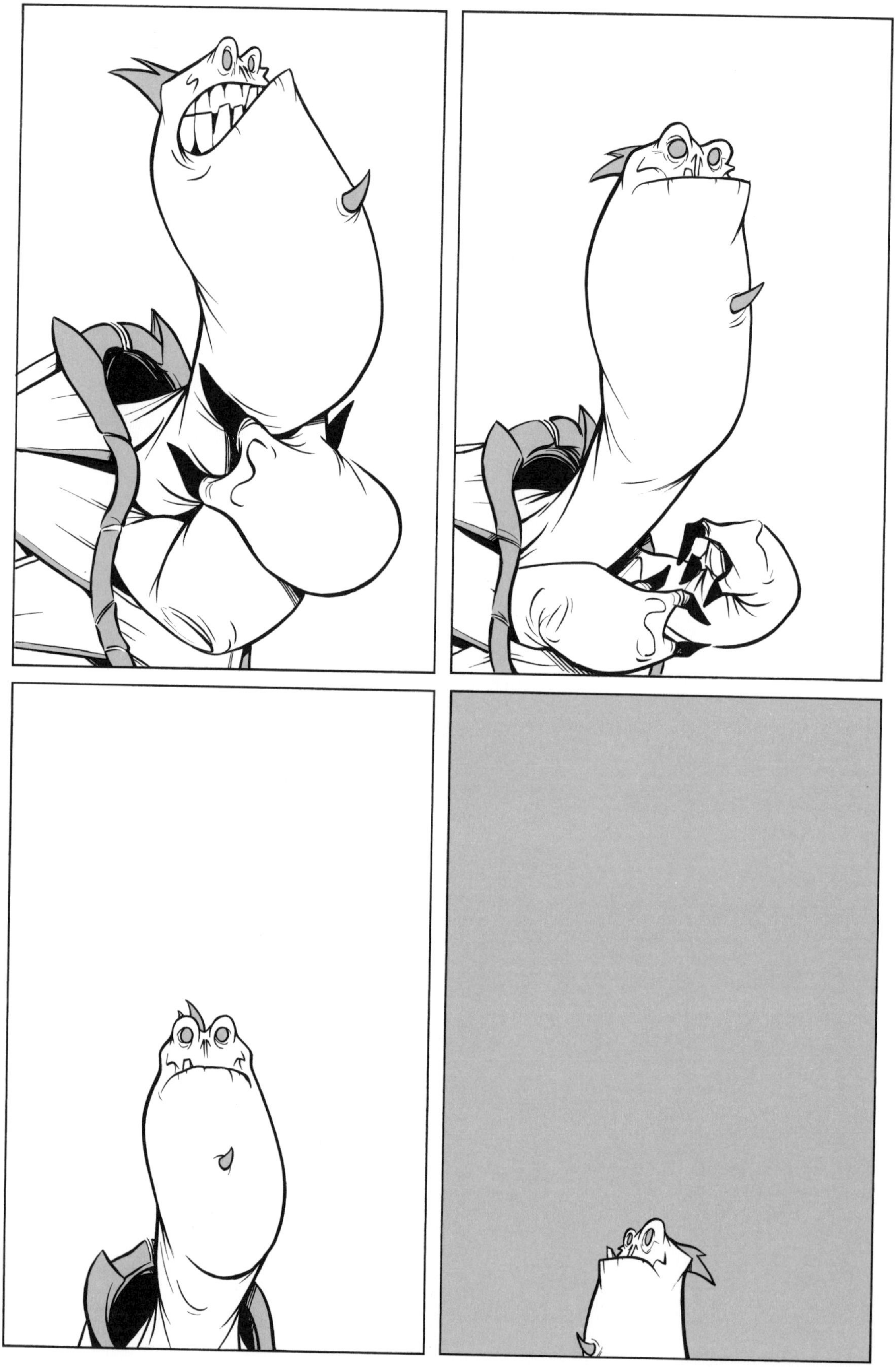

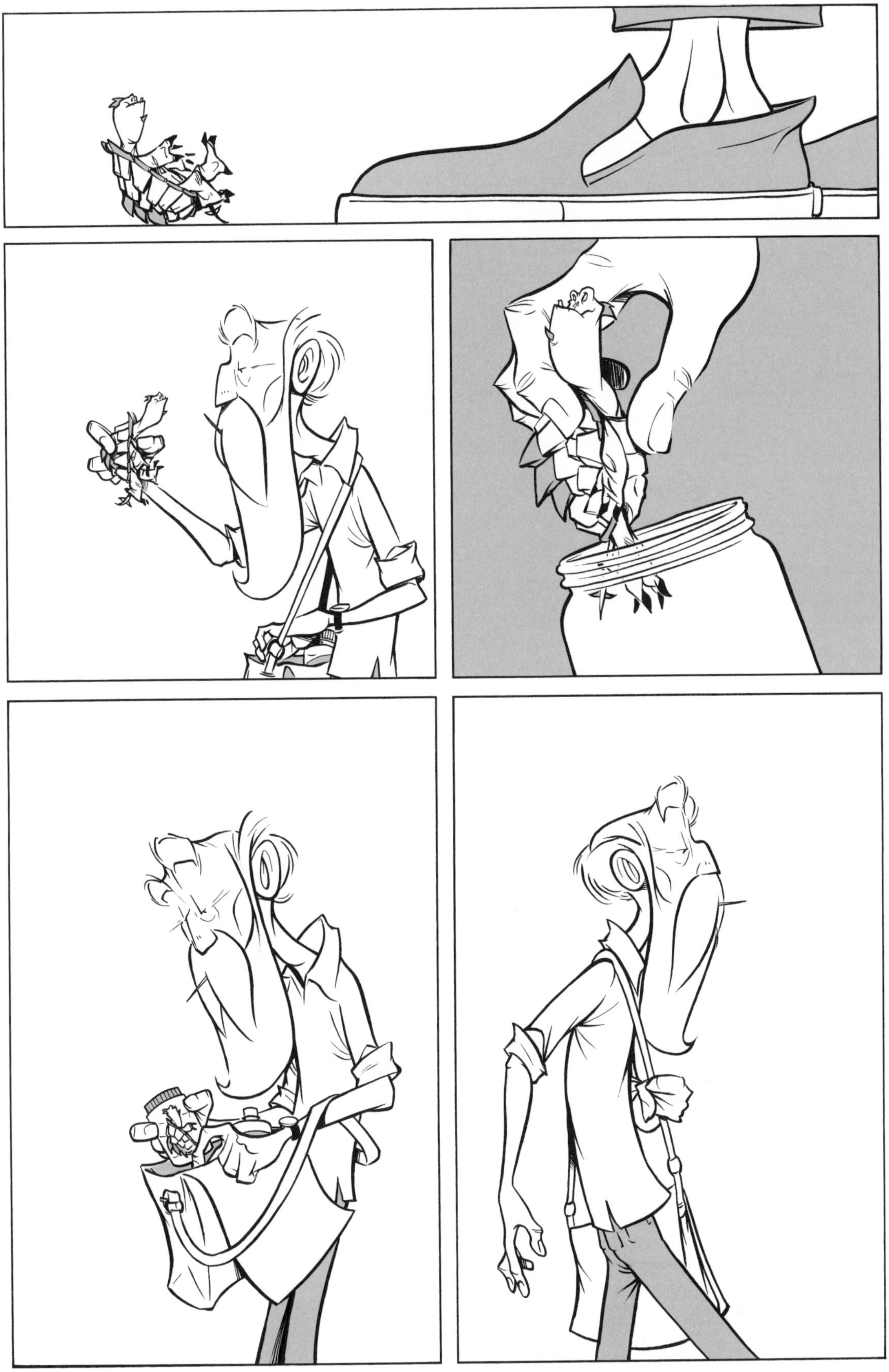

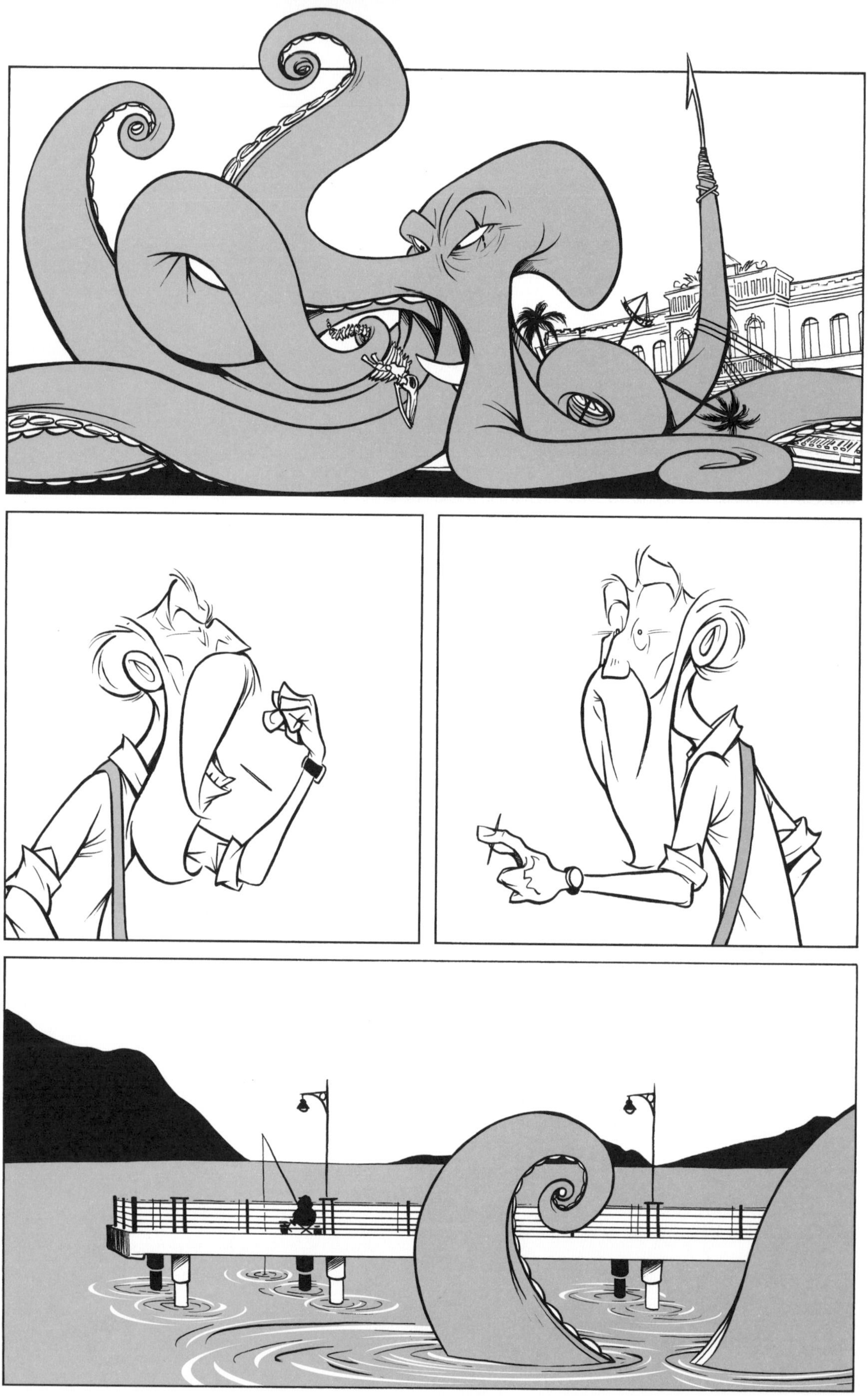

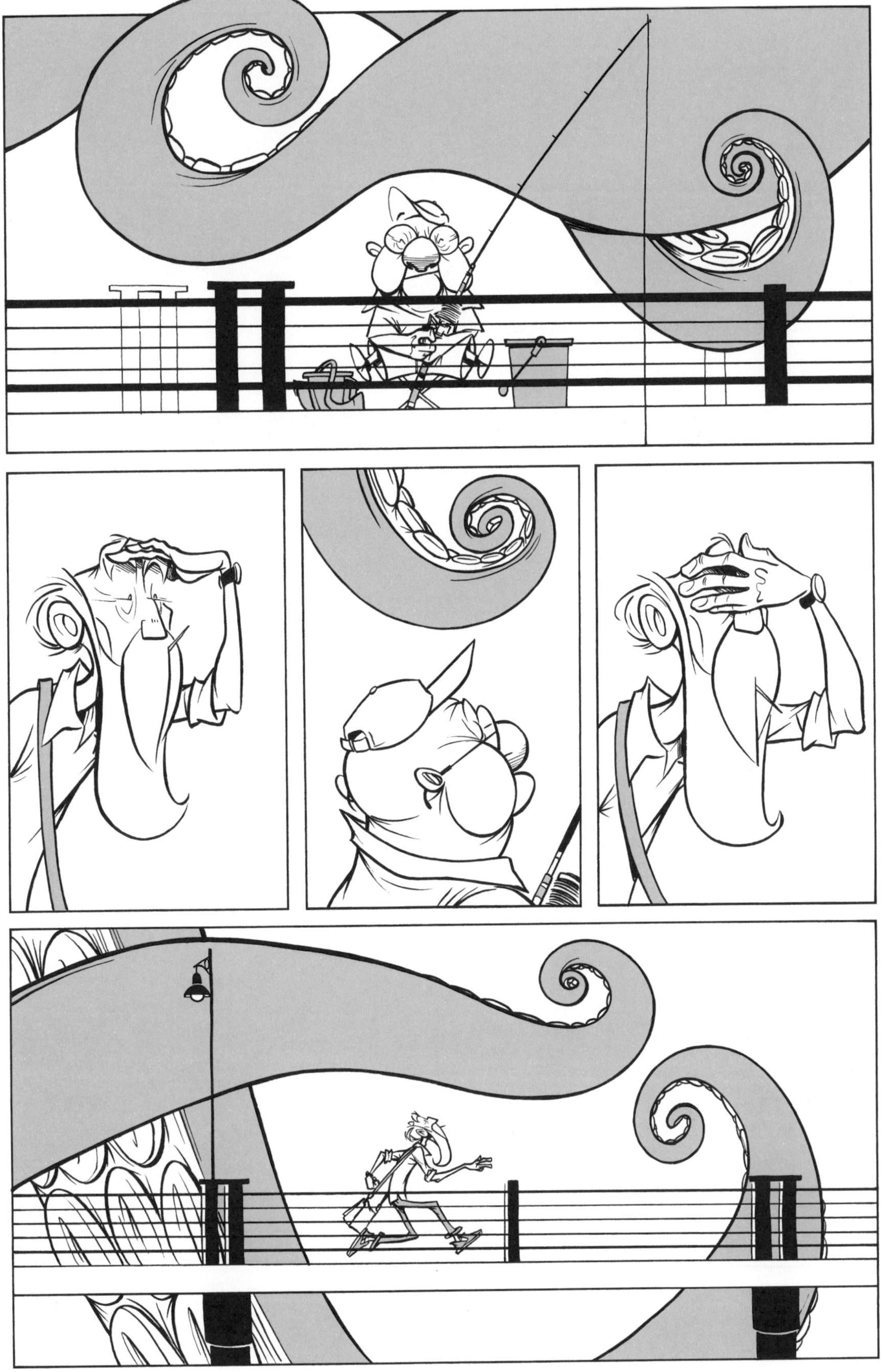

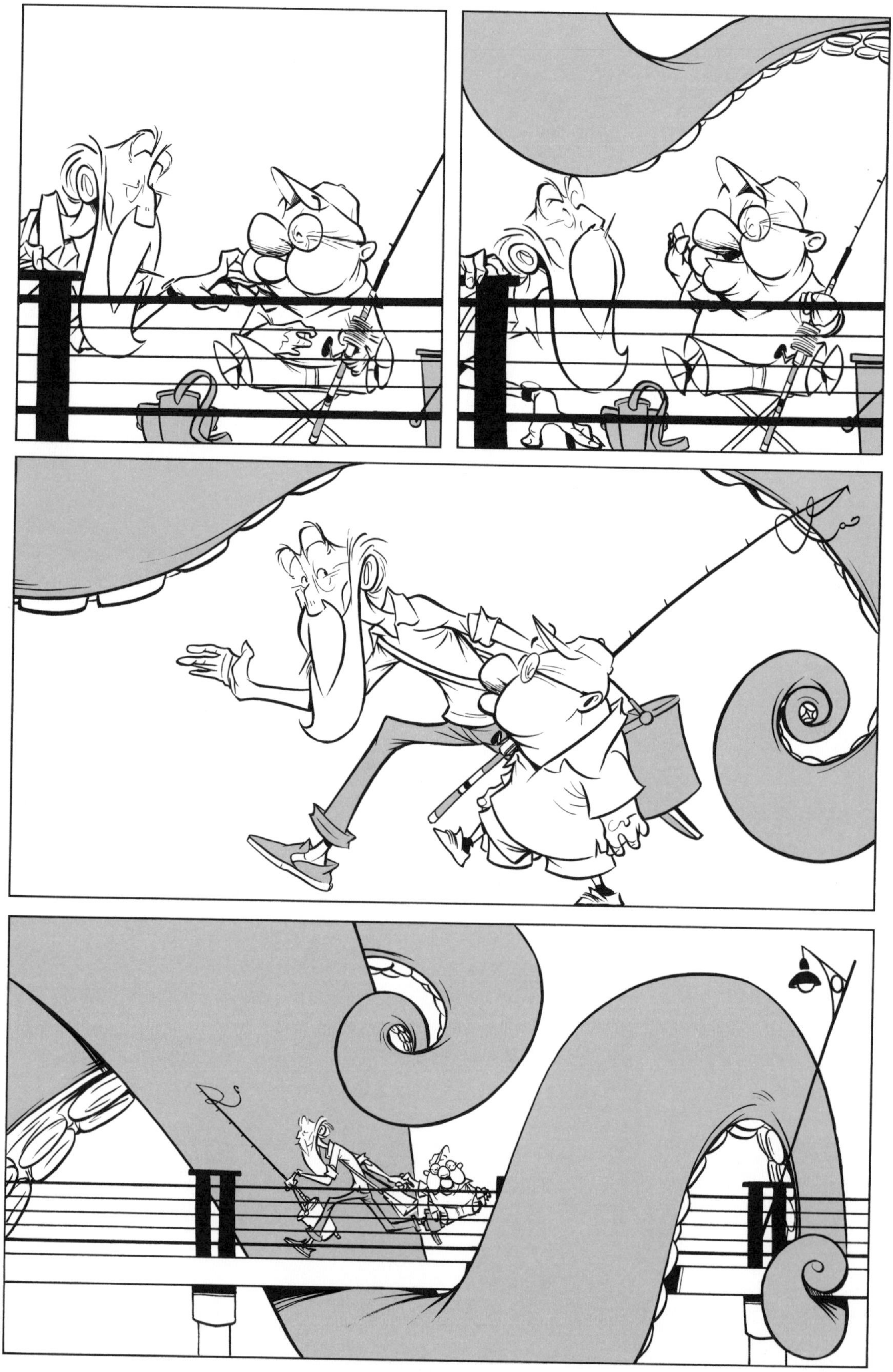

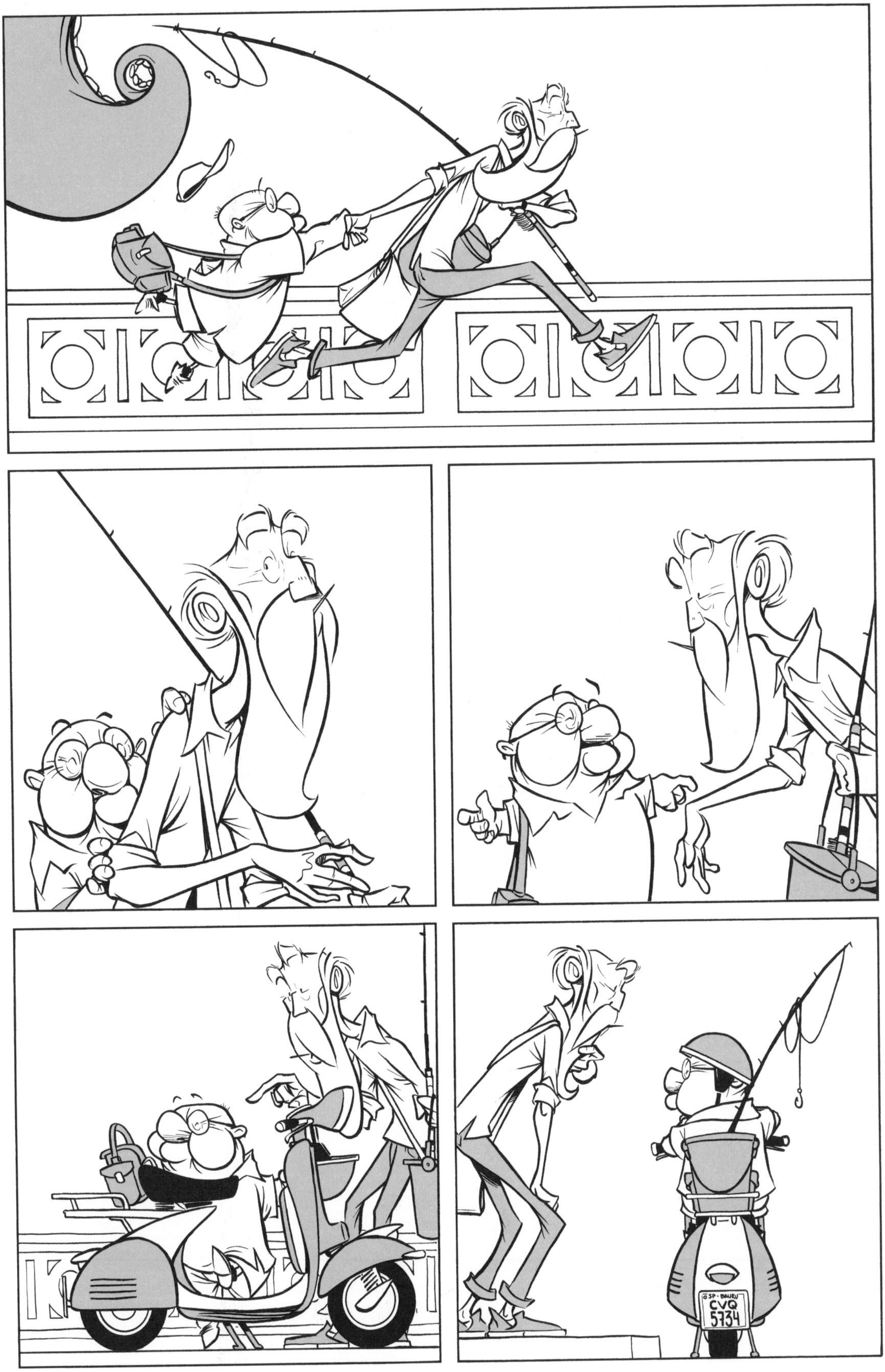
SP · BAURU
CVQ
5734

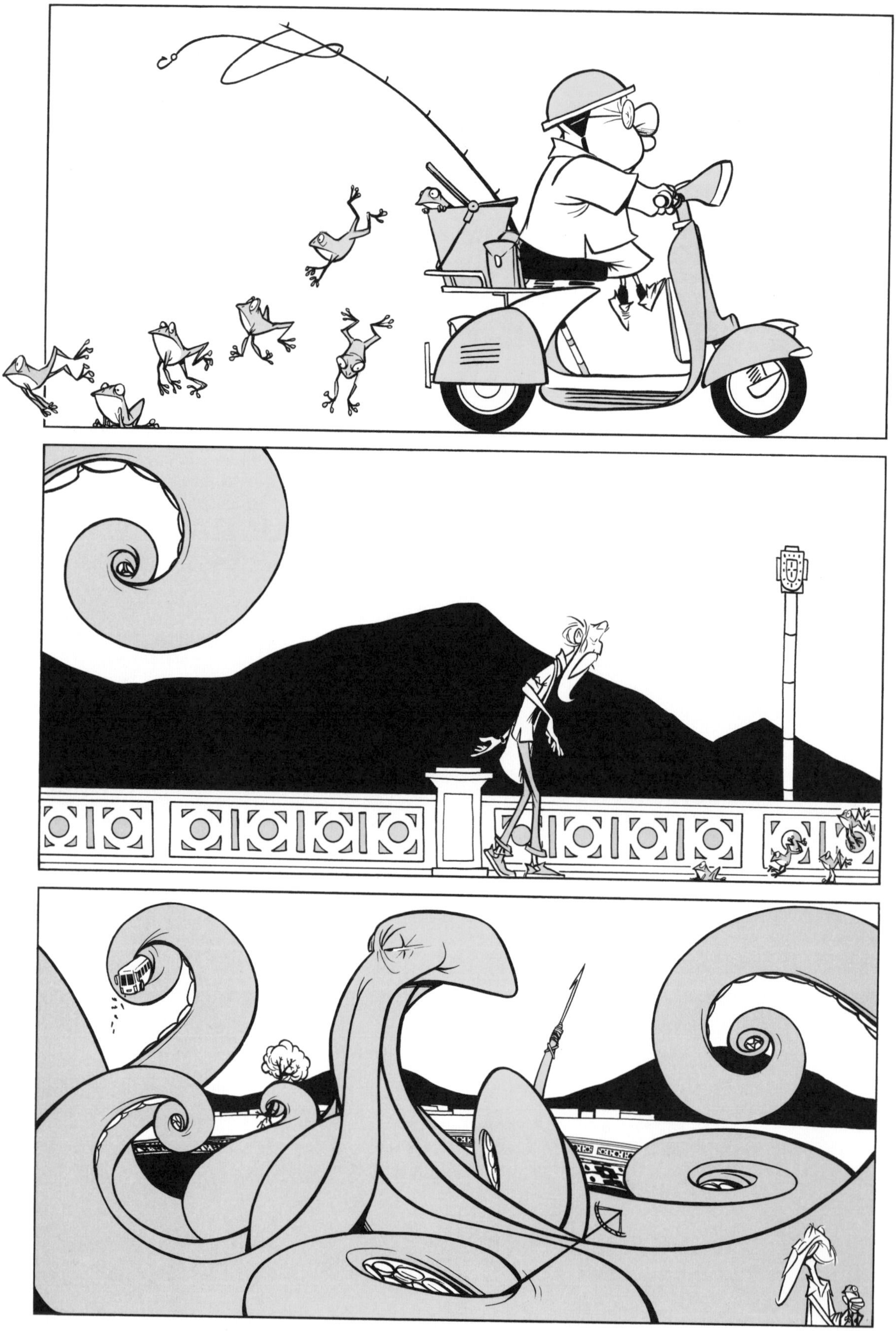

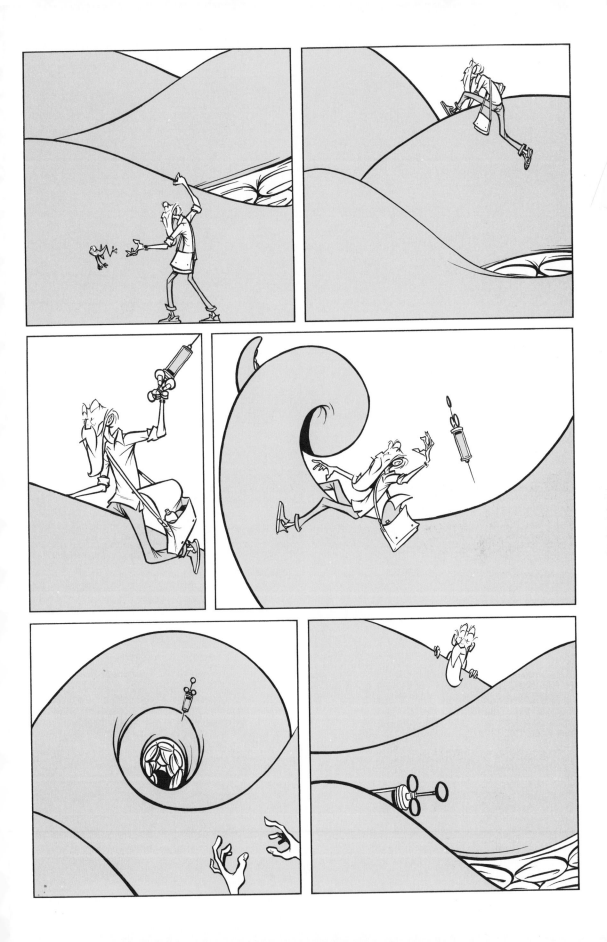

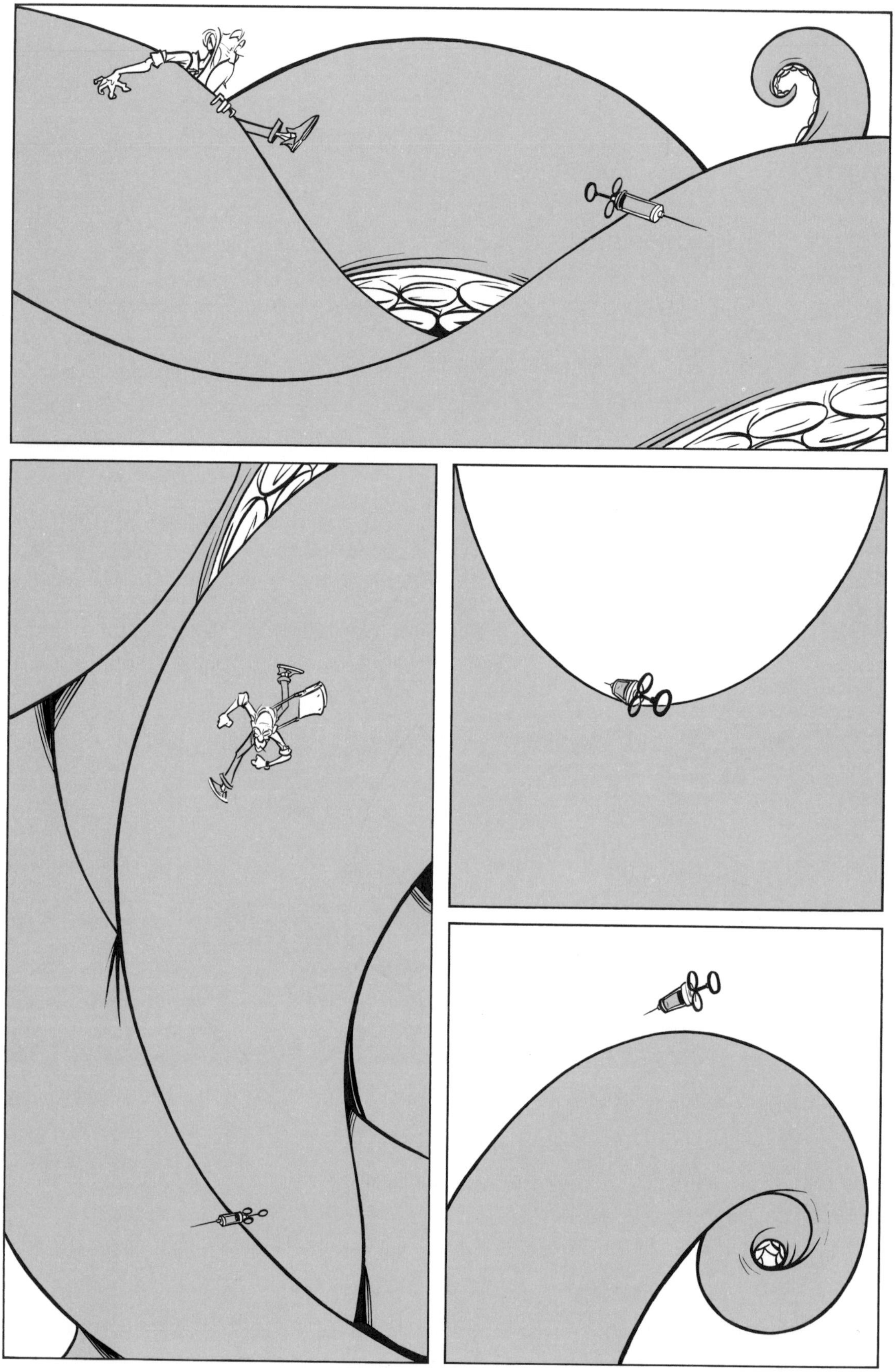

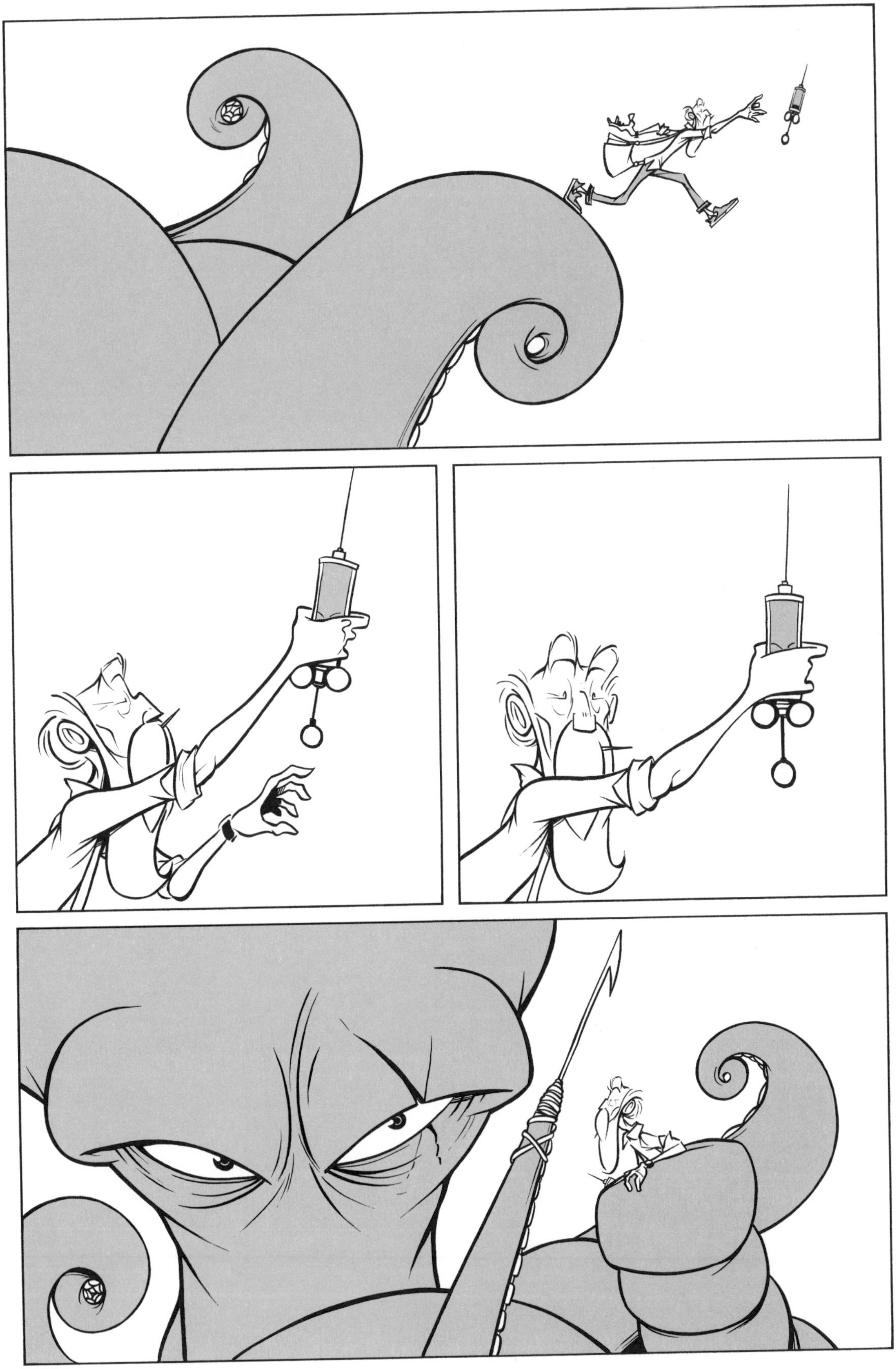

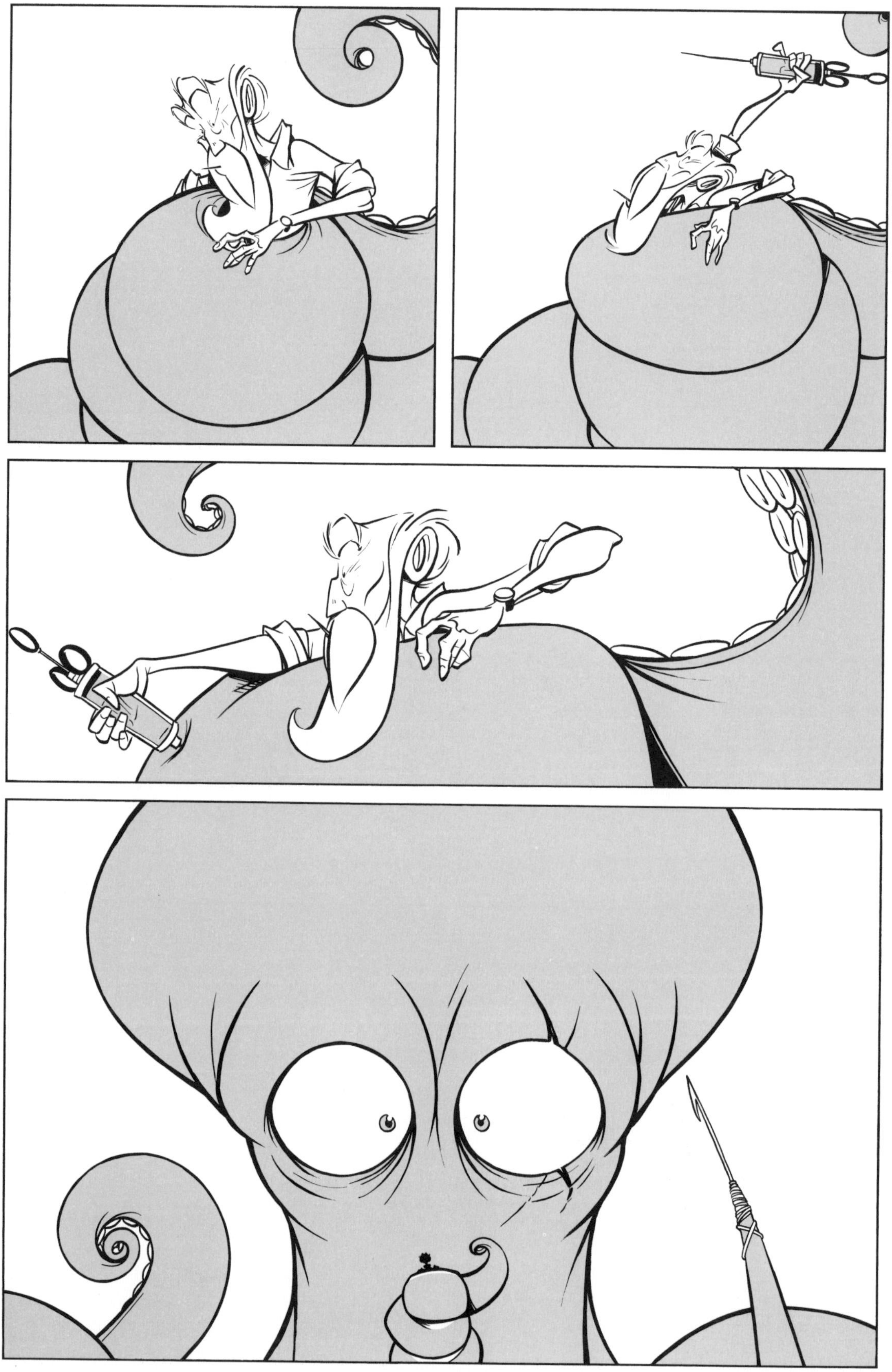

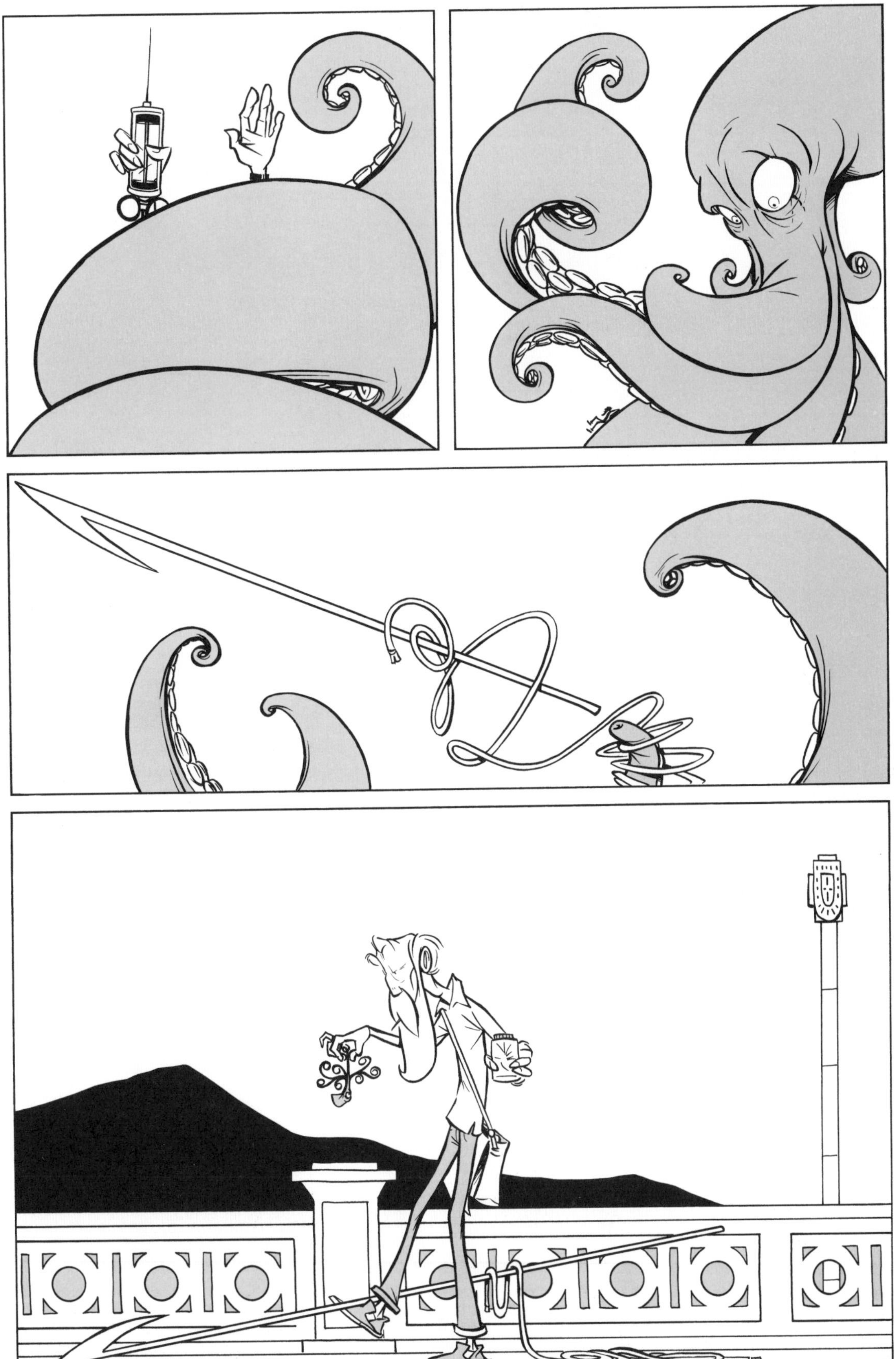

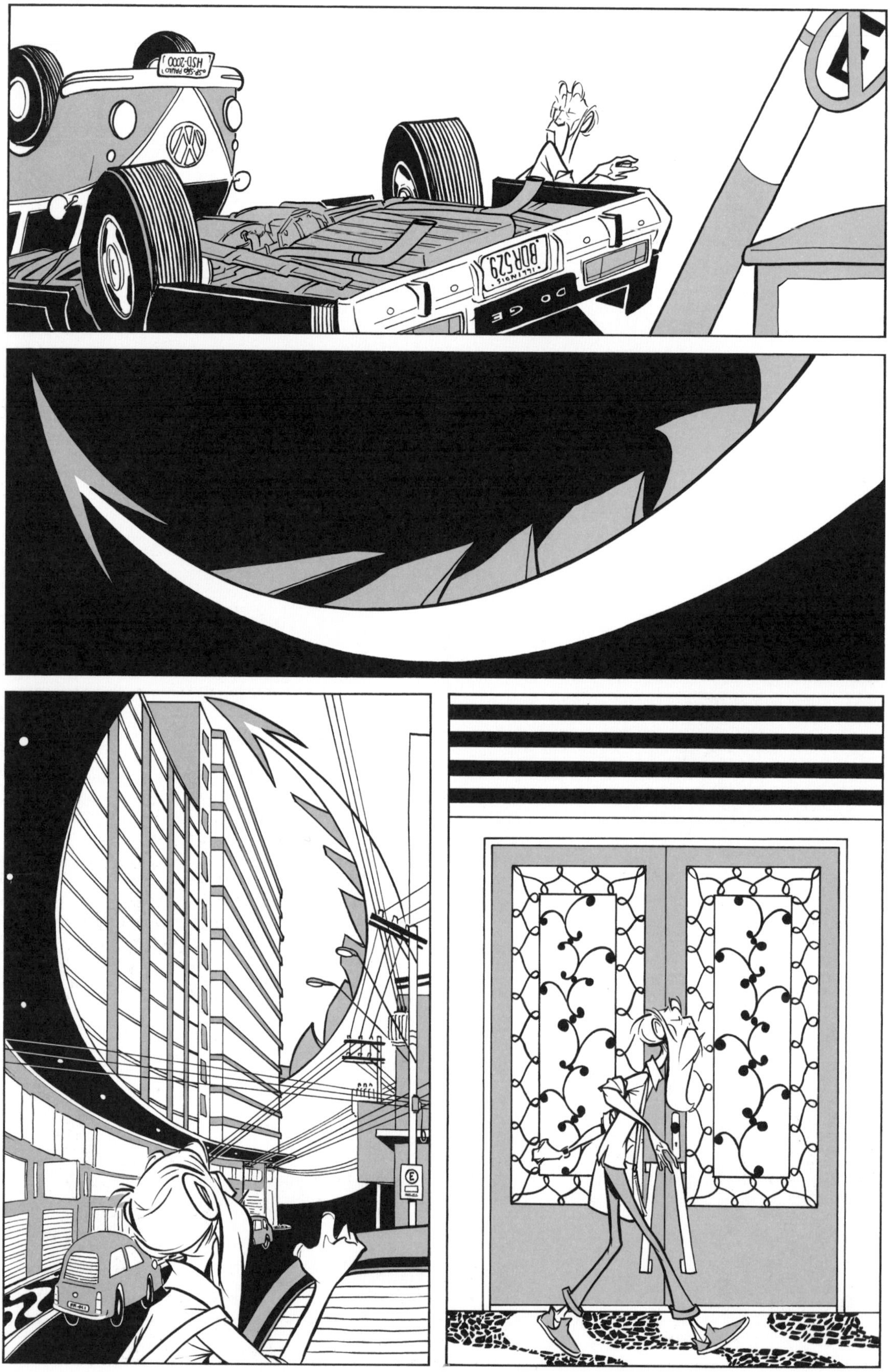
SP-SÃO PAULO
HSD-2000
ILLINOIS
BDR 529
DO GE

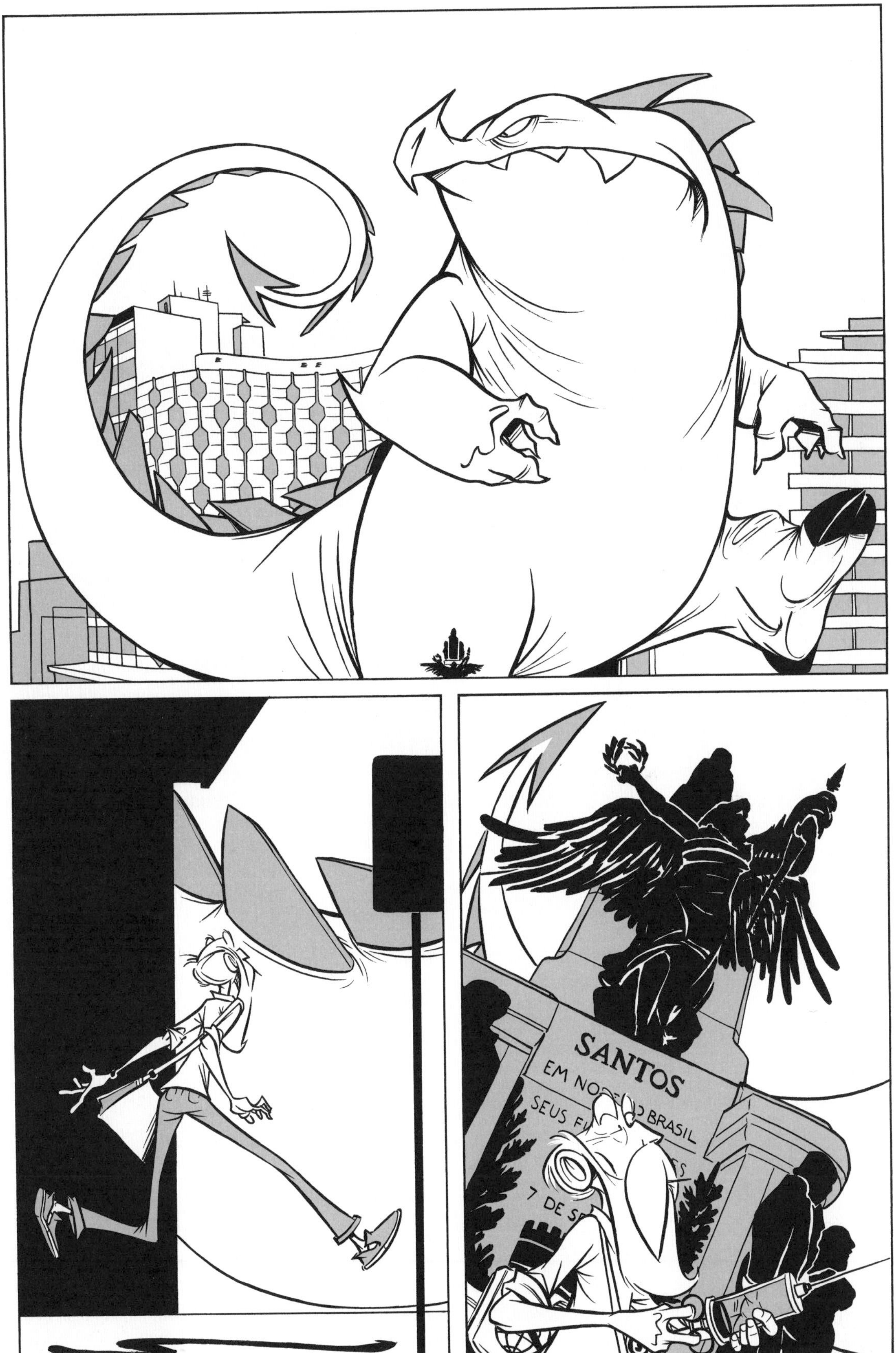
SANTOS
BRASIL

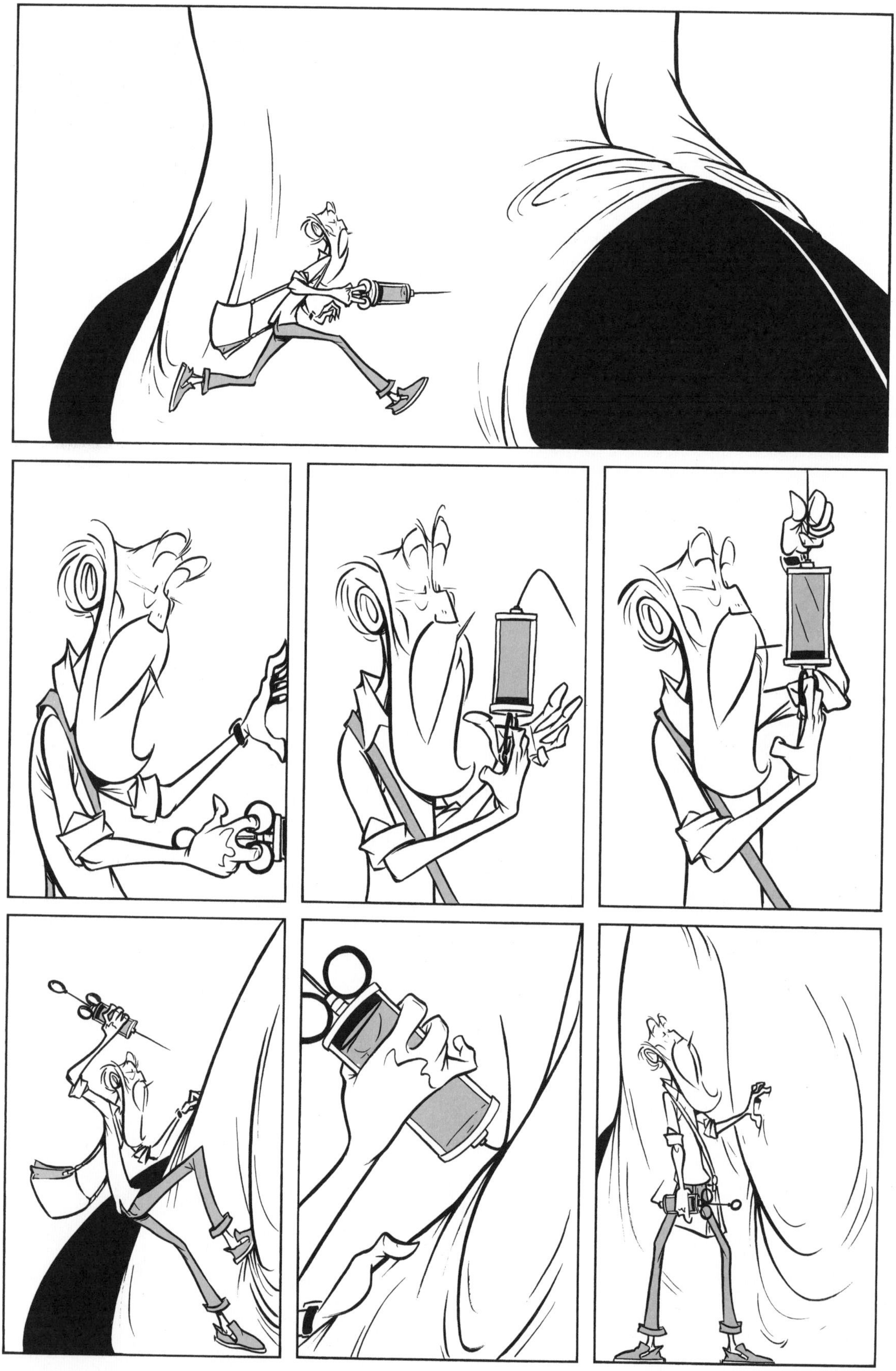

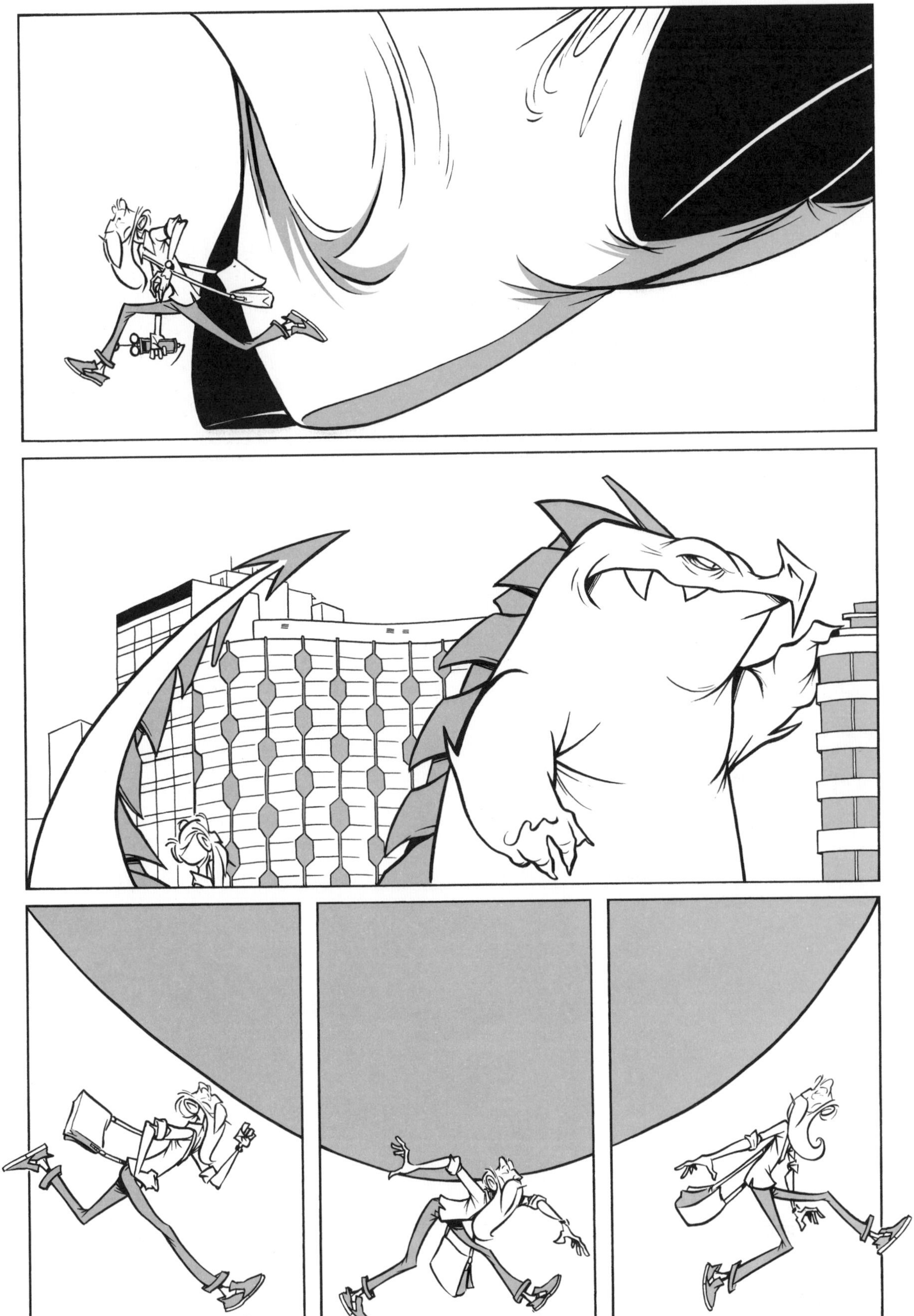

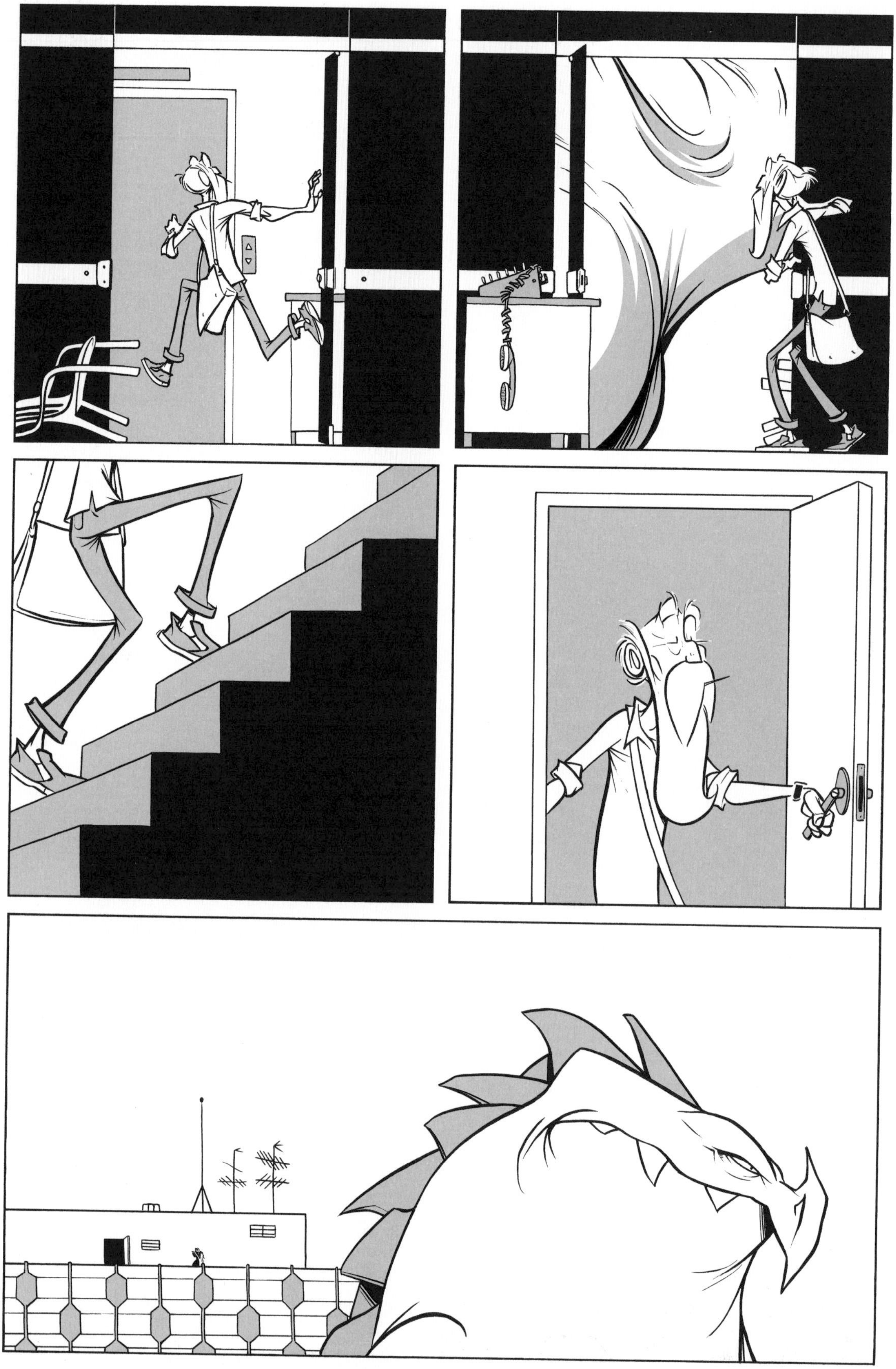

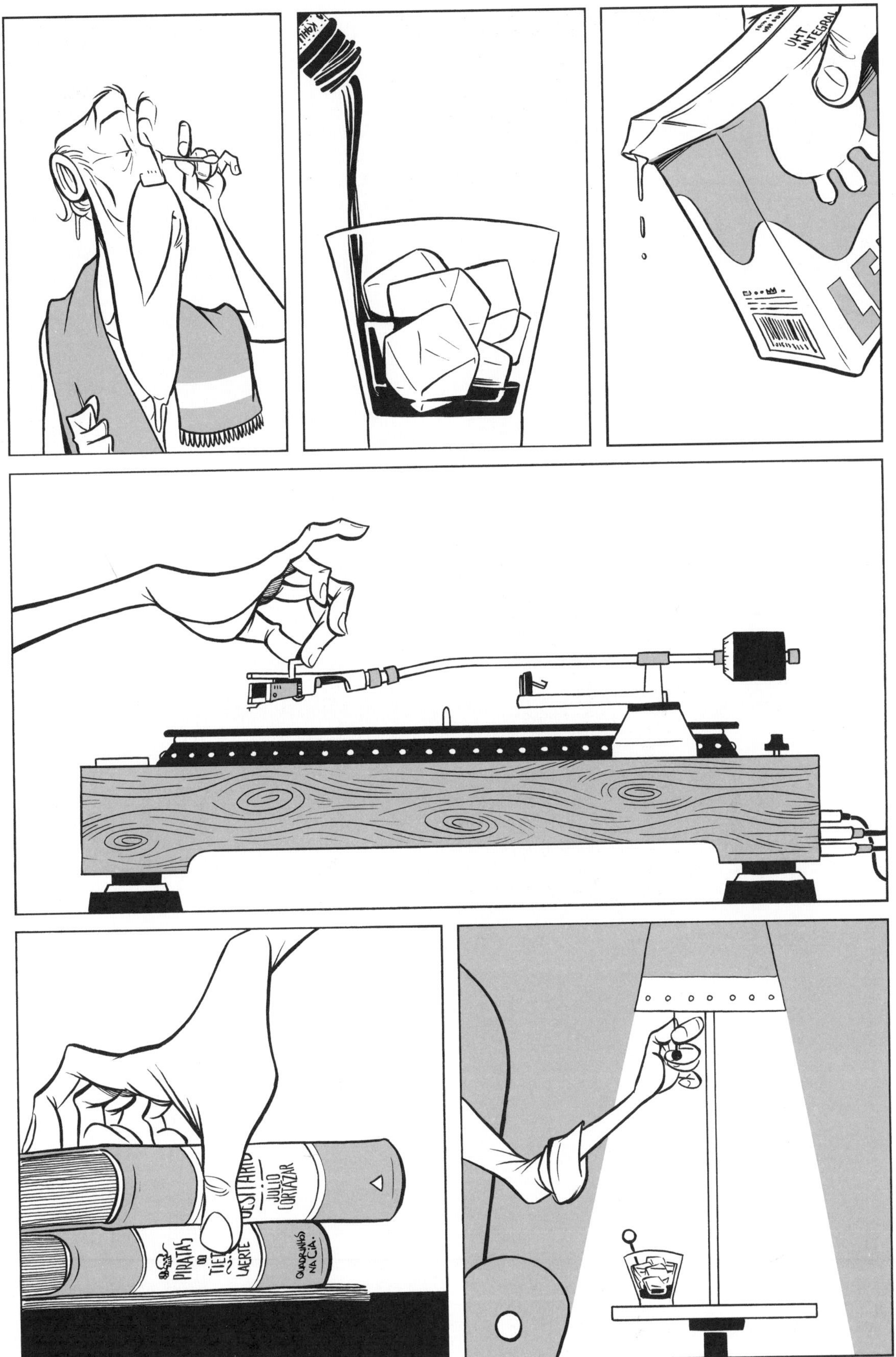
UHT
INTEGRAL
JULIO
CORTAZAR
PIRATAS
LAERTE
QUADRINHOS
NA CIA.

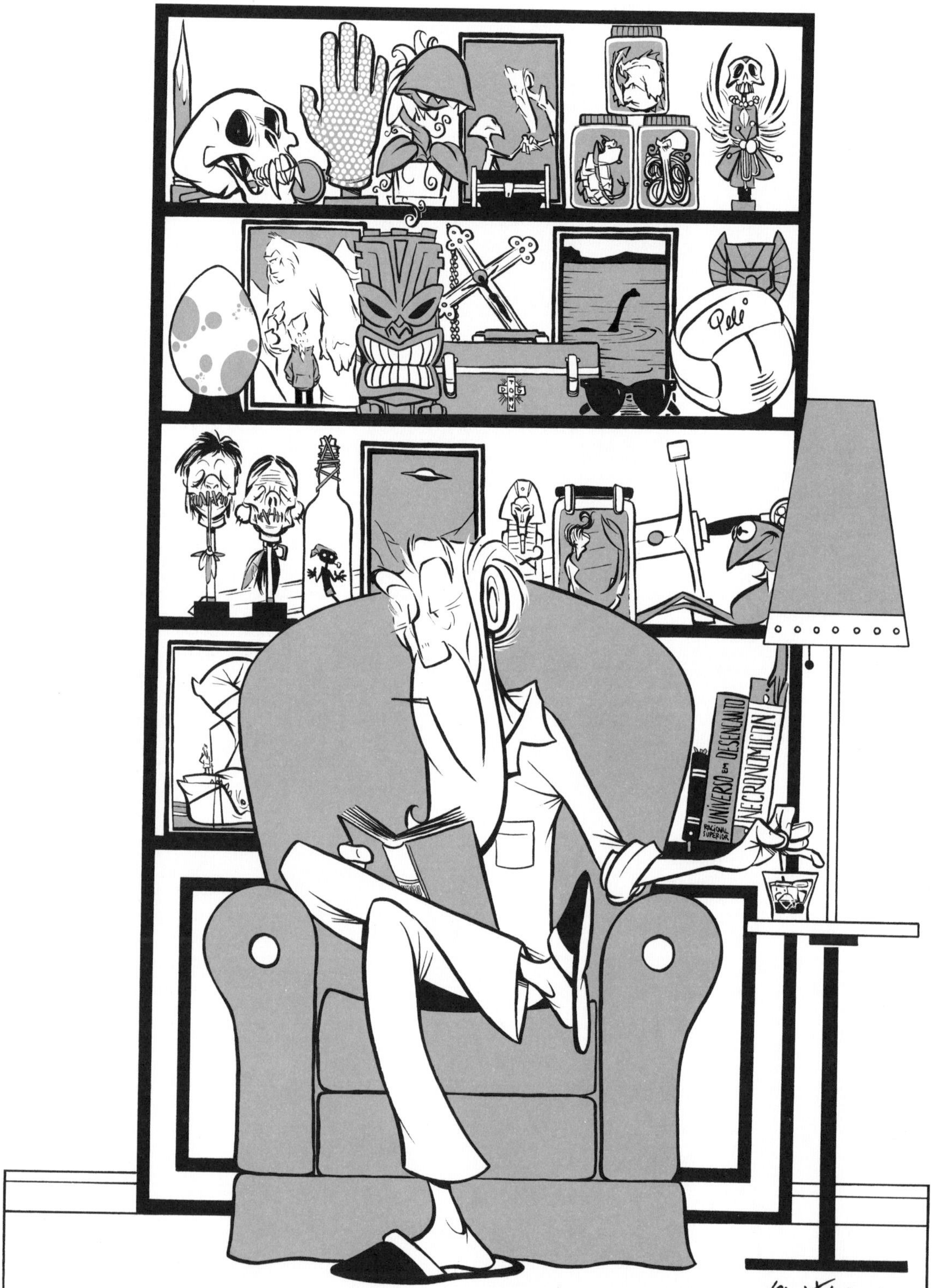
Pelé
DOG TOWN
UNIVERSO EM DESENCANTO
RACIONAL SUPERIOR
NECRONOMICON

Gustavo Duarte is a Brazilian cartoonist born in São Paulo in 1977. He grew up in Bauru, where he eventually graduated from São Paulo State University with a degree in graphic design.

In 2000, Duarte returned to São Paulo, where he began working as a cartoonist and illustrator for publications such as *Folha de S.Paulo*, *Lance!*, *Playboy*, *Le Monde diplomatique*, *Forbes*, and many others. He has published five graphic novels in Brazil: *Có!* (2009), *Taxi* (2010), *Birds* (2011), *Monstros!* (2012), and *Chico Bento: pavor espaciar* (2013). He is also the recipient of eight awards from HQMIX, the most prestigious comics awards in Brazil.

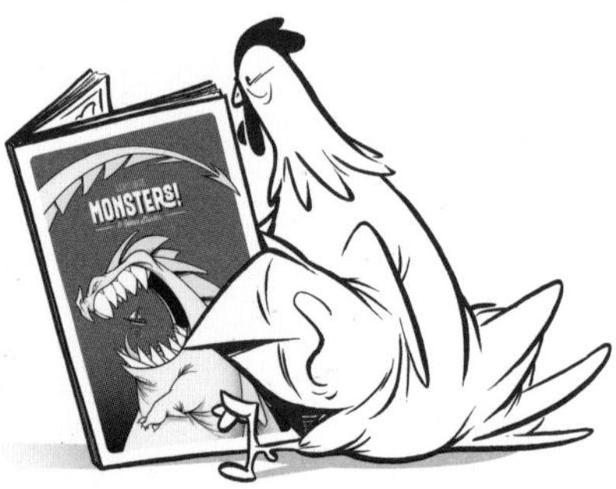
MONSTERS!